@–Marketing Strategy

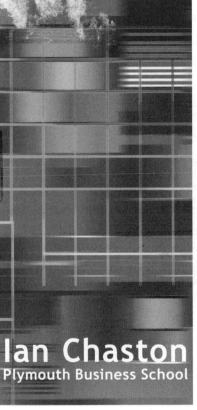

Ian Chaston
Plymouth Business School

McGraw-Hill Publi...
London • Auckland ... ...mpur • Lisbon • Madrid
Mexico • Milan • M... ...Paris • Santiago • St Louis
San Francisco • San ... ...yo • Toronto

Published by McGraw-Hill Publishing Company
Shoppenhangers Road, Maidenhead,
Berkshire, SL6 2QL, England
Telephone: 01628 502500
Fax: 01628 770224

Website: www.mcgraw-hill.co.uk/textbooks/chaston

British Library Cataloguing in Publication Data
A catalogue record for this book is available from the British Library.

Library of Congress Cataloguing in Publication Data
Library of Congress data for this book has been applied for and may be
obtained from the Library of Congress, Washington.

Sponsoring Editor	Tim Page
Publisher	Andy Goss
Development Editor	Caroline Howell
Senior Marketing Manager	Jackie Harbor
Production Manager	Penny Grose

Cover and text design by Ian Foulis and Associates

Typeset by Dexter Haven
Printed and bound in Great Britain by Bell & Bain Ltd., Glasgow
ISBN 0-07-709753-X

SUMMARY OF CONTENTS

FULL CONTENTS

FULL CONTENTS

Preface

The economic fortunes of the world at the beginning of the twentieth century were strongly influenced by the advent of electricity and the internal combustion engine. As the world enters the new millennium, some forecasters are predicting that the World Wide Web and e-commerce will have an even larger impact on the world economic order. Some have been prompted to suggest that the Internet will result in organizations being driven by a completely new management paradigm.

For students of marketing and the academics preparing them for future employment in e-commerce, claims that e-business will totally change the way organizations are managed is a little worrying. For if such claims are true, how can anybody be in a position to offer guidance on exploiting this new technology if the required management models are yet to evolve?

However, as a number of case examples about success and failure in an e-commerce world become available, a common theme is beginning to emerge; namely that many of the basic principles of management applied to existing off-line businesses remain entirely valid when one enters the world of cyberspace trading. To illustrate this claim, one only has to look at activities within the on-line shopping market. Traditional retailers have long recognized that promotion is necessary to attract new customers to their stores. As of Christmas 1999, the largest spenders on traditional mass market promotional campaigns such as TV advertising in the US consumer goods market are Internet companies seeking to attract new customers to their on-line retail outlets.

In view of this situation, the specified goal of this text is to assist students and managers to recognize how existing marketing management concepts can be utilized to guide the effective operation of e-commerce.

The text aims to equip the reader with an understanding of the current e-commerce environment, the unique nature of e-buyer behaviour, on-line information and distribution channels. It then seeks to illustrate that despite the different nature of the e-commerce world, traditional marketing management techniques can produce successful e-marketing strategies. With an awareness of the increasingly competitive e-marketing environment, the e-marketer can employ basic principles of positioning, promotion and pricing to construct successful e-plans. The book also focuses on the importance of establishing real time, computer-based, integrated information systems to supply transaction facilities that are unique to on-line trading. The final chapters focus on business-to-business and services sector marketing on the Web.

Readers of the text are assumed, either as students and/or as practitioners, to have already received some grounding in the basic principles of marketing management. The purpose of this text is to build on this knowledge, thereby assisting the reader to comprehend how, by utilizing existing marketing theories, models of practice can be evolved for guiding the e-marketer in fulfilling their managerial responsibilities.

Outline of the Text

Chapter 1 describes how the e-commerce industry has evolved and how the traditional planning concepts designed to deliver customer satisfaction can be used to define objectives and strategies for companies involved in cyberspace trading. Chapter 2 examines how understanding customer behaviour can have an important influence over evolving appropriate e-commerce marketing plans.

Chapter 3 examines how the flow of information and channels of distribution differ from off-line markets and reviews those variables that impact on organizational performance within on-line market systems. Chapter 4 covers the important internal organizational competences that influence the successful development and implementation of e-commerce strategies. In Chapters 4 and 5, it is shown how, by linking together an understanding of external and internal market circumstances, organizations can evolve and select appropriate strategies for surviving in the face of ever increasing competitive pressures.

Chapter 7 reviews the critical role of innovation management in developing new products and e-commerce organizational processes that can sustain competitive market position. Chapters 8 and 9 cover management of the promotion, price and distribution elements of the marketing mix in on-line markets.

For those organizations that have moved beyond using the World Wide Web as a promotional channel and offer customers on-line transaction facilities, success is critically dependent upon the development and operation of real time, computer-based, integrated information systems. These are necessary in order to deliver the flexibility, speed of response and service quality now demanded by the cyberspace customer. Hence Chapter 10 examines the issues associated with the development and operation of e-commerce information and process management systems.

A major proportion of accepted theories of marketing are grounded in the management of tangible, consumer goods products. Therefore Chapters 11 and 12 respectively examine how e-commerce marketing philosophies may need to be revised to satisfy more appropriately customer needs in on-line business-to-business and service markets.

How to Study Using this Text

To assist you in working through this text, we have developed a number of distinctive study and design features. Each chapter includes chapter learning objectives, integrated illustrative examples, key terms and definitions, chapter summaries, end-of-chapter review questions, and further reading/references.

Importantly, for a text on e-marketing, we have illustrated the text with screenshots from active websites, and listed numerous website addresses (URLs) to enable you to research independently on the web. Throughout the text, real life case studies based on real companies serve further to illustrate the key concepts covered in the text, and are followed by questions that encourage you to analyse e-marketing strategy in action.

To familiarize yourself with these features, please turn to the Guided Tour on pages x and xi.

On-Line Resources

To further assist and enhance your studies, we have provided a variety of Web-based learning resources to accompany this text. These include a downloadable 'Strategy Simulation', additional web exercises with URL links, lecture materials and revision notes as PowerPoint Slides, and further case studies that will be regularly updated to reflect the rapid development of e-commerce. Visit the site at www.mcgraw-hill.co.uk/textbooks/chaston.

Guided Tour

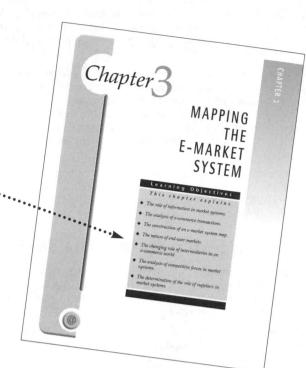

1 The opening page of each chapter states its learning objectives

2 The 'favourites' icon identifies a key term where it is first mentioned in the text

3 Screenshots from active websites help to illustrate the actual implementation of e-marketing

4 Boxed text contains real life examples to illustrate points made in the text

5 The 'search' icon indicates website addresses

6 Each chapter summary reviews and reinforces main topics covered in the chapter

7 Study questions encourage you to review and apply your knowledge of the chapter

10 There is a glossary of key terms at the end of each chapter and a master glossary at the end of the book

8 Each chapter concludes with a case study illustrating the issues covered in each chapter

9 Case studies are followed by questions

---

2 Conservative–relationship-oriented customer needs
— Product/service combinations that deliver complete customer-specific solution.
— Product solutions based on standard specification for industrial sector.
— Customers know their supplier is obsessed with finding even more effective solutions to customer problems.
— Access to information systems that rapidly identify errors in solution provision.

3 Entrepreneurial–transactional-oriented customer need
— Product offering outstandingly greater performance than competition.
— Orientation towards seeking products which offer even more innovation and better performance than existing products.

4 Entrepreneurial–relationship-oriented customer needs
— Product contributes to ensuring customer output delivers superior performance relative to their competitors.
— Supplier able to help customers achieve even more innovation and extend the performance boundaries of existing products.

Although high standards of competence across all areas of activity is the goal of every world class business, it is extremely unlikely that any organization has either the time or resources to achieve this aim. Under these circumstances, the Internet marketer will need to assess carefully the needs of key customers and then decide which competences should receive most development to support the organization's marketing strategies.

Thus the conservative-transactional-oriented Internet company producing standard products and seeking to deliver a strategy of offering the best possible price/quality combination would probably be well advised to give priority to the organization's information management systems and optimizing internal productivity. These competences will also be of importance to conservative–relationship-oriented Internet firms, but additionally attention to service quality competence will be needed in order to deliver a strategy based around working in close partnership with the customer (Chaston 1999a).

Entrepreneurial-transactional-oriented Internet firms should probably give the highest competence priority to the managing of innovation in order to fulfil the strategy of always offering superior products. Given that customers in this sector of the market are more concerned with product performance than low price, this type of company can probably not be as concerned about concurrently achieving high ratings for employee productivity. Similarly entrepreneurial–relationship-oriented Internet companies will also need to pay attention to innovation competence. In this latter case, however, the philosophy of working in close partnership with customers will also demand high levels of competence in the area of service quality (Chaston 1999b).

88   E-COMMERCE COMPETENCE

Summary

In recent years it has been increasingly accepted that as most firms have a complete understanding of market opportunity and use the same technologies in the production of products or services, gaining a competitive advantage is often dependent upon the internal competences that have been acquired by the organization. This concept is known as the resource-based view. Attainment of higher levels of competence will be reflected in superior market performance. The primary competence is that of managing strategic positioning. Effective delivery of a chosen strategy is influenced, however, by operational competences across areas such as innovation, employee productivity, quality and HRM practices. It is proposed that the competence-based model of market performance is applicable to the management of e-based operations. Possibly the most critical operational competence for e-commerce operations is in the area of information management. Internal competences must be developed, prioritized and managed to ensure that they support those actions needed to meet the specified needs of customers.

STUDY QUESTIONS

1 HRM is usually the responsibility of an organization's Personnel Management Department. What new 'people management' issues might confront this department once an organization becomes heavily involved in e-commerce?

2 What are the problems that an on-line company faces in ensuring that customer expectations over service quality are totally fulfilled?

3 Compare and contrast the marketing practices of an on-line company which exhibits a transactional marketing orientation with those that might be expected of one with a relationship marketing orientation.

SUMMARY   89

Case: More of the Same, or Diversification?

Brush Ltd, a UK company, and one of the dominant suppliers of accounting software systems to small and medium-sized companies around the world. The proportion of its sales made in different world regions is: UK 50 per cent, mainland Europe 30 per cent, US 10 per cent, Australia and New Zealand 10 per cent. The company offers a broad portfolio of systems, ranging from simple one terminal book-keeping systems for very small companies through to multi-terminal complete financial management packages capable of supporting automated management accounting and manufacturing costing systems. The company markets the product range through distributors, accountancy practices and office equipment retailers, and operates training centres and an on-line customer support service operation.

Approximately a year ago, the company established a website providing information about its product range and an on-line ordering facility. The experience was useful, and the company is now considering its future on-line market positioning strategy. There are two prevailing views. One seeks to concentrate on the accounting software market and offer an in-depth relationship-oriented operation linking the on-line selling system into the company's existing tele-support department. The other view sees accounting software as too limited a market because over the longer term the company will end up competing with on-line office equipment retailers and distributors. Supporters of the latter perspective feel the company should move to a transaction orientation, and offer, on-line, office hardware, software and supplies.

QUESTIONS

1 Prepare a report reviewing the merits and drawbacks associated with each of these possible on-line market positions for Brush.

2 Use the report to formulate a reasoned argument to justify which of the two positions you think the company should adopt.

(You may wish to visit some on-line office supply operations—www.officedepot.com, www.officemax.com and www.staples.com) and then contrast these with some accountancy software websites (www.sage.com, www.accpac.com, www.bestware.com, www.quicken.com and www.peachtree.com).

114   E-MARKET POSITIONING AND COMPETITIVE ADVANTAGE

Chapter 5 Glossary

Favourites

Customer relationship management, or CRM (p. 101)
Using data about customers to ensure a company offers an optimal product proposition, prices the product to meet specific customer expectations, and tailors all aspect of service quality such that every point of contact from initial enquiry to post-purchase service is perceived by the customer as a trouble-free, 'seamless' service.

Data warehousing, or data mining (p. 99)
Using computer-based statistical analysis to identify clusters and trends in large volumes of customer purchase data.

Inventory turn (p. 100)
The speed with which inventory is acquired and then sold on to the customer.

Lean manufacturing (p. 99)
The concept of operating highly flexible production facilities using machine tools programmable for a range of tasks.

One-to-one, or mass customized, marketing (p. 99)
A philosophy of creating products or services designed to meet the specific needs of an individual customer.

Universal product codes, or barcodes (p. 99)
The numerical codes printed onto product packaging that permit automatic identification.

CHAPTER 5 GLOSSARY   115

About the Author

Ian Chaston is Reader in Management at Plymouth Business School and Professor in Entrepreneurship at UIT, New Zealand. His primary research interests are small business management and marketing. As Vice President of the Institute of Small Business Affairs, he is closely involved in linking output from the UK research community with government bodies responsible for the development and delivery of small business support policies. Publications include 8 texts and over 70 papers in academic journals. Prior to joining the University of Plymouth Ian was Marketing Director for a Division of Consolidated Foods based in Chicago, Illinois.

Acknowledgments

Thanks to the following organizations, which granted permission to reproduce screenshots of their homepages:

AccPac, Barclays, Buyitonline, Caliber, Carnival Cruise Lines, Ecollege, Fedex, Hewlett Packard, IMX, Iboats, Land's End Inc., Millward Brown, Neoforma, NuAuction, Pharmacy2U, Pomexpress, Popwall, Pricescan, QXL, Staples, Travelocity.com, W.H. Smith and Zing.

I would also like to thank the following lecturers who kindly contributed to the market research and reviewing during the text's development: Christine Domegan, NUI, Galway; Debbie Gilliland, University of Staffordshire; Lisa Harris, Brunel University; Kevin Johnston, University of Derby; Wendy Robson, Hull Business School; John Vickers, University College Northampton.

Ian Chaston
Plymouth
July 2000

Chapter 1

MANAGING IN AN E-COMMERCE WORLD

In 1969, the Pentagon's Advanced Research Projects Agency specified the modest aim of wishing to allow computer scientists and engineers working on military contracts across the US to share computers and software resources. The solution was to find a way of communicating information in the form of small packets that could travel independently of each other along a telephone line. In this way, if a telephone connection were broken, the packets of data could be switched to another line and communication would not be interrupted. The technique would work because each packet of information would carry with it the address of its destination and a definition of where it fitted into the sequence of data being sent.

Favourites

The solution, known as Arpanet, had the added advantage that since there were no direct lines between the participating computers, the calling party only had to pay for the first packet switch, in most cases the cost of a local telephone call. Another important breakthrough in the early years of the project was that two individuals, Vint Cerf and Robert Kahn, developed **TCP/IP** (*a computer operating protocol that enables different machines using different operating languages to communicate with each other*). Ray Tomlinson, who was employed by a company that had an Arpanet contract to find a way of sending messages, then developed the concept of e-mail. He was also the individual who selected the @ symbol for defining addresses.

By the end of the Cold War, Arpanet was in widespread usage in the US academic community. In 1991, the National Science Foundation was assigned the responsibility for opening up the system, renamed NSFNET, to the general public. The NSFNET system is the main backbone of what most of us now know as the Internet. At the beginning of the 1990s, however, few people had ever heard of the Internet. More significantly, even fewer people realized the potential impact that the technology was likely to have on the way the world would be doing business by the end of the millennium.

● The Technology

The Internet as we know it today consists of small area networks belonging to individual organizations (local area networks or LANs), networks spread across large geographic areas (wide area networks or WANs) and individual computers. To connect to the Internet, a computer or network uses the TCP/IP protocol. Inside the Internet, the most popular computer platform is an operating system called Unix. Within the Internet there are more networks. These include backbone networks (for example the NSFNET system), commercial networks (which are businesses with direct links to the Internet), service providers that offer smaller companies an Internet connection, non-commercial networks belonging to educational or research organizations, and gateway networks that provide their subscribers with access to the Internet (for example America Online or Compuserve) (Gielgud 1998).

Most Internet sites have an address or 'domain name', the equivalent of a telephone number. Transfer of information uses FTP (File Transfer Protocol). Files can contain images, video clips, sound recording, text or graphics. A person reaching a site encounters an on-line menu or gopher. The World Wide Web can best be described as a gopher in disguise, in that the menu has been made more visually interesting by the addition of graphics, pictures and sound.

● False Gold or Goldmine?

The scale of the Internet's potential influence is dramatically illustrated by a research project commissioned by the US corporation Cisco Systems and undertaken by the University of Texas (Internet Indicators 1999). The researchers concluded that during 1999, within just the US economy, the Internet generated an annual revenue of $332 billion and supported almost 1 400 000 jobs. These figures are rendered even more dramatic when it is realized that revenues on this scale put this sector among the top 20 economies in the world, almost equal to the entire GDP of Switzerland. Another observation that can be drawn from these data is that although the World Wide Web was only launched around five years ago, its total market size already rivals well established sectors such energy, car manufacturing and telecommunications.

Evidence of the apparent potential of the Internet was also demonstrated by a study undertaken by the Boston Consulting Group (1999). It concluded that by the end of 2000 revenues to US retailers marketing goods on-line would exceed $36 billion, and that for the next five years this sector would grow by 145 per cent per annum. Interestingly this research demonstrates that it is not the pure Internet outlets like *www.amazon.com* that are enjoying the real benefits of the Internet. This is because traditional retailers with a website earn 62 per cent of all revenues. One reason for this situation is that it is much cheaper for a multi-channel retailer to attract Web customers than for **on-line only operations** (*organizations with no premises for customers to visit*). The former are spending about $22 per customer to attract visitors to their websites, the latter $42.

The Cambridge, Massachusetts market research company Forrester Research Inc. projects that by 2004 annual on-line retail sales will reach $184 billion (*www.forrester.com*). This figure is dwarfed, however, by its estimates for **business-to-business markets** (*markets in which companies trade with each other rather than with consumers*), in which annual sales have already reached $109.3 billion and by 2004 are projected to hit $13 000 billion.

Despite the amazing growth in the number of websites opened between 1995 and 2000, plus the strong support the Internet has received from individuals such as Larry Ellison of Oracle, Bill Gates of Microsoft and Louis Gerstner of IBM, some industry observers have remained sceptical about this new technology. In 1995, Churbuck presented a series of cases of companies that had invested in creating a Web presence and received no real return from their investment. He concluded that 'the exalted information highway will one day be used by Everyman. But don't hold your breath. Or bet your company.'

A very similar conclusion was reached by Romano (1995), who compared the Internet to the 1849 California 'gold rush', in which the people who made money were not the prospectors but the individuals providing products such as tools, food and clothing. In today's 'Internet gold rush', she concluded that the only people making money are the suppliers of computer hardware, telecommunications equipment and software.

Although some years have passed since these comments were made, even now some people remain unconvinced. To make their case they point to major companies that are still running at a loss (for example *www.freeserve.com* in the UK). Others point to the market capitalization of some of the leading e-commerce companies, such as Netscape, and claim these are financially unjustifiable. In 1999, for example, Alan Sugar, chairman of the UK computer company Amstrad, in his article 'Show us the money', wrote 'So, Yahoo, Amazon, Psion and all the others riding on the Internet and high-tech bandwagon, I invite you to "Show us the money"'. His view is that the new technology needs significantly more streamlining and simplifying before the world is ever to see any real commercial benefits from it.

The mid-1999 temporary collapse of the quoted stock prices of e-commerce companies in the US, and the peaking of the Nasdaq share index at 5000 points early in March 2000 before dropping by 25 per cent in the same month, clearly demonstrate that this is an unpredictable and volatile market. But this volatility is typical of any new technology: quoted share prices of British railway stocks in the nineteenth century fluctuated wildly when many lines failed to deliver expected profits. The railway industry survived and played a critical role in the success of the industrial revolution.

A more reasoned approach to the question of whether there is money to be made on the Internet was presented by an anonymous writer in *The Economist* (1997), who points out that the consumer is being offered a bewildering choice of on-line stores and electronic shopping malls. He proposes that it will take time before the market stabilizes, consumers begin to exhibit loyalty to certain providers, and the market has grown to a scale sufficient for investment to be recovered. The article points out, however, that major profits are already being generated from on-line transactions in the business-to-business market. This is because suppliers and customers of both tangible goods and services have recognized the time and cost savings that can be achieved by using electronic systems to manage their market supply chains. The author closes by quoting Andy Grove, the chairman of Intel who was asked about return on investment from Internet ventures. His response was 'What's my ROI on e-commerce? Are you crazy? This is Columbus in the New World. What was his ROI?'

The other thing to bear in mind when commenting on the Internet is that rapid advances in new technology can often demolish even the most logical of conclusions. Churbuck (1995) quotes Lee Levitt, an analyst at International Data Corporation; 'Consumers won't put up with the slow speed and unpredictability of the Internet…It won't happen. Coca-Cola won't take orders for six-packs on-line.' In September 1999, Pizza Hut UK announced that consumers could now use their interactive digital TV to place home delivery orders for pizza and drinks.

● More than Just a Website

Although in the popular press emphasis tends to be given to the World Wide Web, it is critical for organizations to recognize that exploiting this new technology goes way beyond just putting a brochure on-line. Essentially what is happening on a global basis is that technologies such telecommunications, satellite broadcast, digital TV and computing are converging. As a result of this convergence, the world is being offered a more flexible, more rapid and extremely low cost way of exchanging information. Thus when discussing this new technology, it is safer not to restrict any assessment of opportunity to the role of the Internet. Instead, the debate should cover all aspects of information interchange. This is increasingly being recognized by organizations that

A Small but Hot Idea

It must be of concern to large consumer branded goods companies that, over many years, have invested millions in building their brands to find small companies with a sense of humour challenging their market dominance. One such example is Web Fuel, which was launched as the first breath mint for the World Wide Web. (*www.webfuel.com*)

Donna Slavitt and Amy Katz, two New York entrepreneurs, dreamed up the idea. The product aims to exploit two trends: in the US breath freshener mints, as a confectionery category, are growing much faster than candy or gum and mints; mints are the most popular confectionery product amongst people surfing the Internet. To add to the power of their idea, Web Fuel also uses 'in-tin advertising'. Advertisements inside Web Fuel's lids communicate the Web addresses for companies such as Amazon and generate over 15 per cent of the company's revenues.

The tin is retailed at $2.95, somewhat pricier than the competition. The two entrepreneurs see their product as more than a mint because they offer fresh breath, a dedicated on-line community of users who visit the site via a chat-room and an in-tin Web guide (Poniewozik 1998).

search

The Shout Approach in E-Marketing Management

The easy access to venture capital to start new Internet businesses has resulted in numerous new Internet companies being launched in the hope that the owners will become millionaires when the enterprise goes public. This situation caused J.W. Gurley (1998) to observe that the four stage marketing plan for new Internet initiatives appears to be:

1 Start a company, define a product and begin production.

2 Declare that your product does not fit any market that has ever existed, but rather is the defining entry in a new and exciting market.

3 Declare yourself the leader in this emerging market.

4 Persuade others to make quotes to the media in which they proclaim you king of this new market.

Gurley sees the shouting as worthless in most cases, because there often turns out to be no new market, so that after a few months no more is ever heard from the new company. The other scenario is that the shouting attracts the attention of the big players who, having realized that a new market has genuinely been discovered, invest heavily in product development and rapidly dominate the new sector. This latter outcome occurred in the outsourced **applications services market** (*a market in which expensive, complex software is located on a remote computer server and users, instead of installing the software themselves, access the server and pay a usage fee when running these expensive programmes*), in which a number of small firms had the idea of offering their services to run sophisticated software on remote servers via an Internet connection. This removed the need for the high level of expenditure faced by companies installing new software systems inside their own organizations. In this case, large players such as SAP, PeopleSoft and Oracle realized the potential of this market. They have used their financial muscle to move in and remove control from the small firms that pioneered the market.

are moving to exploit the huge diversity of opportunities now offered by e-commerce. Seybold and Marshak (1998) support the idea that marketers should extend their thinking beyond the Internet, to encompass all platforms that permit a company to do business electronically. They propose that electronic business involves applying a wide range of technologies to streamline business interactions. Examples of these technologies include the Internet, **electronic data interchange** or **EDI** (*a pre-Internet concept that uses specially developed computer software permitting companies to exchange electronically large volumes of data between their respective computers*), e-mail, electronic payment systems, advanced telephone systems, hand-held digital appliances such as mobile telephones, interactive TVs, self-service kiosks and **smart cards** (*plastic cards that contain a microchip on which information is stored electronically, and can be used, for example, to pay for travel on public transport without the need to carry money, or to store a person's medical records*).

Once a company decides to embrace e-commerce to exploit new, entrepreneurial opportunities, then an immediate outcome is that the organization's knowledge

MANAGING IN AN E-COMMERCE WORLD

platform becomes much more closely linked with other knowledge sources elsewhere within the market system, such as suppliers and customers (Seybold and Marshak 1998). This occurs because once buyers and sellers become electronically linked the volumes of data interchange dramatically increase as trading activities begin to occur in real time. The outcome is very dynamic, rapid responses to changing circumstances in both customer and supplier organizations.

The degree to which e-commerce is likely to change the way organizations operate in the future is effectively illustrated by Andersen Consulting's 1999 research project on e-commerce trends in Europe. From this study the consulting company propose the following 'five basic truths':

1   Vertical Disintegration
    In the past, companies sought to be self-reliant by maximizing their ownership of aspects of their role within their **supply chain** (*the description applied to all of the members of a system in which raw materials are acquired and products manufactured, distributed and sold to the final customer*), such as operating their own IT departments, logistics fleets and warehouses. The speed with which information and decisions can now be made using e-commerce means that in many cases costs can be reduced and flexibility of response enhanced by collaboration with outsiders.

2   The Vale of Intangibles
    In the past companies measured success by the value of their physical assets, such as land and buildings. Although financial markets have always recognized that intangibles such as company reputation and brand names have value, analysts have tended to use the fixed assets in the balance sheet to actually value companies. In a rapidly changing world, however, physical assets can be a barrier to rapidly restructuring a company and/or adopting a different, more flexible response to emerging new market opportunities. As a result there is growing support for the idea that the real value of the company in the future will be based on the knowledge resources and technological skills contained within the organization.

3   Increasing Returns
    In traditional manufacturing industries, expansion of the business usually requires new investment in additional production capacity. The world of knowledge management follows a very different path. As demonstrated by the computer software sector, once the initial investment in product development has been made, ongoing costs to support market expansion are almost zero. Petty cash covers the cost of copying more CD-ROMs from the master disc.

4   Perfect Information
    Economists often talk about the theory of perfect markets in which price equilibrium is rapidly achieved because both customers and suppliers have total knowledge. Through on-line services that offer price comparisons and **on-line auctions** (*websites where people can bid on-line for products and services featured on the site*), the world of perfect information may have almost arrived. The outcome will be that suppliers will find it increasingly difficult to retain control over market prices because this power will shift into the hands of the customer.

Favourites

Favourites

<u>5</u>   Instant Supply Chains
The ability to link all aspects of business, from ordering materials from suppliers through to automatically shipping goods to customers, means that the e-commerce supply chain is one in which actions will not be delayed because employees are slow to pass information to each other. Those companies, however, that fail to create integrated electronic communication channels and undertake the right action off-line (for example manually checking customer credit before accepting an order) will soon find themselves being overtaken by competitors that have realized the necessity of offering instant response to the customer.

⬤ Putting E-Commerce into Context

When managers are first confronted by e-commerce, it is not unusual for them to be overwhelmed, both by the apparent complexity of the technology and the diversity of alternative routes to the e-commerce world. It is useful, therefore, to attempt to synthesize exactly what is on offer from e-commerce. As illustrated in Fig. 1.1, there are two dimensions to the application of e-commerce available to an organization. One is the role of e-commerce in the provision of information to customers, such as price, product availability and delivery terms. The other is the role of e-commerce in the management of the purchase transaction.

As proposed in Fig. 1.1, the degree to which an organization uses e-commerce to deliver information and/or support transactions can be classified as high or low. This

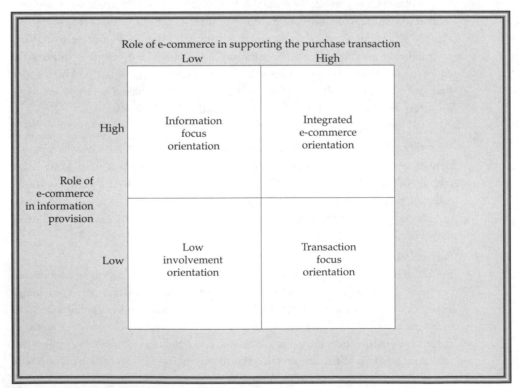

Figure 1.1 *An e-commerce alternative orientation matrix*

taxonomy then yields four alternative choices. The organization can opt to have low involvement in both information provision and transaction management. For example, many fast moving consumer goods (f.m.c.g) companies have created somewhat static websites to communicate a limited degree of additional information about their products. Alternatively, some organizations avoid using e-commerce to support transactions, merely exploiting the technology as a major element in the process of communicating with customers. This approach has been taken by a number of publishing companies that have created free on-line versions of their newspapers and magazines.

A third alternative is to use e-commerce to assist transactions, but concurrently only offer a limited amount of on-line information. Typically this scenario will be found in industries in which the information provided to customers is extremely complex, but the product or service simple to distribute electronically. A number of computer software houses have taken this approach in those cases where the primary customer contact point is dialogue with the supplier's technical sales force. Having determined the appropriateness of the software, the customer then orders on-line and in some cases also takes delivery that way. The last option in Fig. 1.1 is high involvement in both provision of information and support of the purchase transaction. On-line retailers such as *www.amazon.com* and *www.etoys.com* provide examples of this latter model. These companies only exist in cyberspace, having no physical retail outlets.

For the company just beginning to evolve an e-commerce marketing strategy, visiting sites like Dell (*www.dell.com*) or American Airlines (*www.americanair.com*) can be depressing, as clearly a massive investment will need to be made before the organization can aspire to match these 'e-commerce excellent' organizations. The first, and possibly most critical, point to make, however, is that the organization should not throw away all the experience and marketing knowledge acquired from business operations over the years. The good news is that as we begin to observe e-commerce in operation, virtually all of the established guidelines about good marketing practice apparently still apply. Cross and Smith (1995) eloquently spelled out this concept in their 'Interactive Rules of the Road', namely:

1 Technology is merely a facilitator for a marketing strategy that focuses upon customer benefits.

2 The marketer must strive to balance the company's marketing objectives against the customer's needs and preferences.

3 Each technology-based programme should provide multiple benefits to the customer.

Eckman (1996) also stresses the importance of a customer-oriented e-commerce marketing strategy. In his article he proposes that the organization should pose these questions: (1) does the Internet change the target or scope of the market? (2) does the Internet help satisfy customer needs? (3) will customers use the Internet over the long-term? Having reviewed these critical questions, the organization is then at the stage where it can begin to determine an entry point into e-commerce.

> ### PrePRESS Solutions Inc.
>
> Cross and Smith (1995) provide a useful example of evolving e-commerce applications in their analysis of case materials about PrePRESS Solutions Inc., a $50 million player in the $2.3 billion image-setting industry. When, in the late 1980s, pre-press publishing capabilities began to migrate to less expensive computer platforms (from mini-computers to desk-top systems), PrePRESS augmented its direct sales force with a catalogue business catering to new buyers looking for lower cost computer hardware and software. When fax-on-demand began to appear in the market, the company adopted this technology to communicate lengthy technical specifications. Then, in April 1995, PrePRESS opened its first commercial website, which took the innovative step of carrying both sector and company-specific information. Contained within an ever evolving site are features such as an on-screen newspaper updated daily, the Cafe Moire chat site, a convention centre covering major trade shows in the industry, a free reference library, the PrePRESS on-line superstore and a print shop, where users can download tips and tools for improving their pre-press processes.

Most organizations soon realize that e-commerce is a technological tool, the use of which will evolve and change as the organization gains experience of trading in cyberspace. McGovern (1998) presents this evolving view in terms of 'e-commerce life cycles' in his analysis of how logistics and transportation service providers have implemented their e-commerce strategies over time. Initially many firms used the technology to provide general information about themselves on a website. They then used e-commerce as a platform to permit customers to access information for tracking goods throughout each phase of the shipment process. The next stage was typically that of offering on-line, customized price quotes. More recently, the leading firms have permitted customers to use an e-commerce platform to initiate every phase of the shipment process, from order to post-delivery problem resolution.

⬤ Internet Economics

In comprehending the potential impact of the Internet on the world economy, one should recognize that the technology has the ability to cut costs, increase competition and improve the functioning of price mechanisms in many markets (anon. 2000). As such it may bring the world closer to the text-book definition of perfect competition in which there is abundant information, no transaction cost and no barriers to entry. Although it is as yet hard to test such theories, certainly studies of some markets (for example books and CDs) seem to support the concept of markets moving nearer to a perfect competition model, with a resultant major decline in market prices.

In business-to-business markets the Internet is also affecting operating costs. Procurement costs are falling as it becomes easier to locate the cheapest supplier and moving purchasing on-line is reducing transaction costs. There is also evidence to suggest that supply chain management is being made more efficient and firms are able significantly to reduce inventory holding costs. Goldman Sachs has estimated, for example, that in the electronics components industry these factors have already contributed to procurement savings of up to 40 per cent. British Telecom estimates that on-line procurement has reduced average processing transaction costs by 90 per cent.

As the Internet contributes to the lowering of operating costs, Goldman Sachs estimates business-to-business e-commerce could cause a permanent increase in the level of output by an average of 5 per cent in developed nations' economies over the next 10 years. This implies an increase in GDP growth of 0.25 per cent per year. Because spending on IT is considerably higher as a percentage of GDP in the US, some economists think that the US will be the prime beneficiary of the Internet revolution. However, a possible counter argument might be made that the Internet offers even greater potential for cost savings and productivity gains in more tightly regulated economies where rigid labour and/or inefficient capital markets exist. Should this latter scenario prove to be the case, then over the longer term the Internet may have greater impact on the economies of the EU and Japan.

It is also possible to evolve the proposition that emerging economies could be prime beneficiaries of e-commerce. As the Internet reduces transaction costs and the **economies of scale** (*the reduction in operating costs that occur as a company becomes larger*) possible through **vertical integration** (*when a company becomes involved in operations either upstream or downstream from itself in its supply chain*), there could be a decline in the

Favourites

Favourites

optimal size of firms in the future. Should this come to pass, then small Asian firms, by working together, may be able rapidly to expand their share of sales in global markets. Emerging evidence to support this perspective is provided, for example, by the computer software industry in India that, by being willing to undertake development contracts at extremely low prices, is now beginning to steal market share from competitors based in the US and Europe.

● Strategic Marketing Planning

Having begun to appreciate the potential role that e-commerce may play within the organization, the manager is now at the stage where it is possible to embark on the formal process of evolving an e-commerce marketing plan. The stages in this process are described in Fig. 1.2.

The starting point of the process is to determine the current market conditions and to assess the role that e-commerce plays in the delivery of customer satisfaction. At the same time, there needs to be an analysis of the organization's competences and the degree to which the current workforce has the skills necessary to operate in an e-commerce environment. The data from this external and internal analysis allow a manager to determine the opportunities and threats confronting the company in the marketplace, and the strengths and weaknesses of the company's internal operations.

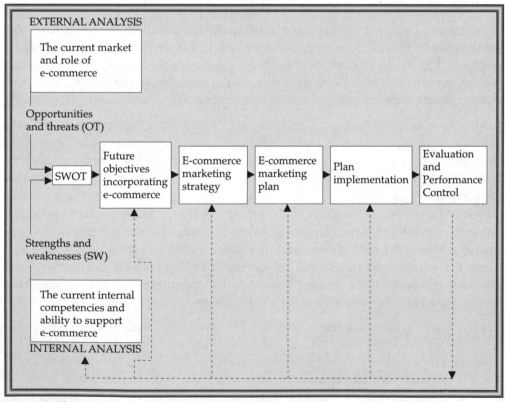

Figure 1.2   The e-commerce marketing strategy planning process

MANAGING IN AN E-COMMERCE WORLD

The next stage is for the organization to determine future objectives by assessing how e-commerce will affect performance. Performance targets are typically related to aims such as market share, total revenue, profitability and return on investment (ROI). These decisions are followed by the identification of the marketing strategy best able to fulfil the specified performance goals. The company can then define the nature of the activities—such as product, promotions, pricing and distribution—which form the basis of the e-commerce marketing plan. Following plan implementation, diagnostic control systems can be used to monitor actual versus planned performance and provide the data necessary to review the ongoing viability of the plan.

Fig. 1.2 presents a 'classicist' model of planning that has been a standard marketing tool for well over 30 years. Some may feel uncomfortable with this approach. They might argue that e-commerce planning is essentially an entrepreneurial philosophy, and that classicist planning models inhibit the manager seeking to identify the opportunities available from the technology. To support their position they might point to numerous examples of new e-commerce ventures in 'Silicon Valley', California that were launched, apparently without the founders paying too much attention to the development of a detailed business plan.

Despite the extensive support received by marketing planning as a business process over the years in the academic literature, Mintzberg (1994) has very eloquently argued that research based upon observation of actual managerial practices across both differing sectors and sizes of company has produced only limited evidence that convincingly demonstrates that structured planning is fundamental to contributing to the success of organizations. Furthermore, in his earlier study specifically concerned with the behaviour of entrepreneurs, Mintzberg and Waters (1982) concluded that in the case of the Canadian supermarket chain Steinberg Inc., since inception Sam Steinberg directed this highly entrepreneurial corporation without any apparent recourse to a formalized business planning process. When, however, the company decided that the future lay with the building of shopping centres, it was necessary to go to the capital markets to raise additional equity. At this juncture the company found that potential investors were not prepared to back the new initiative unless they could be provided with a detailed plan. Hence it was necessary for the company to appear to adopt a planning-oriented culture, although in reality this behaviour was only exhibited in order to satisfy the desires of potential new stakeholders.

Venture capitalists from as far apart as London, Silicon Valley and Auckland will confirm that many of the e-commerce entrepreneurs who they meet have rarely prepared any detailed information about their new business proposition prior to beginning their search for external funds. Hence the usual opening move in the funding application negotiations is to arrange for the preparation of a detailed marketing plan. Furthermore, the experience of these venture capitalists is that although their own organizations will use these plans to monitor the subsequent performance of their investment, their entrepreneurial partners can rarely be convinced of the benefit of using these plans to assist them in the day-to-day management of their businesses.

Migrosbank (www.migrosbank.ch/German)

The Migros Group is the biggest retailer in Switzerland, controlling 50 per cent of the retail market. It also operates Migrosbank, one the 10 largest retail banks in the country (Andersen Consulting 1999). As a bank, the company faced the long-term threat of needing to survive in the face of intense competition from larger banks. Its solution was to examine how e-commerce might be used both to attract new customers and generate new sales from existing customers. One of its discoveries was that customers wanted greater convenience of access to banking services. The company, therefore, developed the concept of mini-branches, containing a private office, an ATM machine and multimedia kiosks. Staff concentrate on resolving complex queries and building relationships with customers, while customers needing more routine, information-based services use e-commerce technology. When these customers enter the mini-branch they can use the touch screens on the kiosks to perform most basic money transactions. The outcome is an approach that offers greater flexibility (mini-branches can be moved if the choice of location proves inappropriate), scalability and enhanced speed of response to customer needs.

Another source of information on the very limited appeal of marketing planning amongst entrepreneurs is provided in the material documenting the development and launch of many of the world's most innovative projects. Thomas Edison appears to have had minimal awareness for the need for planning while developing the electric light-bulb. Frank Whittle, when working on his jet engine in the 1930s and 1940s, clearly had little interest in quantifying the commercial implications of his radical new approach to aircraft propulsion. Similarly it seems that Steven Jobs had few concerns about the need to develop detailed proposals for the future market opportunities for personal computers while working on the first Apple computer in his garage at his home in California.

In trying to persuade e-commerce entrepreneurs of the advantage of having a well documented marketing plan, possible benefits are:

1. It forces an assessment of the external environment.
2. It forces an assessment of the organization's internal competences.
3. It quantifies the expected performance goals for the new venture.
4. It identifies the scale of required resources and the degree to which these will have to be met through the attraction of external funds.
5. It creates a 'road map' that can be used to monitor actual performance against expectations at the launch of the venture.

Although such arguments will be accepted without question by a graduate of any business school, the reader should not be surprised to find that it will often be almost impossible to convince most entrepreneurial, e-commerce company founders of the merits of diverting themselves away from working on their 'big idea' to spend time writing a marketing plan. Nevertheless, on the basis of the author's experience, one can probably hope more easily to gain acceptance for the merits of planning in situations in which:

1. An e-commerce project is at the stage in the development life cycle where further progress cannot be made without significant external borrowings and/or equity capital.

2. An existing e-commerce enterprise has grown rapidly, managerial staff have been recruited (or employees promoted to managerial positions) and the entrepreneurial founder wishes to increasingly delegate downwards the company's 'future visioning' activities.

3. A company founder is engaged in succession planning and wishes to ensure their nominated replacement is capable of sustaining the company's entrepreneurial e-commerce vision.

4. A large company has established 'a new ventures e-commerce centre' to stimulate all employees to consider developing new entrepreneurial ideas and needs to ensure that individuals generating ideas are capable of presenting a detailed proposal to the venture centre staff for evaluation.

5. A large organization's external environment is undergoing rapid change due to the impact of e-commerce. In order to survive, the company needs to move away from an operating philosophy based upon current strategic practices towards one that promotes a high level of e-commerce orientation among all employees.

6. A diversified conglomerate with a mix of entrepreneurial and conservative operating divisions is seeking to determine how best to share financial resources between activities associated with new e-commerce projects and existing off-line operations.

For those managers who still feel uncomfortable with the linear, sequential appearance of the model shown in Fig. 1.2 it is important to recognize that in practice the entry point can be anywhere in the model. Hence an entrepreneur with an exciting new

Lloyd 1885

Lloyd 1885 is a subsidiary of RAS, a leading Italian insurance company owned by the German Allianz Group. The company operates in the low-cost sector of the car insurance market out of call centres based in Milan (Andersen Consulting 1988). The company's analysis of the market was that e-commerce offered a new route by which to reach a wider customer base operating as a 24-hour, 7-day-a-week service provider. The other attraction of e-commerce was that the concept supported a further reduction in transaction costs, which would allow the company to lower its prices. This vision was finalized in 1997 and within 12 months the company had established an interactive Internet site. The speed with which this move was implemented was greatly helped by the fact that the company had previously developed an automated policy quotation engine to support its tele-sales operation.

Marketing Before Technology

The following materials are an extract from an interview given to *Fortune* magazine (Adler 1999) by Larry Pearl and Sandeep Thakrar, who were involved in launching the first US on-line national grocery operation in the US, *www.netgrocer.com*. They now run their own consultancy business, Ecom Advisors (*www.ecomadvisors.com*).

1 Problem: unrealistic expectations

Too many firms expect their e-commerce operation to make money immediately. Even the most successful ideas will usually take some 12–24 months to reach profit.

2 Converting visits into sales

The first move is to generate visitors using links to other sites, **banner advertising** (*small advertisements embedded into Web pages*) on other sites and e-mails. To convert the visitor to a buyer in consumer goods markets, free samples will usually be required.

3 Advertising to build a customer base.

Most new sites will need to invest in advertising in traditional media channels such as magazines and radio to generate awareness of the site address. In the US, radio advertising seems to be the biggest area of expenditure by new consumer websites. Other effective media can be posters on static sites and public transport vehicles. Banner advertisements on other websites appear to be decreasingly effective in attracting visitors to new sites.

4 Affiliate programmes

Many websites are willing to participate in programmes whereby charges are made for links to other sites. For example, Amazon's logo can be placed on a site, directing visitors there to buy books. The source site receives 15 per cent commission from Amazon on every book sold as a result of the link.

5 To be avoided at all costs

Overall site management must be in the hands of people who understand marketing. Often websites fall into the hands of 'techies'; although they may be brilliant feats of software engineering, communication effectiveness is often badly impaired.

Source: Adler (1999)

product idea may select the 'planning the marketing mix' phase as an appropriate entry point. It is advisable, however, is that the individual then move back through the model checking issues such as the current market situation, organizational competences and potential market entry strategies. It is also necessary to highlight to all users of the model, whether or not they are comfortable with a classicist planning approach, that as they progress through the phases of the decision determination process they must expect to encounter new information that requires a re-assessment of the validity of earlier decisions. For example, capability assessment may reveal that the organization lacks certain critical competences, in which case it will be necessary to return to the entrepreneurial e-commerce idea assessment to generate an alternative concept more compatible with identified capabilities. To underline the fact that model users will have to repeat processes, Fig. 1.2 contains a feedback loop to show the importance of not becoming locked into a liner, sequential mind-set when developing entrepreneurial e-commerce plans. In addition, where limited information exists

Managing in an E-Commerce World

and/or there is the need to acquire a higher level of market experience prior to finalizing a detailed map, the company may decide to implement a small scale market entry in order to acquire a greater understanding of the actual e-commerce opportunity.

Whether a company implements a full scale plan or a limited market entry, speed is of the essence. Bicknell (2000) has noted that because e-business is a rapidly changing landscape, firms cannot afford to spend too much time deliberating over the best possible plan. He quotes Andy Hosbawm, the creative director of Agency.com, who believes that 'the largest companies' biggest problem is speed—they are too slow'. In some cases Bicknell believes market conditions are changing so rapidly that companies may have to revise totally their e-business plan every few months. One of the obstacles in this process can be senior and middle management. Their lack of understanding of e-commerce may mean that they fail to realize the importance of staying abreast of new technologies in order to incorporate them into an organization's e-commerce operations.

● Summary

The origins of the Internet can be found in a US defence industry project to communicate research data between scientists. The solution that was evolved for rapid electronic data exchange provided the basis upon which to develop the technologies that underpin the Internet. When companies began to use the Internet to create commercial websites some industry observers were not convinced that the technology provided a genuine commercial opportunity other than for 'techies' to market complex products and services. Over the last few years the convergence of telecommunications and computer technologies has resulted in electronic commerce (or e-commerce), now the fastest growing industrial sector within the world economy. Initially some management theorists saw e-commerce as a completely new way of doing business, one that totally demolished existing management paradigm. Analysis of actual commercial operations would suggest, however, that some existing management theories can be transferred into the world of e-commerce. This means that managers can use their previous experience to develop and implement e-commerce marketing strategies.

1 Review whether you feel e-commerce is a 'completely new way of doing business' or merely a dream of firms wanting to sell more computer technology.

2 How does e-commerce differ from existing, traditional ways of running a business?

3 How might e-commerce threaten firms not yet involved in cyberspace trading activities?

Guidance for undertaking e-commerce research and and generating information to supplement case materials

The Internet offers a very powerful tool through which to generate rapidly more information about e-commerce. It can of course be used to supplement the data provided in the case studies at the end of each chapter. Very useful sites for business news are *www.ft.com*, *www.fortune.com*, *www.usatoday.com* and *www.forbes.com*. All these sites offer free access to their on-line archive service.

If you want to find more magazines and newspaper Internet sites, then use a search engine on a site such as *www.yahoo.com* to locate these additional sources. Additionally, if you are currently studying for a qualification at a college, you will find that most college libraries offer free on-line access to search engines that will link you to a range of sources including many academic management journals.

Case: *An Unfulfilled Promise*

Sports History Ltd is a retail operation with a total of five outlets offering a range of sports memorabilia such as paintings, photographs, books, films and clothing. Annual sales are in the region of £15 million. The operation is a family-run business and the current Managing Director, Andrew Bolt, is the eldest son of the company's founder.

Last year Andrew attended a seminar organized by an advertising agency, Flyer Design, promoting the benefits of on-line trading. As none of his own staff had appropriate technical expertise, Andrew decided to hand the task of developing a Web presence to Flyer Design. This agency, working in collaboration with a small Internet service provider (ISP), goodshopping.com, agreed to jointly undertake the assignment of designing and establishing the Sports History website for a fee of £20 000. As Andrew explained, 'we were in their hands. The only conversation about website content focused on me being asked to identify 50 items that were easy to explain in words and pictures and easy to ship.' The agency then took photographs of these items and wrote some sales copy.

Once established, the website soon ran into trouble. Few people visited the site and those that did easily got lost. In addition, to place an order customers had to download an order form and then mail or fax this back to Sports History's head office. After some discussion, Flyer Design agreed at no charge to (1) improve the site design, (2) increase the number of featured items to 100 and (3) add a 'shopping basket' facility so that customers could place orders on-line.

Sports History pays goodshopping.com a fee of £20 a month for hosting the site. As time has gone on, Andrew has become somewhat concerned that the site still does not attract many visitors and is very inflexible in its ability to respond to Sports History's desire to make fundamental changes. For example, under the terms of the agreement, Sports History is limited, at any one time, to promoting only 100 of the company's over 5000 in-store items.

Sports History has not been advised to consider any form of off-line advertising to build site awareness. The company does, however, carry the site address on its letterhead, business cards and on in-store merchandising displays. No formal research has ever been undertaken into the nature of the socio-demographic profile of Sports History's off-line or on-line customers. Some of this latter group have contacted the company to ask whether it offers a mail-order catalogue service. The agency's advice was 'Why bother? The on-line store provides all the information that customers will ever need.'

QUESTIONS

1 **Prepare a report for Andrew Bolt outlining the possible mistakes made, both at the outset and during the operation of the e-commerce venture.**

2 **Prepare a report proposing possible courses of action that might turn this sad story into an on-line trading success.**

(In preparing your answers you might gain some additional insights on e-retailing by visiting various sites that offer guidance and software tools to the retail industry. Example sites include **www.boomerangsoftware.com**, **www.imagecafe.com**, **www.vstore.com**, **www.bigstep.com**, **www.earthlink.com**, **www.econgo.com**, **www.macromedia.com**, **www.business.mindspring.com** *and* **www.buyitonline.com**.*)*

Case: *Planning with the Vortex Model*

J.W. Gurley is a partner in a venture capital company. Based on extensive experience of successful e-commerce launches, he has concluded that the most successful new website propositions fulfil his criteria of being 'vortex businesses'. His vortex model has four characteristics.

Firstly, site content should be competitive with the leading trade magazines in the sector. Secondly, the website design must reflect extensive understanding of the information a customer would use to reach a purchase decision. Thirdly, there must be an understanding of the flow of goods or services within an industrial sector (for example how goods are ordered; how goods are delivered; whether products can be customized) and a willingness to take physical ownership of the goods to be marketed via the website. Lastly, the website must be used to collect and distribute sector information by creating chat-rooms, bulletin boards and surveys that permit customers to comment on product quality.

Source: Gurley (1998)

QUESTIONS

1   Between accountants, dentists, lawyers, dog breeders, funeral services and sporting goods select one category that you think would make a good vortex business. Prepare a report justifying your selection.

2   Between accountants, dentists, lawyers, dog breeders, funeral services and sporting goods select one category that you feel would NOT make a good vortex business. Prepare a report justifying your selection.

Chapter 1 Glossary

Applications services market (p. 6)

A market in which expensive, complex software is located on a remote computer server and users, instead of installing the software themselves, access the server and pay a usage fee when running these expensive programmes.

Banner advertising (p. 16)

Small advertisements embedded into Web pages.

Business-to-business markets (p. 4)

Markets in which companies trade with each other rather than with consumers.

Economies of scale (p. 11)

The reduction in operating costs that occur as a company becomes larger.

Electronic data interchange, or EDI (p. 6)

A pre-Internet concept that uses specially developed computer software permitting companies to exchange electronically large volumes of data between their respective computers.

On-line auctions (p. 7)

Websites where people can bid on-line for products and services featured on the site.

On-line only operations (p. 3)

Organizations with no premises for customers to visit.

Smart cards (p. 6)

Plastic cards that contain a microchip on which information is stored electronically, and can be used, for example, to pay for travel on public transport without the need to carry money, or to store a person's medical records.

Supply chain (p. 7)

The description applied to all of the members of a system in which raw materials are acquired and products manufactured, distributed and sold to the final customer.

TCP/IP (p. 2)

A computer operating protocol that enables different machines using different operating languages to communicate with each other.

Vertical integration (p. 11)

When a company becomes involved in operations either upstream or downstream from itself in its supply chain.

Chapter 2

E-BUYER BEHAVIOUR

The dominant influence in the literature about US consumer goods marketing has led many marketers to be oriented towards a concentration on management of the **four Ps** (*the variables of product, price, promotion and place*) to optimize organizational performance. Implicit in this approach is the idea that buyers are passive, and only react to seller stimuli by purchasing or not purchasing. The seller is seen as the active manager of process and furthermore the relationship is posited as one in which the seller interacts with a generic market rather than individual customers (Ford 1990).

An unfortunate outcome of this is that buyer behaviour as a marketing discipline has paralleled developments in strategic marketing management theories without much interaction. The danger of this situation is that e-marketers may fail to appreciate the importance of understanding the buyer during the creation of appropriate e-commerce strategies and evolving effective e-marketing plans.

This conclusion is reinforced by the views expressed by Engel et al. (1986). They, in commenting on consumer marketing, propose that 'marketing starts with the analysis of consumer behaviour which are those acts of individuals directly involved in obtaining, using, and disposing of economic goods and services, including the decision processes that precede and determine these acts'. These authors also state that 'understanding consumer motivation and behaviour is not an option—it is an absolute necessity for competitive survival'. Although such views were being expressed before the electronic era, they have now become critical because acceptance of the proactive role of the customer is fundamental during the development of e-commerce marketing strategies: customers decide which websites to visit and the nature of the information they want in deciding what to buy.

Spar and Bussgang (1996) have identified another factor of e-commerce that is also altering consumer behaviour. Under the classical trading rules of **mass marketing** (*making available a standard product to the market*), the marketer tends to consider consumers as anonymous, poorly informed and not empowered. As consumers begin to interact electronically with each other, virtual communities form within which individuals who have experienced better or worse offers are pleased to share this knowledge with each other. Having recognized this trend, some electronic intermediaries are now creating sites where the visitor can rapidly compare product offerings from a vast range of alternative suppliers. The implication of such trends is that now more than ever the marketer must develop a detailed understanding of customer behaviour as a critical antecedent in the development of an effective e-commerce marketing strategy.

● Modelling Consumer Buying Behaviour

Over the years academics and market researchers have developed a vast array of techniques for studying customer behaviour. These range from simple attitude and usage studies through to the development of complex multivariate equations that define the relationship between sales and all of the variables within the marketing mix. Possibly one of the most powerful tools available to the researcher is observation of all phases of the purchase process from need identification to post-purchase evaluation as the basis for constructing flow models of the buyer behaviour process. Such models can provide the e-marketer with:

1   An explanation of all of the underlying variables that might influence the customer's product usage patterns.

2   An understanding of how the customer acquires the information used in reaching a purchase decision.

3   A frame of reference within which to build a more effective e-commerce marketing plan.

4   Knowledge of the information that should be used by the organization to track customer purchase patterns and assess the effectiveness of the organization's e-commerce marketing activities.

One way of approaching the modelling process is to assume that buyer behaviour can be divided into five distinct phases. As shown in Fig. 2.1, these are recognition of need, search for information, evaluation of alternatives, the purchase decision and post-purchase evaluation. For the e-marketer, the objective is to determine the degree to which electronic platforms might be used to move the customer successfully through all five phases of the purchase process.

For the customer, the entry point into the purchase process is need recognition. This can result from either internal (for example hunger or thirst) or external (for example observing the latest model of car in a dealer's showroom) stimuli. Until need recognition has occurred, the potential customer will not invoke any of the later steps in the purchase process. This is one of the reasons that many e-commerce companies

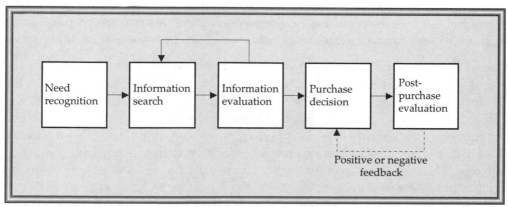

Figure 2.1   *A five-phase customer purchase process*

are now having to spend vast sums of money on conventional forms of promotion. For example, an e-commerce life insurance intermediary may establish an extremely powerful website that permits clients rapidly to select the best policy for them from a wide range of competitive offerings. Yet until the potential customer has (1) decided that he or she needs a new policy and (2) accepted e-commerce as a platform through which to make this purchase, the site will be of no benefit to the company. Hence it is extremely probable that having created the website the company will need to concurrently implement a promotional programme involving activities such as TV advertising or a direct mail campaign.

Once the customer enters the information search phase, the e-marketer must determine whether all the information that is required can be delivered through electronic technology. Clearly the ultimate objective is to ensure that customers are totally satisfied with the information available on the supplier's electronic platform, and that after completing their data search will move onto evaluating the information provided. One of the best known examples of this approach is an early entrant into e-marketing, the on-line bookstore Amazon. Visitors to the site are offered a powerful search engine, links between titles covering similar topics, book reviews from the top literary magazines, and in many cases the frank opinions of other customers who have already bought a given book.

The degree to which potential customers are prepared to use electronic platforms to acquire information will have significant impact on a company's marketing budget. In the early years of the Internet, customer user profiles tended to be limited to young 'techies' familiar with the technology through exposure to it in the workplace. They were followed by customers with graduate-level education who lived in urban areas and had up-market occupations. In his analysis of customer profiles in the US market, Judge (1988) identified heavy users from groups such as (1) the 'Fast Forwards', early adopters of new technology for both office and home use, and (2) the 'Techno-Strivers', those already exploiting technology such as cell phones, pagers and other on-line services to gain a career edge.

It is also not surprising to find that usage patterns vary across the world. Garton's (1999) study of world markets, for example, shows that the US contains the world's largest group of Internet users. Canada is ranked second with 38 per cent of the population on-line. In most countries, however, the Internet remains predominantly male, with heavy users drawn from the management and white-collar strata of society.

One of the current major usage constraints in consumer markets has been in-home access to a PC. This situation is, however, on the brink of rapid change. For with the advent of digital TV even the most 'technophobic couch potato' can shop electronically using the handset that until now merely functioned for switching channels and programming the family's VCR. It is perhaps interesting to discover that it was not Silicon Valley that first appreciated the potential market impact of digital TV. For as noted by Weinberg (1996), while Oracle's Lawrence Ellison was preaching about the need to build low cost Internet terminals, the Japanese, with an uncanny ability to understand future trends in entertainment technology, were already beginning to build

Kids On-Line

One section of society which is already computer literate and experienced in the use of the Internet is children. In the US alone it is estimated that 22.4 million children in the 2–18 age group use the Internet. One of their favourite activities is game playing (anon. 2000). Hence it is not surprising to find that in recognition of this toy makers such as Hasbro and video-game companies such as Sony have established Web portals offering on-line games. The latter companies are very aware of the attraction of offering children the opportunity to game with on-line opponents. A recent Sega machine has a 56K modem to link players via the Internet. Sony's Playstation 2 offers the user the facility of connecting to broadband providers such as the US cable TV companies.

Lycos, a major force in adult on-line gaming, is now also seeking to build market share in the 3–12 year age group. Its strategy is to generate revenue from advertisers using the site. Given growing concerns amongst parents about protection of children on the Internet, Lycos ensures that all commercial messages are clearly marked 'ad'. Additionally, the company does not ask children to register on its site and will not provide advertisers with profiles of website visitors.

Dallas-based Radica Games, a small toy maker with only $134 million annual sales has launched a range of hand-held game controls which link the user to the company's website. This site lets users download free games, puzzles and e-mail. The company has decided against charging a subscription for site access. Instead the company's strategy is that the sale of the hand-held devices will be the main source of revenue. This can be contrasted with Electronic Arts, which charges users a monthly subscription. For example it charges $9.99 per month for access to Ultima, its most successful gaming product.

As a more traditional toy company, Hasbro has been late into the world of on-line gaming. The company launched its site in June 2000. Revenue is planned from a range of sources, including the sale of advertising space, monthly subscriptions for on-line gaming, and an on-line shop offering CD-ROMs, video games and other merchandise.

TV sets that could be used by consumers to enter the world of electronic shopping. Hence with the US leading the world in personal computers and the Japanese dominating the manufacture of electronic entertainment systems, it will be interesting to see who will be the eventual winner in this race to bring the Web to the world's mass consumer markets.

For the consumer, the acquisition and evaluation of information was a very time-consuming process in a pre-electronic world. The consumer had to visit different shops, review a variety of brochures or talk to a number of sales people. The advent of e-commerce has dramatically altered the information evaluation phase of the purchase process. Now at the click of a button, from the comfort of home, the consumer can have access to a seemingly infinite amount of data with which to assess the relative merits of product and service propositions. Customers can go to websites that offer unbiased opinions on these relative merits. Armed with such knowledge, the customer in an e-commerce world is often now in a much stronger position to persuade suppliers to make goods available on more favourable terms.

Although initially many consumers were suspicious about the security aspects of the Internet, this attitude is changing, and most are now willing to purchase on-line. Nevertheless a new potential obstacle to the expansion of consumer use of the Internet is the growing concern that some companies are collecting website user information that might be considered an invasion of privacy (anon. 1999). This is because companies are analysing their user databases to evolve digital dossiers about the product search and purchasing behaviour of website visitors. In 1998 concerns about privacy in the US resulted in legislation being passed regulating the use of the Internet to market products to children. Currently the Federal Trade Commission is examining the issue of whether legislation may be required to protect consumers from using customer profiling technology. Already the privacy lobby in the US has been able to persuade the Intel Corporation to disable an identification number on its Pentium III processor that let companies track consumers on the Internet.

For the supplier, a key attraction of persuading customers to accept on-line transactions is the massive reduction in operating costs. For example, in the case of financial services, one UK industry observer has estimated that a transaction costs 65p in a branch, 32p on the telephone and 3p on the Internet. For the customer the advantage of on-line purchasing is speed. Anybody who wants to demonstrate this has only to compare using the Internet or e-mail to purchase an airline ticket with the alternative options of visiting a travel agent or waiting for the airline reservations department to answer the telephone. Nevertheless, even in the world of direct marketing, where the consumer is happy to make a purchase without ever visiting a retail outlet, there still remains a strong preference for having some degree of human contact with the supplier. As a result, even pioneering direct marketing firms such as the US clothing group Lands' End (*www.landsend.com*) early into Internet use, still rely on a tele-sales operation to manage customer ordering.

In a recent review of trends in direct marketing, Booth (1999) has concluded that for the foreseeable future the telephone will remain the platform of choice for managing complex requests or to answer questions that are not easily resolved using website-based enquiry systems. However, the current trend among many service providers is to offer a variety of platforms to handle customer responses, including mail, fax, e-mail and a web presence. In many cases the heart of these integrated communications systems is a telephone call centre that orchestrates and co-ordinates all aspects of customer service as individuals progress through the purchase decision process. To optimize the operation of such centres, increasingly firms must provide technology which permits activities such as **Internet call back** (*the customer uses the website to request a telephone call from the company*), **Internet chat** (*an instant interactive written exchange with the supplier*), **Voice over net** (*an audio conversation while the customer is using a website*) and **Video over net** (*a videoconference with a member of the supplier's staff*).

While progressing through the early stages of the purchase decision process, the consumer will be forming expectations about the quality and performance of the goods or service being purchased. These expectations are then tested against actual experience in the post-purchase evaluation phase. For all firms, whether or not they are involved in e-commerce, there is little point in ensuring that all phases of the purchase decision process are effectively managed only to disappoint the customer at the consumption stage. Thus all of the conventional techniques which marketers have evolved over the years to ensure post-purchase satisfaction—such as timely delivery, performance to specification, and the provision of adequate post-purchase service quality—are just as applicable in an e-commerce world.

In presenting a product purchase process model of the type shown in Fig. 2.1 it must be understood that the model is based upon the assumption that the customer is acting rationally and makes systematic use of available information. Some academics, however, have expressed concerns about the validity of using buyer behaviour models to assist the marketing process. East (1990), for example, holds the view that the models are of little use because the relationships between variables are often poorly specified and therefore cannot be tested. He also argues that the actual sequence of decision-making in the real world may be different from the one assumed, and that problem-solving is probably better explained as 'a series of associations of thought and feeling, rather than as a logical inference.'

Clearly all such criticisms are partly valid, and certainly in the case of purchase decisions involving a series of feelings, the 'buyer modelling' school of thought would totally accept that other research techniques would be needed for insights to be gained into those factors which are key influencers of behaviour. For example, SRI Consulting have undertaken an in-depth study of attitudes, preferences and behaviour of on-line services and Internet users. From this they have evolved a multi-segment categorization of consumers, using classifications such as **wizards** (*people who have complete mastery of the technology*) and **immigrants** (*people who are recent arrivals in cyberspace, only using the technology because they have been forced to by very specific circumstances at work*).

In view of these types of comment, it is apparent that the e-commerce purchase process model builder does need to recognize that during research of the market attention should be given to how the factors of involvement, **differentiation** (*the creation of clear difference between a company's product and competition*) and time pressure may influence customer behaviour. Munch and Hunt (1984) propose that 'involvement is the level of perceived personal importance and/or interest evoked by a stimulus (or stimuli) within a specific situation'. From this definition it can be concluded that in cases of low involvement purchases (for example the decision to order a sandwich from a sandwich bar by fax) the customer rapidly progresses through the problem-solving model in Fig. 2.1. Over time, however, the repeated use of the sandwich bar will evoke memory patterns that create feelings that may ultimately influence future purchase patterns. This scenario, however, does not invalidate logical problem-solving models; it merely suggests that in reviewing possible future marketing programmes, in some cases the e-marketer should use intuitive common sense rather than a customer purchase behaviour model.

In relation to the issue of differentiation, when the customer perceives that available alternatives offer a wide array of different benefits, the potential buyer is likely to

Customer Profiling

The huge number of visitors to an Internet site provides a data-set that can be analysed to identify segments of common behaviour (McHugh 2000). A US company, Engage Technologies, has built a database of customer preferences based upon an analysis of over 42 million Web users. This information has been generated by monitoring over 900 websites on which the company is contracted to provide market research data. Engage's acquired knowledge is now used by its clients to classify new site visitors into one of the 800 customer behaviour profile categories in the statistical model. The profiles provide the website with guidance on products that the new visitor is likely to buy over the Internet. For example, the website Flycast uses the profiles to display banner advertisements about products which will probably be of greatest interest to a site visitor. Another provider of visitor analysis tools is Younology. Their system is based around the application of artificial intelligence algorithms to model probable behaviour patterns among on-line shoppers. The behaviour model is linked to a software system capable of helping websites to tailor their pages to the tastes and tendencies of each site visitor.

undertake both an extensive information search and spend time in the evaluation of alternatives. Where there are no real differences between offerings, however, the customer is most likely to use a single factor, such as convenience, in reaching a decision. For example, a traveller is likely to opt for an airline which departs from the local airport rather than one flying from further afield.

A customer under extreme time pressure is unlikely to embark on an actively reasoned decision process. For example, someone who suddenly has to visit a strange city because a relative is sick will probably select the first hotel that appears on the website, not bothering with a detailed search of other accommodation. Hence some of the views expressed by the anti-modelling fraternity are valid. However, in those cases where the customer is (1) considering a high involvement product category, (2) can differentiate between alternative offerings and (3) is not facing extreme time pressure, then it does seem reasonable to suggest that the e-marketer can obtain valuable insights by examining the rational problem-solving process at work in both existing and potential customers.

● Modelling Customer Satisfaction

In order for the customer to progress through the phases of information search, evaluation and purchase described in Fig. 2.1, he or she must experience satisfaction. Furthermore, a customer who is to become a loyal user must also experience satisfaction during the post-purchase evaluation phase. Thus to manage successfully the purchase process the e-marketer will need to develop an in-depth understanding of the factors that contribute to customer satisfaction.

One way of acquiring such knowledge is to draw upon the customer satisfaction model developed and validated by Kristensen et al. (1999). As can be seen from Fig. 2.2, these authors suggest that four key factors are fundamental determinants of influence. They are the existing product or company image, customer expectations, perceptions of the product or service's benefit, and perceptions of service quality. The combined influence of these factors causes the customer to reach conclusions about both perceived 'value for money' and, ultimately, overall level of satisfaction.

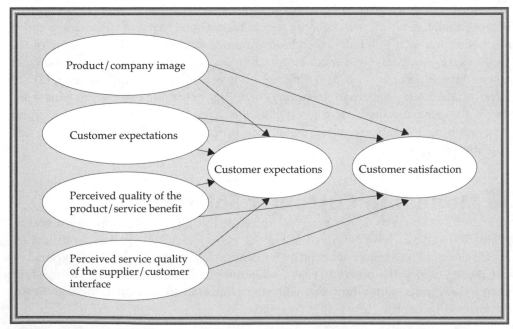

Figure 2.2   Factors determining customer satisfaction (modified from Kristensen et al. 1999)

It is important to note that the degree to which each variable contributes to satisfaction will vary by product type and market sector. For example, customers in an up-market fashion goods sector will probably place greatest emphasis on image and service. In contrast, for a low income household purchasing children's clothes the factor dominating satisfaction will probably be perceived product value. Even in this latter scenario, however, the e-commerce supplier should not just hope that competitive price will dominate the satisfaction process, because there is growing evidence of the need to pay attention to product image. The reason for this is that it appears that consumers rely heavily on the reassurance provided by a known brand when shopping on the Internet. This is demonstrated by the fact when one examines visitor patterns, excluding browser sites such as ***www.netscape.com*** or ***www.yahoo com***, the sites which enjoy very high visitor rates are companies like Sony, Disney and Time Warner, namely those brand names already well established in their respective non-electronic markets (anon. 1998a).

Come Fly with Me

An added complication for e-commerce firms is that customers are so used to technology simplifying their life that they can have high expectations that on-line purchasing will be a smooth and seamless process. Hence when things wrong, as of course they must with virtually any new technology, the outcome is a very dissatisfied customer. Mardesich (1999) provides an example of this. A customer was attracted to the United Airlines website (***www.ual.com***) by the offer of heavily discounted fares purchased one day before departure. The problem she encountered, however, was that 'the site didn't seem to want to sell me the tickets'. Each time she attempted to enter her name, the site refused the data. Eventually she succeeded, but by now was in such a state that she mistakenly selected an a.m. instead of a p.m. departure. The system did not allow her to rectify her error, and she had to telephone a local company to which United outsources Web support. She was then informed that the United computer would automatically charge her an additional $75 to change the booking. It was only after many hours on the telephone that she managed to get this decision revoked. Having eventually arrived at the airport, she discovered the computer had not entered her frequent flier number and hence she would not qualify for any air miles. This was despite the fact that to purchase the ticket on-line she had had to enter her frequent-flier number.

For the e-commerce marketer, the lesson to be learned from that example—which of course in this case was communicated to thousands of *Fortune* readers—is that customer satisfaction is only achievable if the back office technology fulfils the purpose for which it was designed. All too often, however, design and day-to-day operations tend to be in the hands of 'techies'. These individuals do not always appreciate that greater priority should be given to achieving user friendliness than to fulfilling personal aspirations to use the latest available technology to remove human contact from all aspects of the purchase transaction process.

● Building Trust

A commonly expressed concern about e-commerce, especially in consumer markets, is the potential security risk of revealing to a supplier personal information such as e-mail addresses and credit card information. Linked to these concerns over privacy are worries over whether the supplier is a legitimate enterprise and how e-contracts can be enforced if there is dissatisfaction with goods or services. Even large corporations have learned to be wary because, through bitter experience, many have found that databases can be invaded by hackers and sensitive information can be intercepted by unscrupulous competitors (Sterret and Shah 1998). In some ways these concerns are paradoxical because the same people are apparently much less concerned about using the telephone to communicate the same information, not realizing that the same security risks apply.

Nevertheless it is very apparent that successful exploitation of e-commerce does demand that firms give top priority to preserving data security for customers. Most systems now support the industry standard SSL (secure socket layer) protocol (Browning 1999). This protocol encrypts every message on a network making it extremely difficult for anyone intercepting the message to unscramble the data. As hackers are always attracted by any new technological challenge, new encryption systems are rapidly being made available which are so complicated that only an extremely large super-computer can break the code, and only after many hours of data analysis.

Mere assurances that the latest encryption technology is being used will not usually be sufficient unless an organization can also demonstrate reliability and integrity, as these are the basis of trust between supplier and customer. In discussing the factors influencing the formation of effective customer–supplier relationships, Hunt and Morgan (1994) posit that there are five precursor variables influencing commitment

Good Promotional Idea or a Potential Invasion of Privacy?

Under their 'draft-a-friend' programme, Fogdog Sports (*www.fogdog.com*) ask their customers to supply the company with the e-mail addresses of up to 25 friends (Olsen 2000). The company sends these people a $10 coupon and the supplier of the name receives a 25 per cent discount on their next purchase. Such schemes are becoming increasingly standard practice for on-line retailers seeking to build customer lists. It must be recognized, however, that the outcome of this type of promotional offer is a great number of unsolicited e-mails.

On-line firms defend this practice on the grounds that the promotion is offering savings to the consumer. Most also claim that if they receive no response from an e-mail address they do not mail the person again. On the other hand, some industry observers suspect that unsolicited e-mails are as dangerous as unsolicited junk-mail (that unrequested e-mails may cause the recipient to form a poor impression of the sending on-line retailer.)

and trust: relationship termination costs, relationship benefits, shared values, effective communication and the avoidance of opportunistic behaviour.

The assumption over termination costs is that where these are high all parties will try to overcome differences of opinion because both wish to avoid the economic impact of severing the relationship. Thus in industrial markets where changing suppliers may involve a significant investment in re-tooling costs, both parties will probably attempt to resolve differences. The same will rarely be true in consumer e-commerce markets, where in most cases at the click of a button, the customer can instantly change their **purchase loyalty** (*the commitment of the customer to continue buying from a specific supplier*).

The mutual benefit requirement is probably applicable in any type of e-commerce scenario. Clearly the customer must perceive advantage in purchasing from a selected source, and in turn the supplier must believe it is gaining commercially if it is to continue with the relationship. Pricing behaviour will only be an effective contributor to the building of trust if both parties perceive real benefits from supply stability and are willing to forgo short-term opportunistic behaviour. This will only occur if both parties have accepted that price-driven opportunistic behaviour is unacceptable because they are seeking to develop a relationship based upon mutual trust and commitment. Thus, for example, the computer manufacturer that has habitually used the Internet to 'shop around' for the best price deals when microchips have been in plentiful supply should not be surprised if it has real problems procuring components during periods of supply shortage.

The role of communication in the customer–supplier relationship is to ensure that both parties keep the other informed of events that might disrupt the flow of goods or services through the supply chain. As suggested by Mohr and Nevin (1990), 'communication can be described as the glue that holds together a channel of distribution'. Thus if the e-commerce marketer keeps customers fully informed of all

Internet-Based Procurement

Intelysis Electronic Commerce (*www.intelysis.com*) a provider of Internet-based procurement solutions, has recently announced that it will work with the Ford Motor Company to build a $16 billion system for the procurement of non-production goods. Ford are making this investment because it will (1) provide a low cost, streamlined purchasing method that reduces waste, paperwork, time and labour, and (2) deliver a 'just-in-time' procurement philosophy that will dramatically reduce the company's supply chain costs (Friel 1999). The potential to make savings through e-based purchasing systems is further evidenced in data supplied by Cisco Systems (*www.cisco.com*). In 1997 the company saved more than $360 million from Web-based transactions. Of these savings, about 33 per cent came from not using traditional, non-electronic sales and service structures, 23 per cent from software distribution and 44 per cent from replacing paper communications with e-mail (anon. 1998b).

National Semiconductors

An example of using knowledge of customer behaviour in the design of an e-commerce system to improve customer service and reduce transaction costs is provided by National Semiconductors (Seybold and Marshak 1998). A review of the existing purchasing process revealed that the people with the greatest influence over actual purchasing decisions are design engineers. The traditional approach of these individuals when developing new or improved products is to consult parts catalogues and data sheets supplied by component manufacturers. Having selected a potential component, the design engineer then talks with the manufacturer's representative and if satisfied with the information received will order samples. By discussing this process with design engineers, the National Semiconductor development team found that these customers did not want a website offering attractive graphics or the ability to download extensive data sheets, but a search engine which rapidly located the product of interest, permitted on-line scanning of a data sheet abstract (with in some cases the ability to download this information) and a system for rapidly and easily ordering samples.

Having created the system, National Semiconductors have continually monitored usage to determine how knowledge of customer behaviour might be used to further enhance site usage. When the site first went live in 1995, the average customer usually 'hit' between seven and eight pages during the search for relevant data. By 1997, site re-design had reduced this hit rate to 2.5 pages per site visit. Once the company had used its e-commerce system to cement a stronger relationship with design engineers, it then embarked on further evolution of the technology to assist purchasing agents and buyers. These latter individuals usually become involved in the procurement process once a new part has been approved for incorporation into a product. They are interested in the supplier's on-hand inventories, and want to be able to monitor the on-time delivery of ordered components. In 1998, system capability was further upgraded to meet the needs of the company's distributors and component resellers. This was achieved by the launch of BizQuote, a front end that permits automated product configuration, price quotes and order placement using the Internet. It is estimated this system will save customers over $20 million per year by reducing the costs of checking stock and placing orders.

and any problems as these arise, it is much more likely that customers will be forgiving and not switch purchase loyalty. A powerful feature of e-commerce systems is that it is relatively simple to link **transaction engines** (*the in-company software systems that manage the customer order placement, order picking, invoice and shipping activities*) to an e-mail system that automatically keeps customers aware of all events associated with product offerings, price changes and any problems that may have arisen in the delivery cycle of the purchase transaction.

As noted by Kreps (1996), one of the most effective ways of building trust is to exhibit trustworthiness. This can be achieved by being prepared not to adhere rigidly to

Favourites

pre-defined corporate policies, but instead to be willing to respond flexibly to unexpected market contingencies. He points out, however, that a subtle difference exists between having a good reputation and being trusted. Reputation will often be based upon being known to act consistently, whereas trust is only generated by action that is in the best interests of the customer. In the face of this critical difference, it is necessary for the marketer to realize that automated e-commerce operations often lack the ability to handle unforeseen contingencies because the required response has not been programmed into the system. Take, for example, the fact that even today not all websites provide a telephone number, an address or an e-mail facility which the customer can use when he or she has made an error placing an on-line order. Clearly the customer with a choice of where to buy will tend to favour those sites that make contact with the company easy. This of course does assume that unlike the United Airlines example quoted above, the e-commerce operation has empowered the human point of contact with the ability immediately to correct the problem and not, as so often is the case, respond with, 'I'm sorry but I can't override the computer; you will have to telephone the customer services department because only they can handle this sort of complaint'.

Seeking Security

Concerns over computer system security have existed for years (Kover and Warner 1999). Back in 1994, for example, US Citibank (*www.citicorp.com*) discovered that a group of Russian hackers had made off with $10 million in illegal transfers. In this case, using the services of a private security company, all but $400 000 was recovered. Of course these examples mean that many companies, when considering the Internet for business-to-business marketing, and attracted by the ability to link customers with suppliers, are often daunted by the scale of the new security risks created.

Wind River Systems a software company in Alameda, California created an Internet site to exchange e-mails with their customers. Unfortunately some German hackers found a way into the system and used the opportunity to access computer databases in both France and the US. With financial losses from computer crime estimated at $10 billion a year, not surprisingly, one of the fastest growing sectors of business-to-business e-commerce is the provision of computer security systems. One beneficiary of this is the Californian company Pilot Test Network Services, which offers companies links to the Internet through one of its service centres. As well as a dynamic five-layer firewall to protect data, Pilot also operates a 24-hour-a-day human monitoring system. Specialist staff are alerted to attempted security attacks by automated alarm systems. They then act to block any attempted entry by the attacker and where possible move to identify the source of the attack.

● Business-to-Business Buyer Behaviour

Despite the extensive publicity given to growing interest in on-line shopping among the world's consumers, currently a much larger proportion of actual on-line transactions are in business-to-business markets. One reason for this is that prior to the advent of the Internet many large manufacturing companies had already automated many of their procurement, production and distribution processes using a technology known as EDI (electronic data exchange). Hence it has been a relatively small conceptual jump to incorporate e-commerce platforms into existing operations.

In seeking to introduce e-commerce transaction systems into new business-to-business markets, the marketer faces the major complication that more than one individual from the buyer organization may become involved in the purchase decision process. Additionally, the demanded level of data interchange will be of a high magnitude. Hence it seems reasonable to propose that modelling customer purchase behaviour is even more critical than in an equivalent consumer market.

One of the earliest attempts at modelling business-to-business markets was undertaken by Webster (1963). He proposes stage process models to describe the purchase process in industrial sectors. Robinson et al. (1967) have also used a similar approach, but suggested an extended form of the basic five phase model based upon an eight step decision process called 'buyphase'. This consists of the following phases:

1. Anticipation/recognition of need and probable solution.

2. Determining the characteristics of the required product/service.

3. Defining the quantity to be procured.

4. Searching and qualifying potential sources.

5. Requesting proposals from potential providers.

6. Evaluating submitted proposal and selection of appropriate source(s).

7. Implementing the formal purchase process.

8. Using post-purchase usage experience to provide feedback for utilization when seeking to place possible future, repeat purchase, orders.

Subsequently Webster and Wind (1972) introduced the concept of risk management within industrial markets. They propose that the purchaser acts to reduced perceived risk using mechanisms which might include (1) the acquisition of additional information from suppliers (for example by requesting the submission of detailed bid documents) and other industry sources such the sector's trade association, (2) extension in the breadth and duration of the information evaluation phase (for example defence contracts negotiations between governments and aerospace suppliers may take between two and three years, and (3) 'source loyalty' (that is favouring suppliers with whom the buyer already has an existing relationship).

One of the primary catalysts for firms moving into e-commerce in business-to-business markets is the recognition that purchasing can provide the basis for achieving competitive advantage. By the mid-1980s, most leading companies had realized that they and their competitors in an industrial sector used very similar management techniques across all areas of operations. For example, all purchased the same components, operated the same machinery in their manufacturing processes, offered products with very similar performance specifications. Thus identifying opportunities for differentiating their offering in the marketplace had become extremely difficult. At this juncture, some of the more far-sighted began to realize that the buyer behaviour process model might provide new sources of competitive advantage. This prompted a massive interest in seeking ways of building efficient, integrated supply chains. However, realization of the theoretical benefits of automated systems—which reduce inventories and permit rapid, flexible response to changing market demand—have often only been realized since the arrival of e-commerce technology (Werner 1999).

● Summary

The tendency of classicist strategic marketing management thinking is to ignore the role of the customer in the purchase process. The buyer behaviour school of marketing theory have for many years argued that understanding customer behaviour should be the foundation upon which all marketing activities are based. As e-commerce represents a very different environment for the customer in most consumer goods markets, probably the importance of understanding on-line behaviour will be critical in the effective implementation of Web-based marketing. Evidence would suggest that existing consumer buyer behaviour models—which ensure effective information flows as the customer moves from search to purchase—can be also be utilized in e-trading consumer markets. Special recognition will have to be given, however, to sustaining customer satisfaction in an environment in which purchase processes have been automated and little opportunity exists for human intervention by the supplier when the customer encounters problems in the transaction process. The newness of Web-based trading also demands careful attention to the building of trust as the basis for long-term relationships. The same principles can also be applied in business-to-business markets. In this case a possible approach is to utilize the well proven business-to-business buyphase model.

1 How can an understanding of consumer buying behaviour assist a company to ensure that it is using the Internet effectively to influence potential and existing customers?

2 How could a company ensure that its e-commerce operation leads its customers to trust the company completely?

3 How can an understanding of the buyphase model in an industrial market help a company to ensure that it is using the Internet effectively to influence their potential and existing customers?

Case: *A Move into E-Commerce Trading*

An ongoing problem in the world of computing is that modern software packages are very demanding of memory. As a result there are a number of companies specializing in the development and manufacture of memory upgrade chips for the PC market. One of these is Dart Technology, a leader in memory level enhancement. Its products are premium priced. Additionally, a large proportion of sales are of chips customized for purchasers involved in very complex technological upgrades. The majority of customers are major PC distributors, systems design consultancy practices and large organizations with their own IT installation and operations departments.

Sales are generated by a sales force, which calls on major national account customers and a tele-sales operation. The telephone staff have the technical competence to handle customer questions about chip selection and how customization might meet a customer's needs.

The combined influence of continuing sales growth and rising operating costs has caused the company to consider whether it could move the entire sales operation onto the Internet. One concern, however, is whether an e-commerce interface would ensure retention of customer trust. The Head of Marketing's answer is that the company simply needs legally binding agreements between itself and its customers. To support his perspective he points to an existing US on-line operation, the Automotive Network Exchange, which is used by car companies to purchase components. All members are required to sign legally binding trading agreements, and where there are disputes, the internet service provider

(ISP), Telcordia Technologies, accepts the responsibility for investigation and, where required, independent arbitration.

Source: Hicks (1999)

The Head of Sales, however, sees this is a somewhat simplistic assessment of the issues associated with the management of trust in an e-commerce environment. In support of his case, he circulates the following memorandum to the senior management team:

> Within the core of a buyer–seller interaction model, variables such as technology, strategy and individual employee behaviour can all contribute towards influencing development of trust. Thus, for example, where the purchase involves complex technology, then the supplier will have to expend effort exhibiting organizational attributes capable of demonstrating their desire to establish a relationship which is founded upon mutual trust and commitment. Typically this will only be achieved if the seller's employees' behaviours are consistent with the long-term relationship formation objective (for example spending time explaining why a specific recommendation is being made and being very open about the strengths and weaknesses of product offering by other suppliers operating in the same market sector). Additionally it is necessary for the supplier to realize that their market system will contain variables which can also influence the level of trust in the buyer–seller relationship. Examples include market structure (for example the degree of supplier choice available to the customer), market stability (for example minimal fluctuations in year-on-year sector sales trends which permit both parties to reasonably accurately forecast near future demand), industry internationalism (for example domestic suppliers and/or customers moving off-shore to

further expand sector sales) and social system (for example the degree to which cultural trends cause customers to favour sourcing supplies from within their own nation).

Trust is more difficult to build in those scenarios where customers perceive any form of uncertainty. Market uncertainty may be seen to exist by the buyer in those cases where there is a diversity of choice because supplier offerings are highly heterogeneous in terms of product, quality and price. Transaction uncertainty involves the issues of ensuring the product is delivered on time and meets the performance specifications agreed during the purchase negotiations phase. Where high levels of uncertainty exists (for example purchasing from an overseas supplier), the buyer may adopt the approach of requiring lengthy contracts to be signed which contain severe penalty clauses for any form of transaction error by the supplier.

As far as the supplier is concerned, it is also essential that the marketing management system contains elements designed to minimize the effects of uncertainty. Firstly there is a need to ensure that the organization has the appropriate equipment, employee skills and production capacity in order that delivered product fully meets the buyer's specification. Where, for example, the contract involves a front-end period of extensive R&D to create a commercially viable product then clearly the supplier must ensure their organization can complete this first phase of the contract on time. Furthermore, in order to meet agreed delivery dates for the product, it is necessary that the final design does not subsequently create problems when the project enters the manufacturing phase.

Another dimension of uncertainty management for the supplier is to effectively handle social interactions with the customer in order that mutual trust and commitment can develop within the buyer–seller relationship. Typically a critical element influencing this variable is the interchange of information (for example keeping the client updated on contract progress; confirming delivery dates; responding to enquiries from the customer's employees who are using the purchased items). If these are all handled efficiently, then customer uncertainty will be reduced. Conversely poor information management can rapidly cause distrust to develop and this can easily result in the customer beginning to consider alternative sources of supply.

Source: Chaston (1999)

QUESTION

1 **The Managing Director of Dart Technology has taken the view that although legal agreements are important, the broader definition of the factors influencing trust as proposed by the Sales Department is more valid. As his Personal Assistant you have been assigned the task of preparing a report describing how, in an e-commerce trading environment, these variables could be managed in order to ensure that customer trust is retained.**

Case: *Military.com*

Chris Michel, a Harvard MBA, realized that the US military market—comprized of active duty personnel, their families, reservists and veterans—represents a group with a collective annual spending power of over $300 billion. To exploit this opportunity he has launched *www.military.com*, part global community meeting house, part one-stop news source, part one-stop information centre and source of a wide array of on-line products and services.

The founder perceives that 'We have an opportunity to cement long-term relationships. We want to be the trusted home for all the people who serve or served in the military who want to connect with friends and families.' Users are offered free e-mail, chat-rooms, Web pages for thousands of military units, links to a multitude of commercial sites and on-line purchasing facilities. Achieving success will not be easy, and there will have to be significant expenditure on traditional media such as print, radio and TV if awareness is to be built. Additionally, the company will have to compete with another recent market entry, *www.maingate.com*, a company originally created as a relocation service provider for the 500 000 military personnel who move every year. It already receives approximately $20 million in advertising revenue, about half of this from over 500 000 businesses which are located around the 240 military bases across the US.

Source: Strauss (2000)

QUESTIONS

1   Chris Michel requires you to develop three customer buyer behaviour models: one for military personnel seeking car insurance, another for military families seeking to purchase a house upon moving to a new location, and a third for veterans seeking investment services.

2   Use the buyer models created to advise companies supplying the three respective providers (of car insurance, houses and investments) how they can use the Military.com website to market their products.

Chapter 2 Glossary

Differentiation (p. 30)

The creation of clear difference between a company's product and competition.

Four Ps (p. 24)

The variables of product, price, promotion and place.

Immigrants (p. 30)

People who are recent arrivals in cyberspace, only using the technology because they have been forced to by very specific circumstances at work.

Internet call back (p. 28)

The customer uses the website to request a telephone call from the company.

Internet chat (p. 28)

An instant interactive written exchange with the supplier.

Mass marketing (p. 24)

Making available a standard product to the market.

Purchase loyalty (p. 35)

The commitment of the customer to continue buying from a specific supplier.

Transaction engines (p. 36)

The in-company software systems that manage the customer order placement, order picking, invoice and shipping activities.

Video over net (p. 28)

A videoconference with a member of the supplier's staff.

Voice over net (p. 28)

An audio conversation while the customer is using a website.

Wizards (p. 30)

People who have complete mastery of the technology.

Chapter 3

MAPPING THE E-MARKET SYSTEM

Learning Objectives

This chapter explains

- ◆ The role of information in market systems.

- ◆ The analysis of e-commerce transactions.

- ◆ The construction of an e-market system map.

- ◆ The nature of end-user markets.

- ◆ The changing role of intermediaries in an e-commerce world.

- ◆ The analysis of competitive forces in market systems.

- ◆ The determination of the role of suppliers in market systems.

A significant number of TV documentaries and articles in business magazines start with phrases like 'E-commerce will totally change the way the world does business'. Such statements must send shivers of fear down their spines of less technologically aware managers. It seems sensible to examine the validity of such claims.

One approach is to turn the clock back and assume the same media commentators are visiting Henry Ford's Dearborn, Michigan plant in the early 1930s. They would be exposed to production concepts imported from the meat processing industry that dramatically reduced the cost of manufacturing. They would be likely to claim, 'This will totally change the way the world will do business in the future'. Yet the Ford operation was executing the same processes that other manufacturing firms had been using for many years, namely acquiring components, adding value through assembly work, marketing the product to customers, and distributing goods through a chain of distributors. The variable that Ford had changed was to introduce the concept of mass production. The outcome was that some car companies that did not recognize the power of this production philosophy went to the wall. Many others, however, learned to adapt to the new approach.

The Ford scenario is applicable to the world of e-commerce. Most firms will continue to acquire inputs, add value during the transformation of these inputs into outputs and generate profits by obtaining a price in excess of operating costs. All that has changed is that e-commerce as we understand it today will alter, to a greater or lesser degree, (1) the information interchange between customer and supplier and/or (2) the mechanism through which the purchase transaction process is implemented. In most cases the e-commerce enterprise will be operating in the same markets, delivering the same product benefits to customers and using the same technology in the transformation of inputs into outputs.

In reviewing options for the provision of information available through e-commerce, the marketer will need to identify how the new technology can:

1   Reduce the cost of information provision.

2   Increase the speed of information provision.

3   Make information accessible on a 24-hour, 365-day-a-year basis.

4   Provide significantly more detailed information than is typically feasible using traditional channels such as TV or magazine advertising.

5   Exploit the ability to analyse customer behaviour as the basis for providing customized information.

A similar analysis of e-commerce transactions will be necessary to see whether it is possible to:

1   Reduce costs and/or increase the speed of product delivery.

2   Enhance purchase convenience and/or quality of service.

3   Expand market coverage.

4   Offer greater product choice.

It is important to recognize that most e-commerce strategies will need to be integrated into an existing operation. If the e-marketer is to be successful, he or she will have to have a very clear understanding of the factors which influence performance within existing market systems. One way this can be achieved is to build a map of the market system, identifying the key variable factors influencing it. This will show how these variables need to be managed in order to implement successfully an e-commerce marketing plan.

The E-Market System

As illustrated in Fig. 3.1, a market system can be considered to consist of two primary elements, namely (1) the core market system, constituted of the organizations and customers that participate in the market sector supply chain, and (2) the macroenvironment (Kotler 1997). As well as understanding the components that constitute the system, the e-marketer will also need to map information and transaction flows, because the evolution of an e-commerce plan will usually involve revising the nature of the customer–supplier information interaction and/or the purchase transaction process.

The macroenvironment, as the outer shell of the system, contains the generic variables that can have an impact on virtually all market systems. The common problem of such variables is that it is often difficult either to measure their current impact on the core market or forecast how impact may change over time. This is a critical issue because the prime objective of mapping a system is to evolve an understanding of the variables in both the macroenvironment and the core system that represent sources of opportunity and threat.

Economics

All market systems are impacted by prevailing economic conditions, because these determine whether customer demand will grow, remain static or decline. One of the reasons that e-commerce is exhibiting such rapid growth in the world's largest market, the US, is that this country's economy is in a growth phase. Consequently, both consumers and businesses feel that they can afford to invest in technological

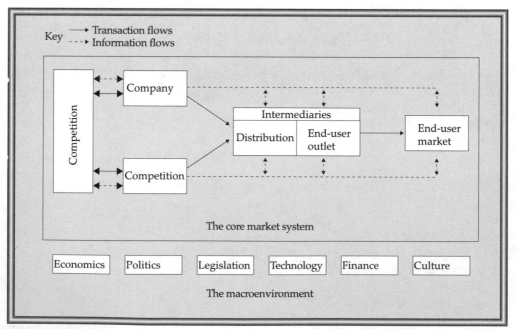

Figure 3.1 *A map of the market system*

infrastructures—such as PCs, mobile phones and faxes—required for access to e-commerce systems. This can be contrasted with the Pacific rim, where e-commerce penetration has, to date, been somewhat slower. To a certain extent this probably reflects the severe economic downturn that countries in the region have faced in recent years in the wake of a major banking crisis.

Politics

The economic policies of most countries are heavily influenced by the policies of their governments. In the US, for example, e-commerce has been particularly supported by Vice President Al Gore. More recently in the UK, a similarly supportive stance has been adopted by the Prime Minister Tony Blair.

Legislation

Legislation is the means by which governments regulate the behaviour of both consumers and businesses. In the face of the exponential growth of e-commerce in world markets, governments are hurrying to ensure that existing legislation is not creating too many obstacles to e-business. One issue that has attracted significant attention is potential tax losses. Within the US these have occurred due to non-collection of sales taxes on e-transactions. In the EU there is a similar problem over Value Added Tax (VAT). Customs and Excise departments in Europe are currently trying to find a way of collecting tax on products which consumers buy electronically from suppliers outside Europe.

Following the 1998 Ottawa ministerial conference, the Organization for Economic Co-operation and Development (OECD) is examining many of these issues with the aim of recommending by the end of 2000, an international agreement on how tax liabilities arising from e-commerce can be managed. Even if all the complexities of these issues can be resolved, however, there still remains the problem of whether the customer or the supplier will be responsible for remitting the collected taxes to the appropriate authorities.

The consultants Ernst and Young estimate that in 1999 tax exemptions associated with Internet trading caused states across the US to lose $170 million in tax revenue. Some states are lobbying Congress to take action over the issue. They are being supported by some 'bricks-and-mortar' retailers that regard the evasion of tax by their on-line rivals as unfair competition. The magnitude of the problem is no smaller in Europe, where VAT can account for up to 40 per cent of a country's tax revenue. This means that European politicians will probably be very supportive of the view that tax should be collected where the customer is based.

Another legal problem facing the e-marketer is that a business activity legal in one country may be deemed illegal in another. For example, in the UK the Financial Services Act strongly limits the nature of the promotional content permitted in the advertising of shares and other financial products. The question then arises of how this

Alcohol On-Line

In the days of 'prohibition', the US federal and state governments enacted laws banning cross-state and direct marketing of alcohol, in an attempt to control the activities of organized crime. Even today, almost 40 States still have laws banning the supplying of alcohol to customers across state borders. This of course creates a major problem for any company wanting to create an on-line alcohol marketing operation (Sandovai 2000).

One way round the dilemma being used by on-line liquor vendors is the contracting of retailers and wholesalers in the customer's state to deliver the product. One Chicago-based on-line operation, *www.drinks.com*, sees this as a slow process. It has, therefore, signed a contract with Drinks America, a national chain that has licensed retail operations in 30 states. In this way, Drinks.com is able to promise delivery within 24–48 hours.

The other alternative is to attempt to get these laws changed. Vintners in California and Virginia, for example, are attempting just this by arguing that the drinks laws in New York state are unconstitutional. The basis of their claim is that the New York law is unfair because it allows Internet sales within the state whilst preventing out-of-state companies from shipping wine to New York.

search

MAPPING THE E-MARKET SYSTEM

regulation applies to offshore advertisers that, in theory, are able to act differently from UK-based financial service providers. Similar problems exist in relation to major differences in consumer protection laws around the world. For example, in the EU there are potentially 15 different sets of consumer, health and safety and other requirements associated with the sale of goods, all of which, in theory, should be taken into consideration by the e-commerce exporter. Thus until these various legislative matters are resolved, the potential exists for both consumers and businesses to find themselves involved in complex cross-border contractual disputes.

Recent court rulings in Europe have not helped build the confidence of on-line traders (anon. 2000). Compuserve had temporarily to close its German operation after a Bavarian court found the company liable for racist material placed on its site by a third party. Lands End was deemed to be breaching German consumer law by offering its normal 100 per cent replacement guarantee for clothing that wore out. On the other hand it must be recognized that governments do attempt to protect consumers from risks during purchase or consumption. It is infinitely more difficult for them to do so, however, if these consumers go to overseas websites. In the US, for example, people are purchasing medical drugs from Mexico that have not been approved for use by the Food and Drug Administration.

Technology

Operating in an e-commerce world, the marketer will hopefully already have a basic understanding of the technologies that operate within his or her core market system. It is also necessary, however, to be aware of emerging technologies—from any source— which have an impact on the future performance of that system. This is no easy task, because e-commerce platforms as we know them have only emerged through the use of a diverse range of technologies from the worlds of computing and telecommunications. In monitoring technology without being overwhelmed with new knowledge, the marketer should generally give priority to the tracking of developments that offer new ways of increasing the speed and/or reducing the costs of data transfer. Thus issues which might be of interest include improvements in the high bandwidth capability of conventional telephone systems, the role of cable modems in providing higher bandwidth, the potential role Radio Fixed Access (RFA) and bandwidth broadening for mobile telephones.

As well as offering opportunities, technological trends can also present potential barriers to cyberspace traders. For example, some on-line retailers have developed graphics for their European sites that have the potential to exploit the advent of interactive digital TV. For the US, however, these companies still need to offer web-pages with less sophisticated visual materials, because for the moment most visitors will be viewing the site via their PCs at speeds of 28.8 bits per second or slower (Chen and Hicks 2000).

Finance

Developing and launching a new e-business is extremely expensive. If one follows the financial press it appears that e-entrepreneurs have few problems attracting investors. When the founder of iVillage (*www.ivillage.com*), Candice Carpenter, took her company public she had this relatively easy task. In fact, upon launching the public share offering the price of the stock immediately rose 233 per cent and by mid-May 1999 the company's market value rose to $1.6 million (anon. 1999a). Similar stories, of such companies as Amazon and Yahoo, abound from the time when new e-commerce start-ups were the 'darlings' of the financial community. However, in mid-2000, as financial analysts began to realize that the actual performance of many of these firms was often much poorer than forecasted in their original business plans, e-commerce share prices fell dramatically. Venture capital companies are becoming more selective about the types of e-commerce start-up companies in which they are willing to invest. These recent trends suggest that in the future, although the founders of many new e-commerce ventures can still expect to be rewarded for their entrepreneurial activities, the scale of the capital gain to be generated from taking their company public will be significantly lower than that available during the 'e-commerce gold rush' days of the late 1990s.

Unfortunately for an established company, the huge investment it needs to create an e-technology infrastructure, and the trading losses that it will probably incur in the early years, usually cannot be covered by exploiting e-commerce investment fever. The company will be treated by its shareholders in exactly the same way as if it had invested in a loss-making traditional proposition, such as the building of a factory for a new product that then failed in the marketplace. The stock will fall and shareholders will be out for the blood of the president or managing director. Existing companies also

---

Mobile Access

In late February 2000, delegates attending the large European trade show CeBIT where provided with forecasts concerning the growing importance of mobile telephones as access points for the Internet. Exhibitors from the mobile telephone sector unveiled their latest products, most of which offer high-speed data transfer based upon the Wireless Applications Protocol (WAP). It is estimated that by 2001 over 80 per cent of manufacturers will offer full Internet access via WAP portals.

The research company GartnerGroup noted that cellular telephone users outnumber Internet users by more than two-to-one, and predicts that the total number of such users will exceed one billion by the year 2003. This scale of difference is seen by the company as having an inevitable outcome, namely that within two years sales of equipment designed to permit remote access will overtake sales for PC-based Internet systems. The company is even prepared to speculate that mobile device penetration could rival that of wristwatches.

MAPPING THE E-MARKET SYSTEM

face the problem that employees want to be paid in currency; in an e-commerce start-up, newly hired employees often gratefully accept a significant proportion of salary in the form of stock options.

The other aspect of the finance variable within the core market is the willingness of financial institutions to led money to end-user customers, and the rate of interest that will be charged on such loans. In a period of healthy economic growth and low inflation, financial institutions will be extremely happy to support high levels of borrowing-based consumption. This is currently the case in both the US and UK economies, which is why sales of e-commerce hardware and software services are continuing to grow. This contrasts with in a non-growth economies such as those in certain Pacific countries, where governments are seeking to dampen consumer spending and financial institutions are less willing to support high borrowing. This in turn has reduced consumer demand for e-commerce products and services.

Culture

Since marketers first began to analyse market opportunity it has always been apparent that different social groups within countries, and the populations of different countries, will exhibit variations in buying behaviour. One of the key variables contributing to this situation is the cultural background of individuals, which determines wants, values, attitudes and beliefs. The e-marketer must monitor carefully how culture may be influencing customer behaviour. For example, an on-line retailer may find young people are happy to purchase via the Internet, but older people, who are less comfortable with new technology, may only be prepared to make a purchase via a traditional retail outlet. Similarly in business-to-business export marketing, one can expect to find countries where customers will utilize on-line procurement systems, whereas in other countries buyers may still insist on face-to-face negotiation before placing an order.

An example of cultural risk was recently provided by Dell Computers in Japan, which discovered that it had inadvertently displeased site visitors by framing the site's content with black borders. In Japan, black is a sign of negativity (Chen and Hicks 2000). Language is possibly the most obvious issue. Chinese and Koreans quite reasonably prefer to buy from sites based in their own countries, because information is presented in their language. Recognition of the need to reflect cultural variations between markets caused the on-line fashion retailer *www.boo.com* in 1999 to open simultaneously 18 different websites around the world. Asia was absent from the first cycle of launches, but the company subsequently developed proprietary applications for the Asian market and had plans to open six sites in this part of the world. Clearly, the front-end investment required to create country-specific websites and then use off-line promotion to build awareness across all these countries was massive. Unfortunately, relative to its high costs, the company's early trading revenues were lower than expected, and it went into receivership in May 2000.

● The Core Market System

The End-User Market

The end-user market is the point of ultimate consumption within the core market system. As shown in Fig. 3.2, it contains two elements, the generic and the core market. Within the core market are those customers who are actively purchasing the product or service. The product's performance and price, and the promotional messages being presented by all of the companies operating in the market can influence this population.

Favourites

Surrounding the core market is the **generic market** (*made up of both potential and actual users*). Actual users are those who have already migrated into the core market. Hence the generic market is a critical influencer of product demand because growth or contraction of this market impacts on the number of customers entering the core market. Thus an e-commerce retailer of children's shoes might define the size of the generic market by the number of households which (1) contain children and (2) have access, via a PC or a digital TV, to the Internet. Thus any change in this generic market (for example a decline in the number of children per household or an increase in the number of households acquiring digital TV) will have a direct impact on the size of the retailer's core e-market.

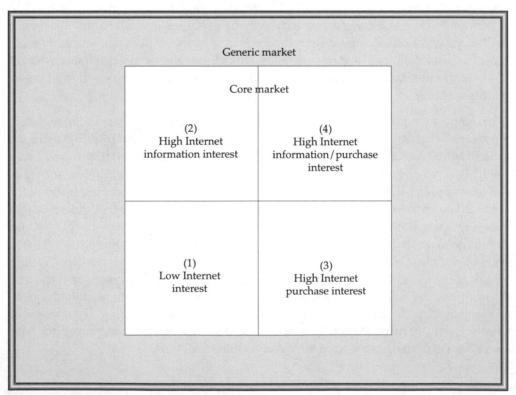

Figure 3.2 *An e-commerce end-user market*

The e-marketer should also recognize that customers rarely exhibit exactly the same purchase behaviour. There are numerous ways of classifying customers. One common approach is known as **market segmentation** (*dividing the market into sub-groups of customers with common, unique product needs*). The e-marketer's approach might be to segment the market on the basis of the degree to which customers seek information and/or use the Internet to make purchases. Drawing upon the conceptual model developed in Chapter 1, it is proposed in Fig. 3.2 that customers might be divided into the following four possible types:

1 Low Internet interest user

This group has minimal interest in e-commerce and might just run a fast simple Internet search for shoes before going shopping. Its main way of acquiring information is through the traditional media and the purchase will be made at a shop.

2 High information Internet user

Members of this group will use the Internet as the primary source of product information but visit a retail outlet to make their purchase.

3 High Internet purchase interest

This group will use traditional information sources to acquire product information. This activity may even involve visiting retail shops in the product search process. Having selected a product, members of this group will then visit an Internet site that they know offers the best possible value and place an order.

4 High Internet information/purchase interest

This group can be expected to implement all phases of the information search and purchase transaction process using an e-commerce site.

Knowledge of these variations in customer behaviour is critical to the successful development of a marketing plan. For if an attempt is to be made to influence customers from all four groups, a plan will be required that (1) contains e-based and traditional media channel promotional activity and (2) ensures distribution is achieved in both e-based and traditional retail outlets. Clearly the complexity of a plan that copes with both traditional and e-commerce market segments will vary depending upon the nature of customer behaviour and the marketing strategy of the supplier.

Intermediaries

The primary role of the intermediary is to act as a link in the transaction chain between supplier and the end-user. In many business-to-business markets—where the value of the product is high, the number of customers relatively low and/or the product customized to meet variations in product requirement (for example civilian passenger aircraft)—the supplier deals directly with the customer and no intermediaries are required. This contrasts with most consumer markets, in which intermediaries have a critical role in managing the final transaction process.

In Fig. 3.1, there are two phases specified for the intermediary; namely distribution and provision of end-user outlets. In the case of some consumer goods these responsibilities are fulfilled by different organizations (for example a clothing

Promotional Spending

As the number of websites has increased, it has become increasingly difficult for companies to attract visitors just by hoping they will be featured as a top ten hit by potential customers using a search engine to find a supplier. More and more e-commerce operations are finding that traditional promotional channels need to be used to communicate the information required to build customer awareness of their website. For example, to attract new e-customers to their on-line facility, in 1998 the San Francisco-based retailer Sharper Image increased its promotional budget to support running print advertising, increasing the level of in-store promotional activity and posting the website address in the company catalogue.

The rapidly rising costs of having to use traditional promotion to attract new e-customers also means that for the start-up e-entrepreneur the Internet no longer represents a zero cost marketing proposition. For example, the two-person business *www.popwall.com*, founded to market dormitory products to students in the US, has been forced to build a network of 70 student representatives around the country to build market awareness. It has also had to hire a public relations firm to get its name across to potential customers (James 1999).

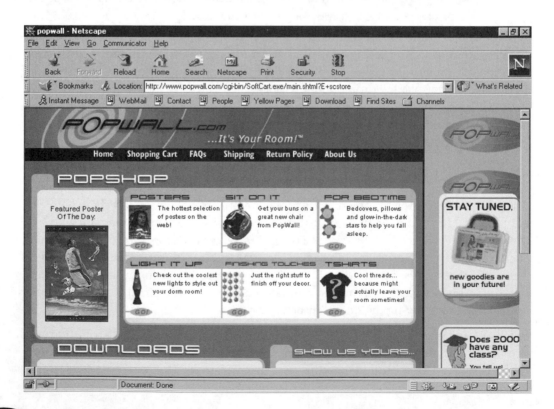

MAPPING THE E-MARKET SYSTEM

wholesaler that supplies traditional high street clothing shops). Over the last 20 years, however, the trend in many market sectors has been for the distribution and end-user outlet role to become the responsibility of one organization, for example the major supermarket chains, which use a centralized buying and distribution system to manage stocks in their own stores.

As intermediaries have moved to integrate the distribution and end-user outlet role, they and their suppliers have tended to take a more integrated approach to promotion. Thus instead of the supplier being the sole provider of promotional campaigns, the intermediary and the supplier form alliances to fund joint promotions. Two examples are (1) in Health and Beauty Aids (HbAs), specific brand names feature in promotions run by department stores, and (2) in the food industry, supermarket chains advertise special offers on national brands of coffee, breakfast cereal or detergent. Thus as well as considering how e-commerce may alter the role of the intermediary in the management of transactions, the marketer must also give consideration to whether e-commerce may impact existing promotional strategies.

In determining the future role of intermediaries, the e-marketer should always base any decision on what the customer wants in terms of both information provision and execution of the purchase transaction. Thus in the supermarket sector, most household consumers still prefer to visit a retail outlet to undertake the weekly shop. Some families are, however, now interested in shopping on-line. In response to this trend, major supermarkets are moving to create websites to service this sector of market need. Hence the manufacturer of branded household goods will need to continue to operate an intermediary management strategy which gives priority to ensuring that distribution is maintained in the major supermarket chains.

Another possibility that may confront the e-marketer is that a new channel of distribution is emerging in their market sector: intermediaries are offering an on-line purchase facility. This is already occurring in many consumer goods sectors such as clothing, music, videos and books. Hence the e-marketer may have to develop a new strategy for its sales force in order to ensure that the company has distribution in this new trading channel.

An alternative option facing the e-marketer is to reduce or cease to use intermediaries, and market goods and services direct to the end-user market. Clearly this decision has major implications both for the company and the intermediaries in the existing conventional marketing operation. For the company, a possible risk in offering goods on-line is that conventional intermediaries will react adversely and terminate the trading relationship with the supplier. The company will need to determine carefully whether conventional intermediaries have a role to play in the marketing process prior to establishing their own e-commerce operation. VIF Corporation, the manufacturer of Lee and Wrangler jeans, decided that the $5–10 million they could make from establishing an e-commerce direct marketing operation was not worth the risk associated with alienating the $5 billion in business obtained through traditional distribution channels. As a result, a consumer visiting the company's website to purchase goods is directed to a vendor further down the distribution channel (Kalin 1998).

For many companies, the future lies in involvement in hybrid channel models in which the customer picks the best opportunities offered by on-line and off-line transaction systems. There is support for this perspective in a research study undertaken by Ernst & Young (Hamel and Sampler 1998). This revealed that currently 64 per cent of Internet users research products on-line and then buy them at stores or by telephone. Thus, in the case of clothing industry, the customer will probably visit a retail store when seeking out a new item. If, however, he or she wants to replace a favourite pair of jeans, the replacement will very probably be purchased from the manufacturer's website.

Expanding The End-user Market

Traditionally the art market has been the preserve of galleries, dealers and the large auction houses. In 1992 it was estimated that the retail art dealer market was comprised of 4500 dealers generating approximately $2 billion in sales. By 2000 there were over 6000, and world-wide sales probably exceed $15 billion (Puente 2000).

A prime cause of this major expansion in market size has been the emergence of a multitude of art websites. These feature everything from mass produced posters through to emerging new artists and old masters. Some sites sell directly to consumers, others are on-line auction operations operated by firms such as Sotheby's. So far the highest known price paid on the Internet is $168 000 for a watercolour by the Italian artist Lucio Fontana sold by Artnet.com in 1999.

In the world of art auctions, bidders have been buying from catalogues and bidding by telephone for many years. Hence for this type of customer a move into Internet trading was a relatively simple conceptual step. What has surprised many art dealers, however, is the speed with which new customers are prepared to visit on-line galleries to make a purchase. Over 2000 people visit *www.artstar.com* every day. This contrasts with a typical 'bricks-and-mortar' art gallery which would rarely expect its total client base to exceed 2000 customers. Two reasons for the on-line success are that on-line galleries are able to offer a much wider choice and can attract world-wide interest.

MAPPING THE E-MARKET SYSTEM

Redefining Market Systems

In an article on changing markets, Jaworski et al. (2000) propose that there are three possible generic strategies for redefining market structures: elimination, player modification, and functional modification. All three of these strategies can be found in markets in which the advent of e-commerce has caused a change in the organizations which constitute the trading system.

An example of disintermediation is provided in the home delivery sector of the flower industry. Traditionally this has been a multi-layered system involving growers, wholesalers and retailers. The approach at Calyx and Corolla has been to train growers in flower arranging and to use Federal Express to ship directly to the consumer. In this way the company has reduced costs and improved product quality. In the process, however, two layers of the system, wholesalers and retailers have been removed.

Player modification involves adding new elements to the market system. In the music industry firms such as Artist Direct and CDNow are using audio-on-demand distributed via the Internet to bring new artists and new record labels to the industry, thereby challenging the role of the major record labels. In functional modification there is usually a shift in the roles played by members of the market system. An example of this is provided by Microsoft's *www.carpoint.com* operation. This is a website where the customer can research new and used cars, compare prices and arrange to purchase a vehicle. Clearly, if this approach is successful it will have a major impact on the status quo in the retail car market system.

Over the next few years it can be expected that as more organizations come to understand the opportunities offered by e-commerce, very significant changes in the role of the intermediary in virtually every market system around the world (Bloch et al. 1996). In some cases within the new systems, manufacturing companies will take over functions traditionally undertaken by intermediaries. The possibility of bypassing existing channel members, with the resultant shortening of channels, is known as 'disintermediation' (Benjamin and Wigand 1995). One example of a sector in which supplier e-commerce strategies are beginning to cause disintermediation is airline travel. Many years ago, the usual way of purchasing an airline ticket was through a travel agent. Even before the advent of e-commerce, the major airlines established tele-sales operations that permitted customers to make direct bookings. Over the last few years, airlines have moved to providing a complete travel service. This has been achieved by creating websites that can be used both to search out and book other elements of a travel package such as car rental and hotel reservations.

Bloch et al. conclude, however, that one alternative is the emergence of entrepreneurial intermediaries that will offer more effective buying services to the customer. They point out that a customer who contacts a single supplier only receives information specific to that supplier. If a new player appears in the market offering to undertake a wider search of alternative offerings, it can offer the customer the ability to evaluate rapidly which is the best purchase option.

GE On-Line Procurement

Even before the advent of e-commerce, major OEMs were utilizing new technology as a means by which to improve communications between themselves and their suppliers. The US corporation General Electric (GE), was a leader in this field, exploiting EDI to launch its Trading Process Network (TPN) to manage both internal and external procurement (Baer 1998). It has now revised TPN to become an Internet-based platform. Annual intra-company purchases via TPN within GE are over $1 billion. The company is now seeking to link all external suppliers into the system with the expectation that eventually it will be purchasing more than $5 billion of products and services electronically. The rationale behind the move is that e-procurement lowers transaction costs whilst concurrently enhancing supplier response times. To date, achievements have been impressive: procurement cycle times have been reduced by 50 per cent, procurement process costs by 30 per cent, and actual material costs by 20 per cent.

Which Way to Go?

GartnerGroup estimate that more than 90 per cent of manufacturers do not sell their product on-line to end-user markets. The main reason is their concern to avoid channel conflict with existing terrestrial wholesalers and retailers (Weinberg 2000). One example is Rubbermaid Home Products which manufactures a diverse range of plastic products. Originally the company had planned to sell on-line. But in 1999 it terminated the on-line purchasing facility. Now when consumers visit the website they are provided with an entertaining array of product choice and then directed to the location of their nearest local retail stockist.

Even some manufacturing giants have also retreated from on-line marketing. Maytag, the US appliance manufacturer, tested an on-line purchasing facility for two years. However, following complaints from its network of terrestrial retailers, the company has terminated the operation. Other companies have avoided the issue by not offering their normal products on the Internet. Black and Decker, for example, sells branded polo shirts but not power tools on their site at *www.blackanddecker.com*. Kawasaki does not sell motorcycles or parts on the Internet but customers can purchase a leather jacket. Others companies have adopted a somewhat indirect approach. GE Appliances does not sell products on its website, but is does supply products and handle the entire shipping operation for another site at *www.xoom.com*.

Unified Marine, a manufacturer of boating products, has also decided not to alienate retailers by operating its own website. Instead the company operates as a **fulfillment house** (*an operation responsible for processing orders, packing goods and managing deliveries*) for other Web operations (*www.iboats.com* and *www.outdoors.com*). In order to provide a full service for these on-line companies, Unified Marine carries inventories of both its own products and those of other boating product manufacturers.

Competition

A vital responsibility of the marketer is the recognition of the nature of competition, the potential threat it may represent, and the development of appropriate response strategies. Possibly the most widely known source of theories on the effective management of competitors is Michael Porter, the Harvard Business School Professor whose first major text (1980) has subsequently been followed by a whole series of writings on this critically important issue. He proposes that competitive threats can be classified into five major types:

1. The threat of other producer firms already operating within the market sector seeking to increase market share.

2. The threat of customers using their purchasing power to dominate terms and conditions of purchase.

3. The threat of a supplier moving downstream using its control over critical resources to dominate terms and conditions of sale.

4. The threat of substitute goods entering the market.

5. The threat of a new entrant which was not previously a major player in the market.

Kleindl (1999), in his analysis of competitive dynamics in the virtual marketplace, proposes that Porter's contending forces model can be utilized by firms seeking to determine the potential source of threat in e-commerce market systems. As posited in Fig. 3.3, the marketer undertaking an e-commerce competitive threat assessment

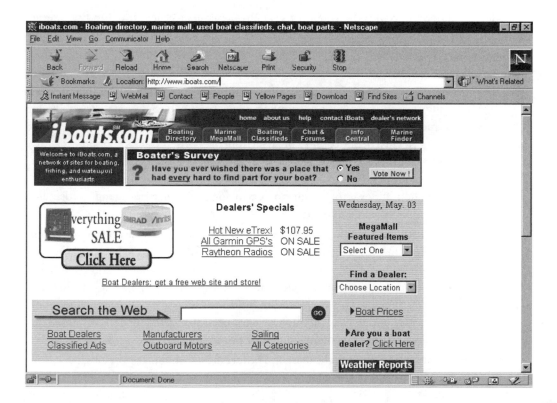

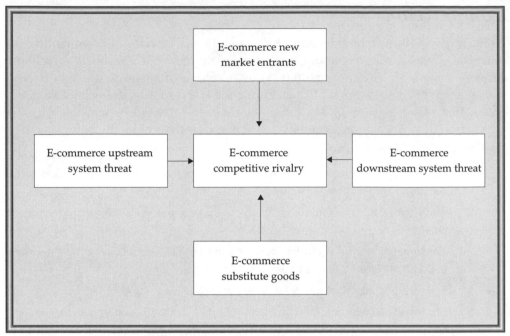

Figure 3.3 *An e-commerce contending competitive forces model (adapted from Kleindl 1999)*

should review the potential impact of each of the following sources of future competition:

1   Competitive rivalry between firms at the same market level within the market system (for example the battle for market share which is beginning to develop between Dell and other PC manufacturers that have begun marketing their product on the Internet).

2   Downstream system threats from groups with sufficient buying power that they can alter the marketing practices of suppliers. One aspect of e-commerce is the ability of consumers to acquire information rapidly on prices being offered by different suppliers, not just in one country but also from overseas. If price variations exist in a market sector, and this fact becomes widely known to consumers, then eventually the supplier can expect these customers to begin to exert downward pressure on prices. This situation, for example, is already occurring in the electrical goods, video and compact disc consumer markets.

3   Upstream system threat posed by a supplier company that has become the one source of products or services critical to e-commerce operations exploiting its power to force downstream customers to accept adverse purchase terms and conditions. This situation, for example, prevailed during the late 1990s in the UK, where small firms have contracted with a software house to construct e-commerce operating systems. After initial installation, these suppliers then demanded excessively high fees for fixing faults and ongoing updating of website front-ends.

4   Substitute goods entering the market. The fact that e-commerce provides a very low cost pathway for firms to enter new overseas markets is likely to mean that in those

MAPPING THE E-MARKET SYSTEM

markets where price, not brand image, is important, companies, especially in Western nations, can expect to face increasing price-based competition from overseas producers based in the developing nations (for example in the furniture and clothing markets).

<u>5</u>   New market entrants gaining a foothold in markets previously inaccessible to them. Prior to e-commerce, for example, it was usually not commercially feasible for large firms to attempt to gain distribution in niche markets that were primarily served by smaller firms. The low costs associated with (1) offering a wide variety of customized products and services via e-commerce and (2) constructing websites customized to fulfil the needs of specialist customer groups means that in future many smaller firms can expect to face increased competition from larger organizations in many market sectors (for example the supply of customized, sector specific software systems).

Suppliers

The restriction of oil supplies by the Oil Producing and Exporting Countries (OPEC) in the 1970s, and this price-setting organization's demand for higher crude prices, triggered a global recession. This event caused marketers, possibly for the first time, to assess carefully the impact of scarce resources on the future positioning of products in respective markets. US automobile manufacturers had to begin to offer their customers smaller cars; construction companies had to improve insulation levels in new houses in order to reduce occupants' energy bills. More recently, however, companies have also begun to realize that suppliers, as well as possibly being able to constrain input resources, can also be a major source of new opportunities. Most of the recent advances in the modern computer's data processing capability have not come from the laboratories of the computer manufacturer, but from the entrepreneurial behaviour of suppliers, for example Intel Corporation's ongoing efforts to produce a computer chips even more powerful than those already available, and the diverse range of Windows products developed by Microsoft Corporation.

Over the last few years, the growing recognition of the importance of working closely with key suppliers has caused many **original equipment manufacturers**, or **OEMs** (*manufacturing companies such as IBM or Ford*) to move from the traditional, conflict-based negotiation style of using purchasing power to drive down input prices towards scenarios based on achieving mutual benefits from supplier–customer relationships. This change in management practice is often described as 'building stronger supplier–customer chains', and usually involves firms mutually determining how to optimize responsibilities for the various stages of the value-added processes associated with the production and delivery of goods to end-user markets (Storey 1994).

The advent of the Internet has accelerated the trend towards stronger customer–supplier links. Virtually every large manufacturing and service organization around the world is implementing e-procurement strategies. Some are building their own systems. Others are linking into third-party procurement **extranets** (*websites closed to the general public that can only be accessed via passwords by approved users*) because the latter are seen by some as offering the buyer much greater supplier choice. Whichever platforms eventually dominate e-procurement, the writing is clearly on the wall for suppliers in most sectors: if a company does not develop the capability to interface electronically with its customers in business-to-business markets, then in the near future there will be no customers.

● Summary

Two of the primary activities within any market are the flow of information and the flow of goods or services. Determining the nature of these two flows is critical because in many e-market scenarios the advent of the Internet may cause either one or both to change. Mapping information and transaction flows can be achieved by constructing an e-market system map. The map will contain the core, constituted of the elements that comprise an industrial sector. The core is surrounded by the macroenvironment, which contains a number of generic influencing variables. The nature of the final customer is usually the factor that determines market system performance. Other critical factors are sources of competition and the nature of the role played by suppliers within the system.

STUDY QUESTIONS

1 How might the variables which constitute the macroenvironment within a market system affect the future performance of the on-line bookstore Amazon?

2 Describe the possible structure and market segments which constitute the end-user market for books.

3 Assume you are the marketing manager for a national chain of traditional high street bookshops. Prepare a report for the Managing Director (1) reviewing how the Internet is changing your company's role as an intermediary and (2) recommending how the company might respond to such changes.

Case: *Trouble at Huddermouth Business School?*

The traditional approach used for many years by business schools has been to deliver programmes by bringing students into the classroom. Although paper-based distance learning and correspondence course approaches have assisted in expanding geographic reach, it has only been with the advent of e-commerce technologies such as the Internet, **groupware** (*computer software such as Lotus Notes which permit a group of individuals to exchange and store electronic information*), e-mail and video-conferencing that fundamental change is beginning to become a reality.

A leading player in videoconferencing technology is Caliber Learning Network (*www.caliber.com*), a company with extensive experience in the development and delivery of 'virtual classrooms' The typical Caliber class has about 500 people, who sit in rooms which have been compared with the bridge of the Starship Enterprise. Materials are created by academics from leading universities and are delivered locally by Caliber instructors. The company is involved in development schemes with some leading US business schools such as Wharton, John Hopkins, Georgetown and the University of Southern California.

Source: Hatlesstad (2000)

QUESTIONS

1 Assume you are the Dean of Huddermouth Business School at the University of Huddermouth. The school has some 2000 undergraduate business studies students and also delivers a small MBA programme. All teaching is done in a traditional 'chalk and talk' classroom environment. Construct a market system model of the current operation.

2 On the basis of the above information concerning Caliber, how might the market system for the traditional business school be changed by the advent of e-education? How should Huddermouth respond these changes?

    (*In undertaking this analysis you might benefit from visiting some educational provision websites such as www.convene.com, www.ecollege.com, www.hungryminds.com, www.unext.com, www.edupoint.com, and www.versity.com*).

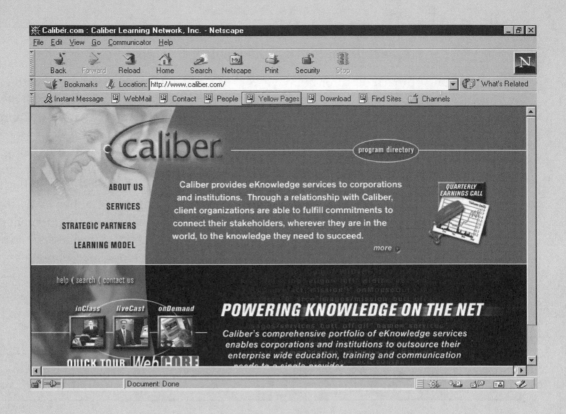

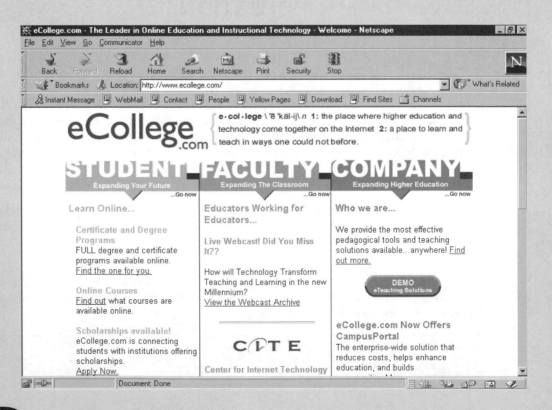

MAPPING THE E-MARKET SYSTEM

Case: *Can Travel Trouble the Mind?*

In the UK vacation market most consumers want to buy a package holiday. National holiday companies create this type of holiday by contracting with hotels, airlines, car rental agencies and coach companies to create a complete travel itinerary and accommodation package. These packages are then marketed in brochures which consumers can obtain from their local travel agent. For those consumers who want customized holidays, a local travel agent will usually be prepared to arrange travel by booking directly with airlines and accommodation by booking direct with hotels at the consumer's chosen location. In the UK business market, the role of most travel agents is to book travel arrangements such as flights, car rental and train tickets by contacting the transportation provider. In the case of the airline market, they may also use 'consolidators', which purchase blocks of seats from the airlines to offer at a discounted price.

Smooth Travel Ltd is a UK travel agent with five in-town outlets and a head office tele-sales operation. The retail sites mainly cater for the consumer market, the tele-sales group handles corporate business. Total annual revenue is £25 million, of which 70 per cent comes from the consumer market, the balance being generated by business travellers. The Managing Director, George Bowling, has not yet read the following two articles recently published in a trade journal.

DIY holidays

More and more consumers are becoming aware that the wealth of travel information on the Internet now dwarfs that which is available in the brochure rack at the local travel agent's office. On-line sites range from terrestrial travel agents who have entered cyberspace to new e-commerce entrants offering full on-line services (for example Internet Travel Network, Microsoft Expedia, Preview Travel and Travelocity). These sites offer flights, hotels and rental car reservations, as well as a wealth of destination information and travel tips. For those who wish to 'do their own thing' then they can also make direct contact with the airlines, go on-line to hotels around the world or book a customized cruise with the leading shipping lines such as Carnival Cruise Lines at *www.carnival.com*.

For those interested in DIY holidays, interesting sites include: *www.abercrombiekent.com* (for exotic safaris), *www.aol.com* (for links to just about anywhere) and *www.amtrak.com* (for US railway vacations), *www.expedia.msn.com* (the Microsoft travel operation), *www.orient-express.com* (for crossing Europe in style) and *www.placestostay.com* (to find those 'out-of-the-way' hotels around the world).

Source: anon. (1998)

Business travel

American business annually spends over $175 billion on travel and entertainment. In the past this business was managed by travel agents offering departments dedicated to taking care of the corporate traveller. However, many firms are now realizing that immense savings can be made by permitting employees to use the Internet to make on-line bookings by themselves, or by using the company's own travel intranet. Brokerage firm Charles Schwab estimate that in 1999 it saved $3.1 million in airfares and agency commission by having employees manage their own travel plans. Two of the catalysts in this travel trend have been (1) the increasing willingness of US airlines to discount fares to keep aircraft seats fully booked and (2) airline on-line booking systems, which often list a whole range of discount options depending upon dates and times of departure.

Source: Rosato and Khan (2000)

QUESTIONS

1 Develop market system maps for Smooth Travel's traditional consumer and business travel market, identifying system participants, information and transaction flows, and variables that may influence performance.

2 Based upon the materials provided in the case, plus any additional data that might be generated by surfing the Internet, prepare a report for Smooth Travel describing how trends in the e-commerce travel market may impact future performance.

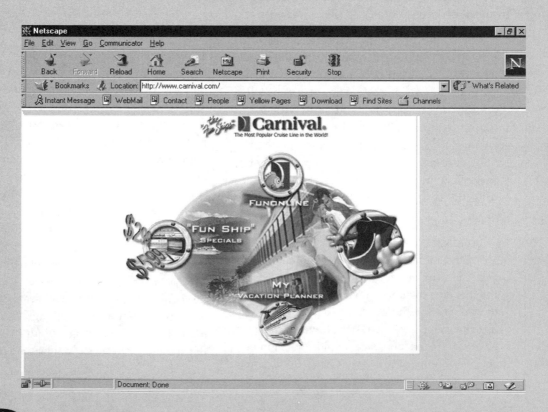

Chapter 3 Glossary

Extranets (p. 63)
  Websites closed to the general public that can only be accessed via passwords by approved users.
Fulfillment house (p. 60)
  An operation responsible for processing orders, packing goods and managing deliveries.
Generic market (p. 54)
  Made up of both potential and actual users.
Groupware (p. 65)
  Computer software such as Lotus Notes which permit a group of individuals to exchange and store electronic information.
Market segmentation (p. 55)
  Dividing the market into sub-groups of customers with common, unique product needs.
Original equipment manufacturers, or **OEMs** (p. 63)
  Manufacturing companies such as IBM or Ford.

Chapter 4

E-COMMERCE COMPETENCE

Learning Objectives

This chapter explains

- *The influence of internal competence on performance.*

- *The role of strategic competence in determining market position.*

- *Organizational competences across the areas of finance, innovation, productivity, human resources management and quality.*

- *The critical role of information systems in e-commerce operations.*

- *Alternative types of customer need.*

- *The priorities for competence development.*

A number of researchers examining the issue of what makes certain firms successful have concluded that they have an outstanding ability to manage internal organizational processes. Peters (1992) has popularized this concept in examples of companies, which have clearly discovered the importance of orchestrating internal activities to deliver superior customer satisfaction. Prahalad and Hamel (1990) conceptualize the importance of managing internal processes better than the competition in their model of firms succeeding through the development of superior **core competences** (*internal capabilities critical to supporting key activities*).

Favourites

Favourites

Goddard (1997) proposes that in successful firms core competences are:

1 Based on experiential and **tacit knowledge** (*understanding among employees of how to undertake effectively organizational tasks*) that competitors would find impossible to replicate.

2 Definitions of what the company does better than, or differently from, other companies.

3 Embedded in the organization's *modus operandi*.

4 Limited to only two or three key activities within the value chain.

5 The source of the company's ability to deliver unique value to customers.

6 Flexible enough to straddle a variety of business functions.

7 The basis for defining market opportunities that the company is uniquely equipped to exploit.

● E-Commerce Competence

For the marketer, e-commerce offers both a new promotional medium and an alternative channel through which to consummate the product purchase and delivery process. In view of this it seems reasonable to propose that success in cyberspace markets will be influenced by the degree to which a company can successfully exploit superior technical knowledge and internal organizational routines as the basis for supporting competitive advantage. This perspective leads to the conclusion that e-commerce provides an important example of how the 'resource-based' view of the company provides the basis for determining whether a company will achieve market success (Hitt and Ireland 1985; Mahoney and Pandian 1992).

Although e-commerce exhibits some unique technological features, the processes, which it supports are not new to the world of marketing. A web-page, for example, delivers promotional information using the same format as a magazine or a newspaper. The key difference is that the former has the facility to provide much more information, and the user who so desires, can undertake interactive searches for more data. Many websites go beyond communicating a promotional message by also offering the additional feature of permitting the customer to place an order. Here again, processes associated with this activity of product identification, provision of delivery information and payment using a credit card are the same procedures that the customer will have already encountered when ordering goods through a direct marketing operation.

It seems that an entirely new resource-based paradigm for e-marketing should not be created; instead an existing organizational performance competence model should be modified. One potentially applicable competence model is that developed by Chaston and Mangles (1997). The attraction of the model is that it was developed through a careful review of the performance literature listed below. This was followed by extensive quantitative validation across a diverse range of market sectors including manufacturing, production of high-technology goods and the provision of services (Chaston 1999a).

By drawing upon the data, it is possible to evolve a resource-based model (Fig. 4.1) of the strategic, financial and operational competences which can have a critical influence on the goal of successfully managing an e-commerce marketing operation.

There are several reports that identify the characteristics of those companies that achieve market success. Coopers & Lybrand (1994) studied UK 'supergrowth' companies, and found that they:

<u>1</u> Perceive their markets as intensively competitive.

<u>2</u> Are flexible decision-makers.

<u>3</u> Seek leadership through offering superior quality in a niche market.

<u>4</u> Deliver superior pre/post-sales service.

<u>5</u> Use technology-driven solutions to achieve a superiority position.

<ol start="6">
<li>Emphasize fast, frequent launch of new/improved products and draw upon external sources of knowledge to assist these activities.</li>
<li>Emphasize application of technology and techniques such as cross functional teams, process re-engineering to optimize productivity.</li>
<li>Recognize the need to invest in continual development of their employees.</li>
<li>Rely mainly on internal profits to fund future investments.</li>
</ol>

A Cranfield Institute of Technology study (Burns 1994) found that successful companies:

<ol>
<li>Seek niches and exploit superior performance to differentiate themselves from competition.</li>
<li>Operate in markets where there is only an average-to-low intensity competition.</li>
<li>Utilize clearly defined strategies and business plans to guide future activities.</li>
<li>Rely mainly on internally generated funds to finance future investment.</li>
</ol>

A comparative study of German and UK food processing companies (Brickau 1994) found that:

The Wal-Mart Story (*www.wal-mart.com*)

Goddard (1997) uses the example of the US corporation Wal-Mart Stores to demonstrate how the composition of competences can lead to market success. The fascinating aspect of this case study is that for many years competence superiority has been based on a philosophy grounded in exploiting IT to build a more efficient retail operation. In 1980 Wal-Mart was a small niche retailer based in the southern US states; yet within 10 years the company became the largest and most profitable retailer in the world. Goddard posits that the fundamental competence driving this success has been its **cross-docking inventory management technique** (*a just-in-time stock control system that keeps inventory on the move throughout the value chain*). Goods delivered to warehouses are almost instantaneously picked for re-shipment, repacked and forwarded on to stores. The result is that Wal-Mart can run 85 per cent of goods through its own warehouse system and purchase full truckloads from suppliers, to the extent that it achieves a 3 per cent inventory handling cost advantage that supports the funding of routine low prices.

The system took years to evolve and is based around investing in the latest available technology. The company, for example, developed a satellite-based EDI system using a private system that sends daily point-of-sale data to 4000 suppliers. The company also worked with Procter & Gamble to develop its 'Efficient Consumer Response', an integrated, computer-based system that provides the benchmark against the company's entire supply chain operation. Finally in order to ensure employees have access to critical information, store and aisle managers are provided with detailed information of customer buying patterns and a video link to permit stores to share success stories.

1 German firms emphasize acquisition of detailed knowledge of external factors capable of influencing performance.

2 German firms can clearly specify their competitive advantages.

3 German firms seek niches exploited through a superiority positioning.

4 German firms use strategies and plans to guide future performance

5 German firms concurrently seek to improve products through innovation and enhance productivity through adoption of new process technologies.

6 German firms fund investment mainly from internal fund generation.

A study of New Zealand exporting companies (Lindsay 1990) found that the best:

1 Emphasize on R&D to achieve continuous innovation and gain control of unique technologies.

2 Are oriented towards achieving 'world class' superiority in specialist niches.

3 Use structured plans based upon extensive information search to guide future performance.

4 Exhibit a very entrepreneurial management style and encourage employee-based decision-making.

5 Strong commitment to using superior quality coupled with high productivity as a path to achieving competitive advantage.

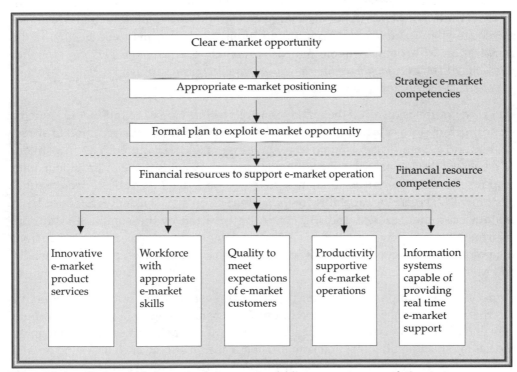

Figure 4.1 *A qualitative model of competences to support and deliver an e-commerce marketing strategy*

Strategic Competence

The long-term survival of all organizations is critically dependent upon their ability both to identify new market trends and to determine how the internal capabilities of the organization can be utilized to exploit emerging opportunities. In the case of e-commerce marketing, Ghosh (1998) proposes that the following four distinct strategic marketing opportunities exist:

1 To establish a direct link with customers (or others with whom the company has an important relationship) in order to complete transactions or exchange trade information more easily (for example Staples, the office superstore chain, selling supplies on-line to large corporate customers (*www.staples.com*).

2 To use the technology to bypass others within a value chain (for example on-line retailers such as the bookstore Amazon).

3 To develop and deliver new products and services (for example the on-line share trading system developed by Charles Schwab in the US (*www.schwab.com*).

4 To become a dominant player in the electronic channel of a specific industry by creating and setting new business rules (for example Dell Computers in the electronic direct selling of computers to large corporate customers).

Financial Resource Competence

To be successful it is critical that the organization has the financial resources to fund the level of investment needed to support any new marketing strategy. To those lacking in Internet trading experience, initial examination would tend to indicate that creation of a website is an extremely low cost proposition. All that seems to be needed is the registration of a domain name and **off-the-shelf-software** (*an existing computer programme that can be purchased from a software supplier*) from suppliers such as Microsoft to construct the organization's web-pages.

This observation is correct if the marketer merely wants to use the Internet to launch a static brochure into cyberspace. Unfortunately, if the website is also required to attract visitors and generate sales, a much larger investment will be required. This investment will be used to (1) establish the hardware/software systems that can provide instant response to the diversity of demands that will be placed on the site by potential customers, (2) create the capability to update the site on almost a daily basis in order to sustain customer interest and (3), ensure integration of the company's internal information management systems such that customers receive a seamless service from the point of initial enquiry through to final delivery of purchased products (Seybold and Marshak 1998).

Even once the company has made the initial investment to establish an effective Internet operation there still remains the problem of sustaining visits to the site by both new and existing customers over the longer term. Merely being able to appear high on the list of sites identified by a customer using a search engine such as Yahoo or Alta Vista is not sufficient. For most marketing propositions the only way to generate a high number of site visits is to invest continually in building customer awareness through expending funds on traditional promotional vehicles such as advertising, public relations and sales promotions (Chaston 1999b).

Innovation

To prosper and grow, all organizations need continually to engage in finding new ways of improving products and process technologies. Unfortunately for the e-marketer, at the 'click of a button' competitors can rapidly gain an in-depth understanding of the operation, as graphically illustrated by the war between Amazon and more recent market entrants from the traditional retail book trade, such as Barnes & Noble (*www.barnesandnoblebooks.com*) and W.H. Smith (*www.whsmithonline.co.uk*). Having analysed a company's Web operation, it is very likely that competitors will offer similar services and use heavy promotional spending and deep price cuts to poach customers. Thus to prosper and grow in cyberspace the e-marketer will need continually to engage in finding new ways of improving e-commerce products and process technologies.

Exploiting innovation as a strategy for staying ahead of competition in e-commerce markets can be extremely expensive. IBM has recently shifted 25 per cent of its entire R&D budget into Internet projects. The objective behind this move is to ensure every IBM product is 'Internet-friendly' (anon. 1999a).

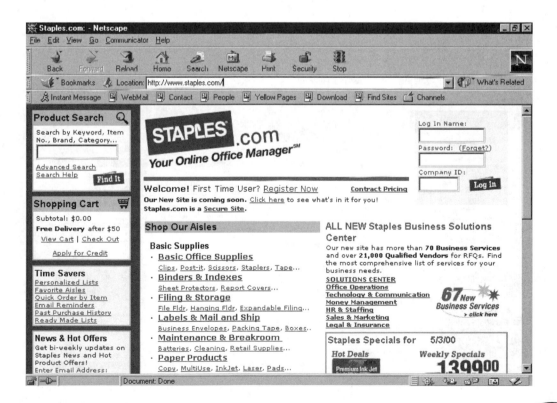

Workforce

In most e-commerce markets—because all firms understand the nature of customer need, and internal operations utilize very similar computer technologies—it is often extremely difficult to achieve a long-term sustainable advantage over competition. Two variables which are clearly critical influencers of customer satisfaction are (1) the speed and accuracy of service delivery and (2) the ability to sustain the technical reliability of all on-line systems (Seybold and Marshak 1998). The importance of these variables does mean that the e-marketer will need to ensure that the human resource management (HRM) practices within the organization are focused on continually investing in employee skills so that all staff are capable of fulfilling roles to a standard that exceeds that achieved by the competition. Furthermore, the e-marketer should seek to understand what causes certain employees to achieve consistently high performance standards within the organization, and then determine how effective management of these factors can contribute to sustaining a market lead over competition.

HRM practices that achieve optimal workforce performance among **back office staff** (*the off-line administrative activities of an organization*) will usually be based around the principles to be found in any type of organization. At the moment, the greatest HRM problem facing the e-commerce industry is **retention** (*ensuring that employees, having joined the company, want to remain there*) and ongoing skills development for technical staff responsible for the development and operation of e-commerce systems. For as recently reported (anon. 1999b), even in Silicon Valley, the greatest constraint facing companies wishing to gain competitive advantage in their Internet operations is the

Strategic Leadership

Despite all the media attention given to the investment opportunities in the latest e-commerce **initial public offering** or **IPO** (*the first time a company offers the general public the opportunity to buy shares in the operation*), there is growing evidence that many of these new firms will enjoy a short life before either failing or being acquired by a larger competitor. If these new shooting stars on Wall Street and the London Stock Exchange are to thrive and grow, they will need to develop a long-term strategic vision. Unfortunately, a range of writings would tend to suggest that this goal can only be achieved if the company has appointed a capable and visionary leader.

Many aspects of the e-commerce world have only been around for a few years. Hence identifying visionary leaders amongst the new breed of Internet millionaires is not an easy task. There are, however, a number of sector examples from within the IT industry which suggest that having a strong, strategic leader at the 'helm' is a fundamental requirement for sustained performance grow over a number of years.

One such individual is Bill Gates, founder of Microsoft. Despite his critics perceiving him as the 'robber baron' of the computer world, this individual has successfully steered the company through a whole series of technological changes and market sector diversifications. Another exemplar is Lewis Platt of Hewlett-Packard (*www.hp.com*). He has moved the company from being number 11 in the PC market to number 3. More recently the former electrical engineer has taken the company into frontier areas of e-commerce through new product developments in the digital image market, and credit and debit-card transaction systems through the $1.3 billion acquisition of VeriFone.

Possibly the most enduring figure in the world of IT is Andy Grove at Intel. Through his envisioning of new opportunities opened up by the Internet, he has carefully found new markets to generate profit growth as older sectors of the chip industry have gone into decline due to excess capacity and price competition. A stark contrast with Grove in terms of age is one of the founders of Yahoo, Jerry Wang, who managed to take the search engine idea and used it to build a massively successful business. The feature he clearly shares with the other examples of leadership in the IT industry is a deep appreciation of how to sustain a long-term vision in the face of technology, which is changing at an exponential rate (Harrington and Solovar 1998).

All of the above examples share the common attribute that they have been deeply involved in the computer industry for many years. An exception to this rule is IBM's Chairman Louis Gerstner, who was recruited from outside the industry to solve the computer giant's performance problems. Initially he focused on restructuring and redefining core values. More recently he has moved to ensure that IBM is a major player in the world of e-commerce (anon. 1999) by generating revenue across a diverse range of activities, including the supply of hardware, software, consulting services and website hosting.

Favourites

search

availability of computer staff with knowledge of the latest advances in network systems operation, telecommunications and programming.

The other main aspect of HRM policy is to create a work environment appropriate for the workforce. 'Techies' are well known for their love of informality, the freedom to work strange hours and immediate access to pizza and Coca-Cola. Even traditional firms such as IBM have been forced to recognize this requirement. At their Atlanta Web design office—more usually known as 'Artz Cafe'—employees bring their dogs to work, massages are available, and there are facilities for playing ping-pong and billiards (anon. 1999a).

Quality

Favourites

Correction-based quality management (*waiting until something goes wrong and then initiating remedial actions to correct the fault*) is founded on what is now considered to be an outmoded concept. By moving to prevention quality, the organization develops processes that minimize the incidence of mistakes that cause the defects to occur (Schonberger 1990). One outcome of the efforts by large multinational companies to improve service quality is that customers now have much higher expectations of suppliers, and furthermore are willing to seek out alternative suppliers.

In relation to the management of quality, e-commerce can be treated as a service business. As with any service business, customer loyalty is critically dependent upon the actions of the supplier being able to totally fulfil the expectations of the customer. As shown by Parasuraman et al. (1988), the critical variables influencing whether the customer perceives that expectations are being met include reliability, tangibles, responsiveness, assurance and empathy.

In many service encounters the customer is forced to accept some degree of supplier failing, and continues to patronize the same service source because that supplier is the most convenient, for example the business person who frequents a poor hotel originally booked via the Internet because it is located next to a customer's office. It is important, however, that the e-marketer recognizes the 'loyalty due to convenience' scenario rarely applies to customers purchasing in cyberspace. For example, if the website visited fails to fulfil expectations, then at the click of a button the potential customer can instantaneously travel to a new location offering a higher level of service quality (Shapiro and Varian 1999).

All of the same issues influencing the perceived service quality of terrestrial companies also apply to on-line operations, namely order fulfilment, customer questions, shipment errors, product returns, guarantees etc. The problem is that the inexperience of many on-line customers is likely to cause then to make more mistakes and therefore need even more help resolving the problems that their errors originally caused (Bartholomew 2000). For example, Ernst & Young estimate that about two-thirds of people abandon their on-line **shopping trolley** (*a visual device that makes it appear that the user is placing products into a supermarket trolley*) because they become confused or concerned about their purchase decisions. The other cause of service problems is that some on-line operations have failed effectively to link their websites to their back office order fulfilment activities.

In response to these problems a number of service companies have started up to which a website operator can **outsource** (*sub-contract a specific role to an external supplier*) the provision of live customer service representatives. LivePerson in New York (*www.liveperson.com*) is one such organization. The company provides a text-based talk-back service for its 450 clients, charges a $1000 start fee and a monthly fee of $250 per operator. A single operator can handle up to four on-line conversations simultaneously. Such services are also used in the business-to-business market, and the San Diego company Equipp.com, which markets metal cutting equipment and forming machines, contracts with eAssist.com to provide an on-line customer support service.

Some firms operate their own customer support systems. For example, Consolidated Freightways in California uses technology developed by New Channel Inc. which connects visitors to *www.cf.com* with Freightways service representatives. The system is based around a dialogue box which permits staff to converse on a one-to-one basis with customers, providing assistance, information and sales help.

Amazon

Service quality is a critically important organizational competence in successful e-commerce marketing strategy. Possibly one of the most effective examples of the service quality that can be achieved is provided by the on-line bookstore Amazon (*www.amazon.com*). Access to the site is extremely fast, the user is presented with search engines, book reviews, a 'shopping trolley' for purchases, a purchase decision review screen summarizing the cost of items in the trolley and a wide variety of delivery alternatives. Once the order is placed, the site automatically confirms the order by e-mail and permits on-line checking of delivery status. Some weeks after order placement an e-mail is sent suggesting other related books that might also be of interest.

Productivity

Productivity is usually measured through the number of value-added activities and/or number of hours worked per employee. By increasing productivity the company can expect to enjoy an increase in profitability (Hornell 1992). Given the major influence that productivity has on organizational financial performance, it is clear that this is an area of internal competence that will have significant influence on any marketing plan. In relation to e-marketing, possibly the two most important elements of the productivity equation are customer interface productivity and logistics productivity. In the case of customer interface productivity, this can usually be maximized by ensuring that through investment in the latest computer technologies virtually all aspects of customer need, from product enquiry through to ordering, can occur without any human intervention by supplier employees. Additionally, however, where human support is needed, this must be delivered by highly trained support staff with the latest on-line assistance tools, so as to ensure the productivity of the **customer interface** (*the contact point between the company and the customer*). Once an order is placed, employee productivity among back office staff involved in order processing, order assembly and product delivery must be high.

Information Systems

For those companies that decide the Internet can provide the primary channel through which to attract new customers and retain the loyalty of existing ones, poorly integrated information systems are not an acceptable option. Success can only be achieved if all data flows are integrated and more efficient than the competition, and this requires continuous investment in upgrading and enhancing company information systems. Without such investment it is likely that one of the most effective strategies for **brand differentiation** (*differences between a brand and competitive offerings which can be used to attract the customer*) on the Internet—the operation of integrated information systems superior to those of the competition—will be impossible (Young et al. 1997).

Alternative Customer Needs

In considering customer needs, over recent years a number of researchers have come to question classic strategic marketing theory on the grounds that it places undue emphasis on the management of single transactions. Studies of the marketing process in service sectors such as finance and retailing have revealed situations in which customers do not behave in a strongly transactionally-oriented way. This situation has permitted supplier firms to exploit opportunities for building long-term relationships based on close partnership with purchasers.

In manufacturing environments, added weight for a move towards closer customer–supplier relationships have been assisted by the managerial philosophies of total quality management (TQM) and just-in-time (JIT). TQM is an organizational commitment to fulfilling customers' expectations over product and/or service quality.

Clearly a large original equipment manufacturer (or OEM) such as IBM or Xerox can only fulfil customer expectations if suppliers are also dedicated to the delivery of high quality components. For this to be achieved, both the suppliers and the OEM have to move away from the traditional, price-based, confrontational negotiation style towards a relationship-oriented style based upon respect for each others' contribution to achieving the mutual goal of optimizing product quality.

JIT is a concept based upon reducing finished goods and work in progress by moving away from the traditional concept of long production runs of single items determined by an **economic order quantity** or **EOQ** (*the size of production run that optimizes manufacturing costs*) formula towards a highly responsive, batch-type manufacturing system based on matching production schedules to recently received customer orders. As with any concept, where achievement tends to be less than stated aspiration, but for companies such as Hewlett Packard JIT has significantly reduced inventory levels and enhanced the company's image of being able to offer a rapid, flexible response to changing customer needs. As with TQM, however, for JIT to be successful the OEM must create a close working relationship with suppliers in order to implement concepts such as same day delivery, willingness to come onto the shop floor to manage restocking of component bins and automated invoice generation using EDI systems.

Favourites

During the 1970s and 1980s there was a massive expansion in companies dedicated to the provision of services in sectors as diverse as finance, fast food and management consultancy. Marketers hired by these organizations encountered significant problems when attempting to apply classical concepts such as influencing customer demand through application of the 'four Ps'. The conclusion of both practitioners and academics was that features such as the intangible nature of goods, the difficulty of separating production from consumption, and the heterogeneous nature of customer need, effective service marketing would require the evolution of new paradigms.

Similar to the marketer in industrial markets, many service marketing theorists have focused on the fact that firms placing emphasis on single transactions should in fact be attempting to build long-term relationships with customers. A strong impetus to this alternative philosophy was provided by Reichfeld and Sasser (1990). They demonstrated that a transaction orientation could result in focusing excessive resources on attracting new customers when in fact the real benefits of marketing come from programmes directed at retaining existing customers (or in their terminology ensuring achievement of 'zero defections').

From studies of the marketing processes employed by both industrial and service companies, a new school of thought has emerged that examines how companies can orchestrate internal resources and processes to create and sustain customer loyalty. Collectively this new orientation, which has both US (Berry 1982) and Nordic (Gummesson 1987) roots, is known as 'relationship marketing'. Supporters of this new form of marketing argue that in order to survive in markets that have become more competitive and turbulent, organizations must move away from managing transactions and instead focus on building long-lasting customer relationships (Webster 1992).

Marshall Industries

Marshall Industries is the fourth largest distributor of electronic components and production supplies in the US. The company distributes 125 000 products manufactured by over 100 suppliers through 38 distribution branches in North America and in Europe, through an equity share in SEI. Over 75 per cent of the company's sales are semiconductor products. For many years the distribution of electronic components has been a highly competitive business, with firms seeking to exploit competences in areas such as product availability, price, customer service, technical expertise and market coverage as attributes upon which to build customer loyalty. In the 1990s, the distribution business needed to respond to a new trend, namely large customers acting to globalize their business and demanding their supplies acquire a global sourcing capability. Concurrently distributors were expected to take greater responsibility for managing the inventories of large customers moving towards optimizing 'just-in-time' manufacturing philosophies.

In reviewing the implications of all of these trends, Marshall recognized that it had become a dysfunctional organization basing its internal processes on outdated assumptions. This situation was exacerbated by a tendency for the distribution branches to operate independently of the company's overall umbrella strategy. The conclusion of the management was that the organization had become fixated with maximizing product sales to the detriment of the more critical goal of responding to the real needs of the customer. The revised vision, enshrined in the phrase 'Free, Perfect, Now', is based upon the reality that customers, given the choice, want everything: products and services at the lowest cost, highest possible quality, maximum customization, and fastest possible delivery times. To fulfil the revised vision, the company recognized that (1) every sectoral and internal operating convention would have to be challenged, and (2) there was a need to embrace totally a philosophy of integrating all aspects of internal knowledge management with the systems operated by customers.

Some of the changes implemented were based upon conventional wisdom (for example flattening the organization to improve response times; replacing the reward systems based upon individual merit with a system in which employee bonuses are linked to overall company performance). Concurrently, however, the company examined how entrepreneurial approaches to the use of IT could win it market leadership in an e-commerce world. To achieve this, the company decided against huge investments in totally new systems. Instead it used the entrepreneurial skills of its own workforce to find ways of linking together existing company IT systems using low cost, commercially available products such as groupware platforms and client servers. In 1992, for example, Marshall launched QOBRA (quality order booking and resell application).

The next stage was to link together all of the knowledge contained within the organization to enable the organization to exploit internal knowledge management capabilities to deliver superior levels of service. All field sales staff were equipped with laptop computers that permitted them, in real time, to check inventory, product specifications, data sheets and orders in process. The system also allowed the sales force to communicate with other employees who had specialist knowledge which might be used in presentations to customers. The core element of this intranet system is Compass, which acts as a marketing encyclopaedia of over 2500 documents about the product lines and suppliers for which Marshall acts as a distributor.

In 1994, Marshall began to implement the next phase of its strategy to become a superior knowledge provider by creating an on-line browser that provided customers with a 24-hour automated order fulfilment process system. This system was complemented by an EDI automatic replenishment channel for large customers plus a fax and telephone-based order entry system. The following year, the company launched an object-relational database that provides customers with a dynamic picture of the products which Industries can supply. Behind the system is a database containing information on almost 200 000 parts, over 100 000 data sheets and a real time inventory system. The site allows the customer to order parts and request samples. To help customers track the progress of orders, Marshall has linked its systems with that of its logistics partner, United Parcels.

The system offers an extensive range of additional knowledge provision services. RealAudio broadcasts news about the electronics industry. Visitors can also talk to Marshall engineers on-line 24-hours-a-day to obtain assistance in product selection, troubleshooting and product design. The NetSeminar element of the system links customers and suppliers to assist with the design of new products. It also offers after-sales training on new technologies. From a studio in El Monte the company broadcasts product information in real time video and audio streams. Viewers and listeners can pose questions of the presenters of these programmes using a GlobalChat system. The success of NetSeminar has led to the company to create a separate consulting business called the Education News and Entertainment Network. This system permits clients to hold real time seminars over the Internet for such purposes as publicity announcements, sales training and after-sales service. Marshall is a graphic demonstration of the principle that the most effective strategy for e-commerce brand differentiation is the operation of integrated information systems superior to those of the competition (Young et al. 1997).

Dell Computers

Possibly one of the best examples of e-commerce productivity is provided by Dell Corporation, the world's largest computer direct marketing operation. Customers visiting the Dell website are provided not just with an effective ordering system, but in additional a multitude of tools for answering technical questions and configuring their own personalized computer design. If a customer has a problem, a click of a button puts him or her in telephone contact with a highly trained Dell service employee. Once an order is placed, the Dell automated procurement, manufacturing and distribution system keeps logistics productivity at a standard that is the envy of the competition.

Advocates of relationship marketing will typically support their views through a comparison of process of the type shown in Table 4.1.

Some disciples of the 'new marketing' have suggested that traditional concepts based around the approach of focusing resources on the four Ps, which may have been appropriate in the North American consumer branded goods markets of the 1950s and 1960s, are no longer relevant. Gronroos (1994), for example, proposes that 'the usefulness of the 4Ps as a general theory for practical purposes is, to say the least, highly questionable'. A somewhat less extreme position, however, has been proposed by Nevin (1994), who feels that companies should adopt a segmentation philosophy ranging from building strong relationships with key customers through to continuing to utilize the traditional four Ps approach for those customers seeking a standardized, generic product proposition. A similarly balanced view is presented by Anderson and Narus (1991), who recommend that firms weigh both customer orientation towards closer relationships and the cost/benefit implications of sustaining close relationships when selecting the most appropriate strategy to suit prevailing market conditions.

Jackson (1985) presents a similar view of the need to recognize that only certain market scenarios permit application of a relationship marketing orientation. For her, transactional marketing is probably more appropriate to cases in which the customer has a short time horizon and switching suppliers is a low cost activity. A customer seeking a standard specification microchip can purchase it from a number of manufacturers, and the purchase decision will be heavily influenced by which supplier is offering terms and conditions perceived as the best at the time of order placement. In contrast, where the customer has a long time horizon and the costs of switching are high, then the purchase decision will involve a careful search for a supplier prepared to invest time and money to build a strong, lasting relationship with the customer. An example of this latter type of situation would be an automobile manufacturer seeking to purchase a 'state of the art' robotic car assembly line, and which will carefully review the project bid specifications and commitment to partnership of potential suppliers.

If Jackson's perspective is accepted, then the debate between transactional and relationship marketing is one of choice. In virtually every industrial and/or service sector situation there are price-oriented customers who respond well to a transactional marketing philosophy and others with whom a strong long-term relationship can be

Table 4.1 Contrasting marketing philosophies

Transactional marketing	Relationship marketing
Orientation towards single purchase	Orientation towards repeat sales
Limited direct customer–supplier contact	Close, frequent customer–supplier contact
Focus on product benefits	Focus on value to customer
Emphasis on near-term performance	Emphasis on long-term performance
Limited level of customer service	High level of customer service
Goal of customer satisfaction	Goal of 'delighting the customer'
Quality a manufacturing responsibility	Quality a total organization responsibility

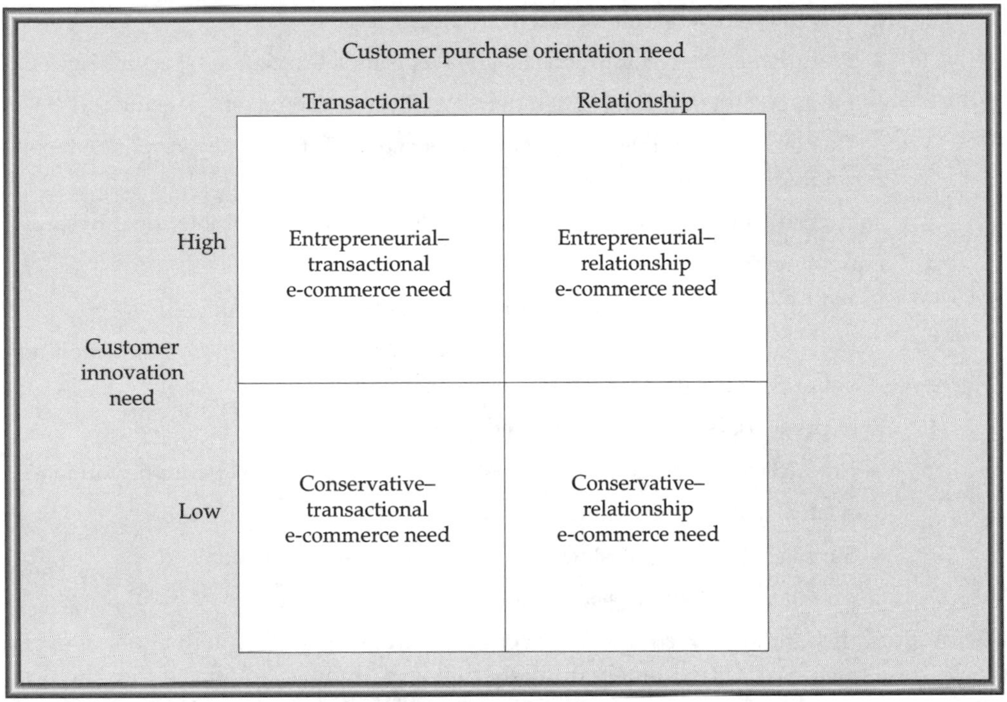

Customer purchase orientation need

	Transactional	Relationship
High	Entrepreneurial–transactional e-commerce need	Entrepreneurial–relationship e-commerce need
Low	Conservative–transactional e-commerce need	Conservative–relationship e-commerce need

Customer innovation need

Figure 4.2 An alternative customer e-commerce market need matrix

created. The objective for the marketer under these circumstances is to select the marketing philosophy for their organization most suited to internal capabilities and/or the nature of the desired product proposition.

The same proposal on internal capability and the nature of the product offering can be made in the context of either entrepreneurial or a non-entrepreneurial marketing orientation. Some companies are best suited to manufacturing standardized goods at a competitive price. Others are extremely competent at managing 'leading-edge' technology, and clearly this skill can be best exploited by adopting an entrepreneurial orientation, regularly launching new, innovative products.

● Alternative Competence Priorities

By drawing up Chaston's (1999a) theory of alternative customer needs, it is possible to evolve an e-commerce need matrix of the type described in Fig. 4.2. This conceptual model suggests that the following need orientations exist in e-commerce markets:

1   Conservative–transactional-oriented customer needs

— Price/quality/value product combination superior to that of competition.

— Standardized products.

— Low prices through access to excellent production and distribution logistics systems.

— Rapid access to information.

2   Conservative–relationship-oriented customer needs

— Product/service combinations that deliver complete customer-specific solution.

— Product solutions based on standard specification for industrial sector.

— Customers know their supplier is obsessed with finding even more effective solutions to customer problems.

— Access to information systems that rapidly identify errors in solution provision.

3   Entrepreneurial–transactional-oriented customer need

— Product offering outstandingly greater performance than competition.

— Orientation towards seeking products which offer even more innovation and better performance than existing products.

4   Entrepreneurial–relationship-oriented customer needs

— Product contributes to ensuring customer output delivers superior performance relative to their competitors.

— Supplier able to help customers achieve even more innovation and extend the performance boundaries of existing products.

Although high standards of competence across all areas of activity is the goal of every world class business, it is extremely unlikely that any organization has either the time or resources to achieve this aim. Under these circumstances, the Internet marketer will need to assess carefully the needs of key customers and then decide which competences should receive most development to support the organization's marketing strategies.

Thus the conservative–transactional-oriented Internet company producing standard products and seeking to deliver a strategy of offering the best possible price/quality combination would probably be well advised to give priority to the organization's information management systems and optimizing internal productivity. These competences will also be of importance to conservative–relationship-oriented Internet firms, but additionally attention to service quality competence will be needed in order to deliver a strategy based around working in close partnership with the customer (Chaston 1999a).

Entrepreneurial–transactional-oriented Internet firms should probably give the highest competence priority to the managing of innovation in order to fulfil the strategy of always offering superior products. Given that customers in this sector of the market are more concerned with product performance than low price, this type of company can probably not be as concerned about concurrently achieving high ratings for employee productivity. Similarly entrepreneurial–relationship-oriented Internet companies will also need to pay attention to innovation competence. In this latter case, however, the philosophy of working in close partnership with customers will also demand high levels of competence in the area of service quality (Chaston 1999b).

● Summary

In recent years it has been increasingly accepted that as most firms have a complete understanding of market opportunity and use the same technologies in the production of products or services, gaining a competitive advantage is often dependent upon the internal competences that have been acquired by the organization. This concept is known as the resource-based view. Attainment of higher levels of competence will be reflected in superior market performance. The primary competence is that of managing strategic position. Effective delivery of a chosen strategy is influenced, however, by operational competences across areas such as innovation, employee productivity, quality and HRM practices. It is proposed that the competence-based model of market performance is applicable to the management of e-based operations. Possibly the most critical operational competence for e-commerce operations is in the area of information management. Internal competences must be developed, prioritized and managed to ensure that they support those actions needed to meet the specified needs of customers.

STUDY QUESTIONS

1 HRM is usually the responsibility of an organization's Personnel Management Department. What new 'people management' issues might confront this department once an organization becomes heavily involved in e-commerce?

2 What are the problems that an on-line company faces in ensuring that customer expectations over service quality are totally fulfilled?

3 Compare and contrast the marketing practices of an on-line company which exhibits a transactional marketing orientation with those that might be expected of one with a relationship marketing orientation.

Case: *Service Quality Competence*

Various forms of human interaction between the customer and the company—through, for example, one-to-one meetings and telephone calls—are a critical mechanism through which to sustain and deliver the organization's service quality message. Additionally, in non-Internet operations the company can provide the customer with a variety of human interactions from different departments, such as sales, production, accounting and shipping to communicate a total commitment to quality by employees across all areas of the organization.

The problem confronting many e-commerce operations is that the website is the only real point of contact between the company and the customer. Hence any weaknesses exhibited by the website will rapidly be perceived by the customer as fundamental service quality problems that may deter him or her from a long-term, loyal relationship. Some common website faults include:

1   A poorly organized site, or one with an ineffective search engine. In both cases this will result in the shopper having difficulty finding the product wanted.

2   The product visuals and/or product descriptions are poor, causing doubt in the customer's mind about the suitability of the offered goods.

3   The operating software is poorly designed, and as a result page download times are extremely lengthy.

4   The site is either slow or totally incapable of responding to customer e-mails.

5   The site does not offer full refunds to dissatisfied customers.

6   The site does not offer a help button requesting a call from a sales person.

7   Privacy policies concerning subsequent use by the company of a customer's personal information are not clearly communicated.

8   The product selection and order placement system is poorly organized.

9   Product delivery charges and expected delivery time are not clearly communicated.

10 The site offers no follow-up service confirming purchase and/or delivery date.

Source: Mardesich (1999)

QUESTIONS

1 Assume you are employed by a large national hardware retail operation that regularly monitors the service quality of competition. Using the above list of service errors and any other factors that you feel are important, develop a measurement tool for assessing e-trading service quality.

2 Visit the sites listed below and use your quality assessment tool as the basis for preparing a report on the e-trading service quality exhibited by competition.

Competitor Sites: **www.sears.com, www.1stoptools.com/ost, www.hardware.com, www.restorationhardware.com, www.cabinetknobs.com, www.thetoolman.com** and **www.grainger.com**.

Case: *Automation to Upgrade Employee Productivity*

It is the annual partners' meeting for Lovell, Grimes and Associates, a multi-office accountancy practice providing a broad portfolio of financial services to both large and medium-sized firms. Over the last 12 months, the partners have become increasingly aware that while billings are rising, costs are rising faster, and a number of clients have expressed concerns about both the speed of response and quality of service. A junior partner, Jim Brent, has been allocated the task of investigating the situation. The summary of his conclusions is that the problems reflect the fact that (1) there is poor communication between staff (in many cases because people are often out of the office seeing clients), (2) communication is slow because it is still paper-based, (3) people are rarely at their desk, so reaching them by telephone is often impossible, (4) younger staff are often forced to 're-invent the wheel' because there is no central system through which to share 'learned knowledge', (5) younger staff find getting access to senior staff to have them review work or resolve problems is difficult because mutually convenient diary dates are hard to identify and (6) team meetings to review major client projects do not occur on a sufficiently regular basis (usually because people have conflicting travel schedules). His closing comment to the meeting is 'we are still operating as if we are a small practice, and furthermore our work methods make us appear to be only just leaving the age of the quill pens and discovering the typewriter'.

QUESTION

1 **Assume the role of Jim Brent. Prepare a report demonstrating how the various technologies associated with e-commerce—such as e-mail, groupware, the Internet and videoconferencing—could be introduced to improve employee productivity while removing the problems currently causing client dissatisfaction.**

To assist you in developing this report it may be useful to visit some of the following websites containing further information on various aspects of e-commerce technology: ***www.lotus.com*** *(groupware),* ***www.microsoft.com*** *(netmeeting software),* ***www.netopia.com*** *(low cost meeting software),* ***www.vocaltec.com*** *(conferencing systems),* ***www.pine.com*** *(on-line video links),* ***www.inovie.com*** *(remote site scheduling software),* ***www.jana.com*** *(e-mail tracking),* ***www.jfax.com*** *(e-mail voice translation),* ***www.instinctive.com*** *(virtual office space building) and* ***www.changepoint.com*** *(intranet building software).*

Chapter 4 Glossary

Back office staff (p. 78)
The off-line administrative activities of an organization.

Brand differentiation (p. 82)
Differences between a brand and competitive offerings which can be used to attract the customer.

Core competences (p. 72)
Internal capabilities critical to supporting key activities.

Correction-based quality management (p. 80)
Waiting until something goes wrong and then initiating remedial actions to correct the fault.

Cross-docking inventory management technique (p. 74)
A just-in-time stock control system that keeps inventory on the move throughout the value chain.

Customer interface (p. 82)
The contact point between the company and the customer.

Economic order quantity, or **EOQ** (p. 83)
The size of production run that optimizes manufacturing costs.

Initial public offering, or **IPO** (p. 79)
The first time a company offers the general public the opportunity to buy shares in the operation.

Off-the-shelf-software (p. 76)
An existing computer programme that can be purchased from a software supplier.

Outsource (p. 81)
Sub-contract a specific role to an external supplier.

Retention (p. 78)
Ensuring that employees, having joined the company, want to remain there.

Shopping trolley (p. 81)
A visual device that makes it appear that the user is placing products into a supermarket trolley.

Tacit knowledge (p. 72)
Understanding among employees of how to undertake effectively organizational tasks.

Chapter 5

E-MARKET POSITIONING AND COMPETITIVE ADVANTAGE

Learning Objectives

This chapter explains

◆ *The philosophy of mass marketing.*

◆ *Segmentation and product customization.*

◆ *Niche marketing.*

◆ *The determination of e-commerce competitive market advantage.*

◆ *The influence of marketing style on the selection of an e-market position.*

The primary reason for the emergence of the US as the leading economic power in the first half of the twentieth century was the country's adoption of mass production processes of the type pioneered by Henry Ford. These permitted the manufacture of standard goods that could be made available at prices affordable by the majority of a population. Having established this manufacturing philosophy, the Americans then went on to develop the concept of mass marketing as a route through which to build brands that could dominate markets.

Richard Tedlow (1990), a business historian at Harvard Business School, has analysed the life history of a number of well known US companies in the automobile, electrical goods, retailing and soft drinks sectors. From his research on company behaviour, both before and after World War II, he formulates some generic guidelines concerning effective strategies for establishing successful mass market brands. These include:

1. Exploiting the economies of scale associated with mass production to generate high absolute profits by selling large volumes of low margin goods.

2. Re-investing generated profits in high levels of promotional activity as a mechanism through which to shape and mould market demand.

3. Creating a vertical system in which raw materials are sourced, production operations managed and products delivered to the final consumer. This vertical system usually involves integration within the company of key steps in the production process (for example Ford owning both car assembly and component manufacturing plants) accompanied by contractual relationships for other elements within the distribution system (for example the move by Coca-Cola to reduce costs by supplying concentrate syrups to bottling companies that manage production and distribution in a specified market area).

4. Having achieved market dominance through being the first company to exploit a high volume/low unit price strategy, creating economies of scale barriers to ward off attacks from competition.

In the early years of the Internet, some of the first entrants into the market were small companies offering specialist goods. This trend caused some industry observers to predict that the low cost of entry into the world of cyberspace trading at last provided a mechanism that could threaten the long-term existence of large companies that had achieved market dominance through mass marketing. However, over the last few years it has become apparent that many major brands are now effectively exploiting the Internet to consolidate further their market position. An analysis of this situation makes clear that e-commerce is a purchase channel that tends to favour the brand leaders in many market sectors. A prime reason for this is that when customers start to use the Internet they are often very concerned about the potential risks associated with this new way of buying. As a way to reduce risk, this type of customer usually selects the company or brand name with which he or she has greatest familiarity.

This trend is demonstrated by UK customers in the world of consumer banking: the majority of individuals who decide to start using on-line banking services are more likely to select a brand they know, for example Barclays On-line (*www.barclays.com*)

search

E-MARKET POSITIONING AND COMPETITIVE ADVANTAGE

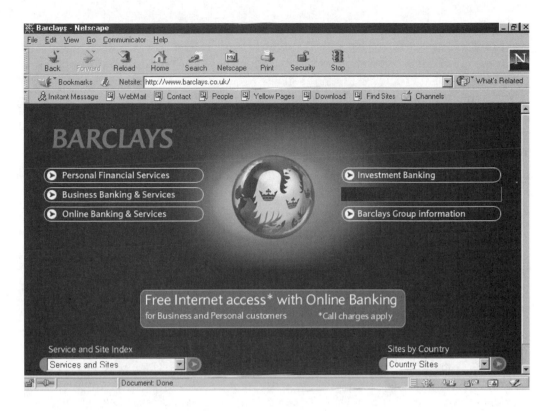

or First Direct, offered by HSBC (*www.banking.hsbc.co.uk*) than one of the new European e-commerce banks operating out of countries such as the Republic of Ireland. Similarly, those shoppers who have gone on-line to purchase household goods without having to visit a supermarket tend to favour well known brand names when selecting items to put into their electronic 'shopping basket'.

● Segmentation and Customization

Despite the long-term success of companies such as Pepsi-Cola and Coca-Cola, which have continued to use mass marketing to sell standard goods, many years ago marketers recognized that in some markets customers were beginning to have varying needs. In analysing this situation, Tedlow (1990) concludes that during the second half of the twentieth century the long-term survival of many leading mass market companies necessitated a move from a profit-through-volume strategy towards a new operating philosophy based around segmenting the market and offering a variety of goods to the now more sophisticated and experienced customer. The higher costs associated with expanding product variety was not a problem, because (1) many market segments are quite large (thereby permitting some degree of ongoing economy of scale) and (2) even more importantly the supplier now had the freedom to 'price in accord with the special value that a particular market segment places on the product, independent of the costs of production'.

Mass Marketing and Cyberspace

Major fast moving consumer goods (f.m.c.g.) brands have extensive experience in developing and executing marketing strategies designed to ensure they can sustain the long-term performance of their branded goods operations (Marsh 1999). It is not surprising, however, to find that apparently they have been slow in seeking to establish a significant presence on the Internet. It is important to realize that these companies rarely attempt to lead customers to make significant changes in purchase behaviour. Instead, they are more likely to tend to monitor emerging market trends and make a move only when they believe the time is right.

One factor influencing f.m.c.g. marketers' strategic decisions about use of the Internet is the degree to which their customers embrace the use of websites as an alternative to more traditional channels of promotion and distribution. Companies marketing transactional brands targeted at housewives, such as detergents or frozen food, are aware that their target customers are still mainly influenced by TV advertising and do most of their shopping in their local supermarket. Such companies will tend to be late arrivals on the Internet.

This can be contrasted, however, with brands aimed at children, because young people are known to be heavy users of the technology both as part of their schoolwork and as a source of entertainment. Thus in Europe, for example, Nestlé has created a website to support promotion of its chocolate milk brand, Nesquick. Using Quicky the Bunny as the promotional vehicle, the company's website offers competitions, games and recipes. Mass marketing companies targeting adult groups such as housewives can be expected to follow Nestlé's lead once digital TV sales reach the point at which interactive message delivery has a market penetration similar to conventional, non-interactive TV channels.

The outcome of this situation is that since the early 1960s most large multinationals have accepted that market segmentation may be more advantageous than merely offering a single, standardized product to all areas of the market. Initially these companies tended to use very simple taxonomies for segmenting markets, such as customer location or socio-demographics. In numerous cases, however, a single socio-demographic variable has been found to be a somewhat crude tool with which to define customer segments. As a result, many organizations now use multi-attribute segmentation, which can involve combining two or more socio-demographic factors (Bonoma and Shapiro 1983). Thus, for example, banks may use the variables of age, income and social class as the basis for developing specific product portfolios aimed at meeting the different needs of customer groups in the consumer financial services market.

Another approach is to divide customers into groups on the basis of their knowledge, benefits sought, attitudes and/or use of the product. The marketer can also consider segmentation based on product usage rates. Many beer companies have found that their heavy usage customers exhibit common behavioural traits (for example a brand may be heavily consumed by 18–25 year old males who are keen football supporters). This knowledge can then be exploited to position the product in the market, and also to select the media vehicles used to promote the beer's benefit claim. In consumer goods markets, as time has gone on and organizations have gained experience of market segmentation, more sophisticated techniques, such as basing segments around the psychographic variables of lifestyle and/or personality have become increasingly popular. To a large degree this change has become necessary because research using traditional measures such as demographics has often revealed that these taxonomies are not sufficiently sensitive to permit effective classification of actual customer behaviour.

In the early days of segmentation, the degree to which companies could offer a range of products to meet varying customer need was often controlled by the fact that inflexible manufacturing philosophies meant that short runs of differently specified products were prohibitively expensive. By the mid-1980s, in large part due to pioneering efforts by Japanese companies in the area of **lean manufacturing** (*the concept of operating highly flexible production facilities using machine tools programmable for a range of tasks*) manufacturing companies have acquired the ability to achieve a dramatic reduction in costs associated with frequent changes on the production line. As this new approach to manufacturing began to be adopted around the world, companies started considering the idea of serving smaller and smaller customer segments. The possibility ultimately offered is that in some market sectors companies could consider the idea of **one-to-one** or **mass customized marketing** (*a philosophy of creating products or services designed to meet the specific needs of an individual customer*).

One of the early disciples of this new marketing philosophy was the American management consultant Don Peppers, who argued that by meeting the individual needs of each customer the company could begin to evolve a long-term relationship based on a much higher level of customer loyalty. Before the 1980s, however, one major drawback to implementing this type of marketing strategy was the limited knowledge that many companies had about variations in customer need. However, two events acted to remove this obstacle. Firstly, companies began to be able to acquire data on individual customer purchases. One thing that accelerated progress in this area was the advent of electronic shop tills that permitted the monitoring of purchase patterns of individual consumers using **universal product codes**, or **barcodes** (*the numerical codes printed onto product packaging that permit automatic identification*). This was followed by companies using data generated from consumer use of credit cards to make purchases and, more recently, the exploitation of the information that becomes available when customers join loyalty schemes which use 'smart cards' that record individual in-store purchase behaviour.

The other factor influencing the ability of companies to research individual purchase behaviour is the increasing availability of lower cost computer hardware and very affordable, powerful software tools, which together have driven down the cost of analysing market data. This trend has sparked off a new concept in market research, known as **data warehousing** or **data mining** (*using computer-based statistical analysis to*

Depth or Breadth?

Some marketers claim that the unlimited shelf space and centralized warehousing available to e-commerce operations means that there is no limit to the range of products that can be offered on a website (Noto 2000). This type of on-line operation has the ability to offer the customer a genuine 'one-stop shop'. Other marketers believe that, as many potential visitors to a website often need assistance in reaching a purchasing decision, that degree of support can only be offered by companies with an in-depth understanding of their market sector.

Although there are merits in both perspectives, it seems very probable that both broad product line and category expert websites will co-exist in cyberspace for the foreseeable future, because they are serving different customer needs. For example, in the case of medical products in the US, some customers who know what they want will probably visit the general web operation, *www.kmart.com*. Other customers may feel that they need some specific guidance about the best available treatment, in which case they will probably contact a website such as *www.planetrx.com*.

Similarly, in the business-to-business market for computer servers, some customers will be happy to buy on-line from the general, value-based supplier Compaq. If, however, the customer feels that there is a need for careful guidance in the design and implementation of a new server-based system, he or she is more likely to go on-line to the leading specialist provider of server technology, Sun Microsystems.

Christensen and Tedlow (2000) suggest that in the depth or breadth debate one should recognize that possible outcomes may be similar to those seen in the battle between department stores and retail discount stores such as KMart in the 1960s and 1970s. By operating on the edge of town and using a high turnover inventory model the latter could offer products at 20 per cent discounts. The response of the department stores was to move up-market. Subsequently, the broad range discounters faced attacks from highly focused, specialist retailers such as Staples and Toys 'R' Us.

The Internet permits on-line retailers to offer a much broader range of products, and have price flexibility because they do not have to make investments in 'bricks-and-mortar' and do not have to worry about their store being in the right location in specific cities. Furthermore, e-retailers are able to enjoy an **inventory turn** (*the speed with which inventory is acquired and then sold on to the customer*) of 25 times per year. This means they only have to make a gross margin of 5 per cent in order to achieve a very high return on investment.

Leading retailers such as Amazon have evolved a department store strategy by offering a broad range of goods accompanied by on-line services to assist the customer in the selection of products. Christensen and Tedlow believe that it is probable, however, that these major on-line retailers will be forced to migrate up-market and offer additional value-added services in order to survive in the face of competition from companies willing to adopt an on-line price discounting strategy. Additionally, the power of Internet search engines makes it easier for specialist retailers to move on-line. In some cases they will seek to enhance

E-MARKET POSITIONING AND COMPETITIVE ADVANTAGE

market impact by renting space in cyber-malls to offer collectively a range of choice similar to that available in today's terrestrial shopping malls. The authors recognize that it is currently difficult to predict which on-line retail strategies will prove successful. They conclude, however, that it is very probable that the outcomes will be very similar to those that have occurred in terrestrial retail markets over the past 50 years.

identify clusters and trends in large volumes of customer purchase data). Baker and Baker (1998) propose that this new approach is based around exploiting information provided by customers to:

1 Classify customers into distinct groups based upon their purchase behaviour.

2 Model relationships between possible variables such as age, income and location to determine which of these influence purchase decisions.

3 Cluster data to define specific customer types.

4 Use this knowledge to tailor products and other aspects of the marketing mix, such as promotional message or price, to meet the specific needs of individual customers.

Customers' increasing use of e-commerce in both business-to-business and consumer goods markets has greatly added to the ability of companies to use data warehousing to gain in-depth insights into the behaviour of consumers. As a result, mass customization has become a practical reality for companies that in the past were positioned as mass marketers. The reason for this situation is that when customers start surfing the Internet they are asked to provide detailed information to potential suppliers. Information on what pages they visit, data provided in answer to questions asked as part of registration, e-mail addresses and data from credit cards can be grouped together (anon. 1999). In commenting on this new world, Jeffrey Bezos, founder of Amazon, used the analogy that the e-commerce retailer can behave like the small-town shopkeeper of yesteryear because large companies can also now develop a deep understanding of everybody who comes into the on-line store. Armed with such in-depth knowledge, like the shopkeeper in a village store the large retailer can personalize service to suit the specific needs of every individual customer across a widely dispersed geographic domain.

Even before the advent of e-commerce, in commenting upon the increasing value of exploiting technology to gain a deeper understanding of individual customers, Porter and Miller (1985) forecasted that the future market winners would be those that recognized ahead of competition the value of managing information as the core asset of the business. As companies have begun to exploit the data-rich environment associated with the e-commerce transaction process, a new term has arisen in the marketing literature, **customer relationship management**, or **CRM** (*using data about customers to ensure a company offers an optimal product proposition, prices the product to meet specific customer expectations, and tailors all aspect of service quality such that every point of contact*

Favourites

from initial enquiry to post-purchase service is perceived by the customer as a trouble-free, 'seamless' service) (Vowler 1999).

In his analysis of the strategic implications of operating in the information-rich world of e-commerce, Glazer (1999) proposes that the current winners are the 'smart' companies. He defines these as organizations that have realized the power of IT to transform totally business practices within their market sector, and are the 'first movers' who exploit every advance in computer and telecommunications technology ahead of their 'dumber' competitors. He suggests that the key objective of the smart company is to offers the benefits of:

1 One-stop shopping to provide all customer needs, thereby saving the customer searching time.

2 A menu of choices concerning types of product and delivery options.

3 Proactive anticipation of changing market needs, and the development of even more effective information systems to satisfy the customer more rapidly and more efficiently.

A critical variable in the execution of a mass customization strategy is an ability to produce the customized product when required by the purchaser (anon. 2000). This has been achieved by Dell Computers, which permits customers to design on-line an individualized computer that is then manufactured. The car industry can only look with envy at this approach. To date all they have managed to achieve is partnerships with companies such as Microsoft to permit the customer to view what is available at the local dealer and what models are scheduled for production. Mimicking Dell's ability to customize cars on-line will be an infinitely more difficult proposition. DaimlerChrysler is experimenting with the Smart car, however, onto which plastic panels of the colour requested by the customer can be attached in the last few moments of production.

Where companies are involved in less complex manufacturing technologies, mass customization is a more feasible strategy. Procter & Gamble, for example, has recently created the Reflect brand. This operation takes customer orders on-line and then offers cosmetics, shampoos and other beauty-care products to meet individual customer requirements. An added appeal of the Reflect brand is that it can offer a much broader range of products than would normally be offered through a terrestrial outlet such as a department store.

● Niche Marketing

A market niche is a narrowly defined market containing a group of customers with highly specialized needs. A niche tends to be smaller than a segment, and consequently the limited scale of market opportunity means that only a limited number of companies seek to offer the distinct product benefits sought by potential customers. The limited revenue offered by many niches is such that this type of opportunity is of little interest to larger companies. As a consequence, niches are often serviced by smaller businesses, for example Devon-based company Creative Learning, which specializes in the provision of computer-based training courses on food hygiene for catering outlets and food processors. Although the company operates on a national basis, the total number of potential competitors can be counted on the fingers of one hand.

It is usually assumed that niche marketers rarely have to worry about being confronted by competition from larger companies. The assumption is based on the idea that these larger organizations lack the specialist skills and flexibility in their manufacturing processes to compete. In recent years, however, the advent of lean manufacturing has meant large companies in some market sectors being able to switch from long production runs of standard goods to limited runs of a range of products without incurring any cost penalties. This has happened, for example, in the car industry, with global companies such as Toyota successfully entering niche markets for both up-market executive cars (with the Lexus) and the sports car market (for example with the MR2).

Another risk facing the niche marketer is the assumption that, having proven the ability to satisfy one group of customers, this expertise can be exploited in expansion into other market sectors. Regretably, what often happens in this scenario is that the company lacks the expertise to manage effectively a growth strategy, and the enterprise fails. A recent example of this is provided by the UK company Laura Ashley, which started life as a specialist producer of up-market fabrics and furnishings. Having successfully established itself in this niche, the company embarked on a massive expansion in the 1980s, broadening the product range and seeking to expand market coverage into many countries around the world. The company soon encountered severe trading difficulties, went through the process of hiring and firing chief executives, and by the late 1990s had become a shadow of its former self.

One of the constraints facing niche players wishing to implement a growth strategy is that the revenue generated on sales is often insufficient to permit the level of investment in promotion and channel expansion required to attract a sufficiently large number of new customers. The advent of e-commerce has clearly changed this situation in that by establishing a Web presence niche companies can now offer

Exotic Niches

Two recent American examples of the exploitation of on-line niches are provided by *www.ostrichonline.com* and *www.mesomorphosis.com* (Kotler 1999). As the name suggests, the former, founded by entrepreneur Steve Warrington, sells ostriches, ostrich meat, feathers, leathers, egg-shells and even ostrich-derived body oils. A short time after establishment, the company was trading an annual turnover of $4 million. Mesomorphosis was founded by Millard Baker, a clinical psychology graduate student at the University of South Florida, to supply food supplements and oils to body-builders.

Similar examples of small companies exploiting e-commerce niches can also be found in the UK. Glenn Hilton produces unusual up-market furniture products carved in stone, wood and steel. In the past, his main way of attracting customers was to attend trade exhibitions, which was both expensive and speculative. In 1998 he commissioned a local software company to build a virtual gallery on the Internet. The site has already attracted customers from all over the world. The other advantage of being on-line is that he can use e-mail to dialogue with potential customers during design selection (Bird 1999).

Anne and Andy Ledbetter inherited a set of beehives when they bought a house in Derbyshire. This prompted them to produce a range of products, from honey to beeswax candles and face creams, which they marketed through their own retail outlet. The scale of the operation, however, meant that sales were restricted to people visiting the area on holiday and residents of surrounding villages. By creating a website, 'The Place To Bee', the couple have now expanded their market to cover the entire UK. Similarly, another retailer, in this case Cookson's, a hardware store selling DIY tools, has expanded its market by going on-line. Initially sales were slow, but initiatives such as offering a 'purchase on account' to business customers, a loyalty reward scheme and the paying of commission to other sites that route customers to the Cookson site have resulted in a rapid growth in new business.

products or services internationally. A reason for the success of the approach is that in many cases it is not necessary to spend heavily on traditional promotional campaigns to build awareness of the company's website. Promotional expenditure can be avoided because customers with very specialist needs are often prepared to spend hours using Internet search engines to find new sources of supply.

● Competitive Advantage

Marketers have long accepted that success demands the identification of some form of competitive advantage capable of distinguishing an organization from others operating in the same market sector. By combining the concepts of niche and mass marketing, and the nature of the product proposition, Michael Porter (1985) evolved the theory that there are four possible generic competitive advantage options available to organizations, namely cost leadership, differentiation, focused cost leadership and focused differentiation.

Cost leadership is based upon exploiting some aspect of internal organizational processes that can be executed at a cost significantly lower than the competition. There are various sources of this cost advantage. These include lower input costs (for example the price paid by New Zealand timber mills for logs produced by the country's highly efficient forestry industry), lower in-plant production costs (for example the lower labour costs enjoyed by Japanese companies locating their video assembly operations in Thailand, or by US mail-order companies locating order fulfilment activities in Mexico) and/or lower delivery costs brought about by the proximity of key markets (for example the practice in the brewing industry of locating micro-breweries in, or near, major metropolitan areas). Focused cost leadership exploits the same proposition, but the company decides to occupy a specific niche or niches, serving only part of the total market (for example a horticulture enterprise operating an on-site farm shop offering low priced, fresh vegetables to the inhabitants of towns within the immediate area).

Porter proposes that focused and overall market cost leadership represent a 'low scale advantage' because it is frequently the case that eventually a company's advantage is eroded by rising costs. For example, as an economy moves from developing to developed, unions are able to persuade employers to pay higher wages and/or improve terms and conditions of employment (for example in Mexican electronics assembly plants near to the US border). Alternatively, a company's market position may be usurped by an even lower cost source of goods (for example Russia's post-*perestroika*

Business-to-Business Niche Opportunities

The tendency of the popular media, when seeking to run a story on e-commerce, is to feature companies operating in consumer goods markets. In reality, however, the volume of e-commerce niche marketing is significantly higher in business-to-business markets (Stackpole 1999). The reason for this is that many business-to-business markets contain highly fragmented groups of buyers and sellers, many of whom encounter problems finding each other due to time or geographical constraints.

An example of this type of market scenario is provided by the construction industry. At the end of a major contract, construction companies are often left with capital equipment. The chance of timing a sales call to coincide with the time when another company has just decided it needs a used bulldozer is very low. The solution that has emerged is that construction companies can now use the 'Industry to Industry' website to dispose of the surplus equipment in an on-line global auction.

Channel Point Inc. in Colorado has created an on-line trading system that insurance brokers can use to generate instant multi-carrier insurance quotes for the freight industry (*www.commercebroker.com*). In the shoe industry, manufacturers and retail footwear chains face major problems getting rid of excess stocks. The solution, developed by iWork Networks Inc. of New York, has been to establish an on-line auction system in which buyers and sellers can rapidly reach agreement on the sale of surplus shoes.

> ### Micro-Niching
>
> As with the mass customization opportunities available to large companies, e-commerce also permits small companies to become involved in the practice of one-to-one marketing. The outcome is that niche marketers now find it feasible to operate as 'micro-nichers', customizing products to meet individual customer needs. Acumin, for example, is a Web-based vitamin company that blends vitamins, herbs and minerals according to the specific instructions of the customer. New York's CDucTIVE offers customers the ability to design CDs on-line that contain their favourite mix of music tracks.

entry into the world arms markets offering extremely competitive prices on the latest military hardware).

The generic alternative of differentiation is based upon offering superior performance. Porter argues that this is a 'higher scale advantage' because (1) the producer can usually command a premium price for output, and (2) competitors are less of a threat, as to be successful they must be able to offer a higher performance product. Focused differentiation, which is typically the preserve of smaller, more specialist companies, is also based on a platform of superior performance. The only difference is that these companies specialize in serving the needs of a specific market sector (for example Ferrari offering high performance sports cars).

The other attraction of differentiation is that there are a multitude of dimensions that can be exploited in seeking to establish a product or service superior to its competition. Garvin (1987), for example, proposes that in relation to quality there are eight dimensions that might be considered: features, actual performance, conformance to quality expectations specified by customers, durability, reliability, style and design. In addition to dimensions associated with the physical product, organizations can also exploit other aspects of the purchase and product use process by offering outstanding service in ease of ordering, delivery, installation, customer training, maintenance, repair and post-purchase product upgrade.

The core attributes of many products and services are often very similar (for example liquid detergents or life insurance), and the customer would be hard pressed to distinguish any real technical difference between the performance of products offered by the various suppliers in a market sector. Under these circumstances, one way to differentiate the company from its competition is to use promotion to create a 'perceived difference' in the mind of the consumer. For example, Fairy Liquid was positioned in the UK as effective and yet mild: 'Hands that do dishes can be as soft as your face'. Commercial Union's commitment to the rapid settlement of claims was communicated in advertising that proclaimed, 'We won't make a drama out of a crisis'.

Although a very useful conceptual tool, a major risk associated with the Porter competitive advantage model is that if users follow the theory blindly they may incorrectly decide that the four alternative positionings are mutually exclusive.

E-MARKET POSITIONING AND COMPETITIVE ADVANTAGE

Available case materials would suggest that in the past many Western nations assumed that a choice had to be made between being either a low cost leader or a producer of superior, differentiated goods. Thus, for example, in the 1980s, in response to the high labour costs associated with the country's social charter, German companies concentrated on premium priced, superior goods market sectors. In Spain, the lower labour costs stimulated the establishment of factories oriented towards serving down-market, price sensitive sectors.

This situation can be contrasted with Pacific rim companies whose Confucian approach to decision-making appears frequently to result in the generation of superior, holistic solutions. In the case of competitive advantage, the advent of developments in flexible manufacturing permitted Pacific rim companies to develop products that offer both high standards of performance and low prices. Their ability to achieve this goal in areas such as video cameras, cars and TVs was a key factor in global market share gains during the 1980s.

As Western companies began to recognize this new threat, their response in the late 1980s was to re-assess internal organizational processes, with special emphasis on manufacturing processes. This involved the application of a bundle of techniques that subsequently came to be known as business process re-engineering (Hammer and Champy 1993). Although initially the orientation of such projects tended to focus on simplifying organizational procedures, over time some corporations found that by revisiting fundamental assumptions about manufacturing processes (for example the time taken to switch production from one product to another), new working methods began to emerge that, in addition to enhancing productivity, revealed new ways of working that increased organizational flexibility. This outcome has permitted some major Western corporations to challenge even the performance benchmarks established by Japanese companies. For example, in 1999 the General Motors Saturn plant in the US achieved the highest level of employee productivity in the entire world car industry.

Nevertheless, despite the 'rave reviews' that process re-engineering has received in the trade press and business magazines, having adopted the concept, many companies have not been able to achieve massive gains in productivity or worker flexibility. A key

On-Line Diversity Management

Andersen Windows of Bayport, Minnesota (*www.andersenwindows.com*), for example, is a $1 billion manufacturer of windows for the building industry. To handle a wide diversity of customer needs the company has created an interactive computer version of its catalogue that links distributors and retailers directly to the factory. With this system, based around an Oracle database and proprietary software, salespeople can help customers customize each window, check the design for structural soundness, and generate a price quote. The company has since developed a 'batch to one' manufacturing process in which everything is made to order, thereby reducing order–delivery cycle times and the finished goods inventory (Harari 1997).

reason for this is that in some cases prevailing sector conventions about aspects of operational processes such as logistics and channel management have severely restricted fundamental changes in approaches to supply chain needs. In the last few years, however, the advent of e-commerce has permitted companies to develop new and more effective ways of responding to customer needs.

It seems reasonable to suggest that e-commerce marketers can significantly increase the number of competitive advantage options available to them by considering the opportunities offered by the dual options of (1) combining cost leadership with differentiation and (2) product customization. As shown in Fig. 5.1, this increases the number of competitive advantage options from 4 to 12.

● Market-Oriented Advantage

Another potential drawback with the Porterian approach to defining competitive advantage is the risk that it may result in excessive emphasis on internal organizational competence. It might be argued that a better approach would be to base consideration of competitive advantage options on a decision model oriented towards fulfilling customer needs (Chaston 1999). If it is accepted that neither transactional and relationship, nor entrepreneurial and conservative, marketing are mutually exclusive concepts, hybrid management models can be considered. This approach seems more likely to benefit the evolution of theories of marketing than an unchanging allegiance to a single, purist philosophy. Acceptance of these alternative views of the world then permits the suggestion that all of these different marketing styles are equally valid strategic choices.

	Product benefit		
	Single competitive advantage		Combined competitive advantage
Mass market	Cost leadership*	Differentiation*	Value and superior performance
Mass customization	Customized cost leadership	Customized differentiation	Customized value and differentiation
Niche market	Focused cost leadership*	Focused differentiation*	Focused value and focused differentiation
Micro-niche market	Personalized focused cost leadership	Personalized focused differentiaition	Personalized focused value and focused differentiation

Market coverage (vertical axis label)

*The original four Porterian options

Figure 5.1 *An expanded e-commerce competitive advantage options matrix*

The other aspect of customer behaviour is the degree to which purchasers seek standard goods or desire products or services that are radically new or different. For example, some individuals buying a mobile telephone may be totally satisfied with a standard product capable of making calls and storing messages. These can be called 'conservative' customers. Other individuals, however, may desire a mobile telephone that connects to other IT systems, permitting them to execute all aspects of work while away from the office. These can be called 'entrepreneurial', and they avidly seek mobile phones that can be used as a complete e-commerce portal.

As with relationship marketing, some academics have argued, especially in relation to the management of small companies, that organizations should only opt to meet the needs of entrepreneurial customers. Like in the debate between relationship and transactional marketing, however, the choice of product offering can be determined by the debate between entrepreneurial and non-entrepreneurial marketing. Some

Alternative E-Market Positioning

In the context of an e-commerce world, examples of companies that have opted for this approach to establish a unique market position are as follows:

1 Conservative–transactional: EasyJet in the UK, established some years ago and now the country's leading 'no frills' airline. Similar to operators in the US, the company uses smaller regional airports and limits the scale of ground and in-flight services offered to customers. The company does not pay commission to travel agents, and hence customers are required to book flights directly with EasyJet. Following the advent of the Internet, the company has created an automated, on-line flight enquiry, booking and ticketing system. Since opening this facility, total flight bookings have risen dramatically, and it is expected that in the near future the system will overtake the existing tele-sales operation in serving customers (*www.times.easyjet.com*).

2 Conservative–relationship: Federal Express has been a global leader in the application of IT to customized delivery services for major corporate customers. The company has built upon its original customer service software system Cosmos by providing major clients with terminals and software so that they link directly into the Federal Express logistics management system. In effect Federal Express now offers customers the ability to create a state-of-the-art distribution system without having to make any investment in it themselves (*www.fedex.com*).

3 Transactional–entrepreneurial: The Modbury Group in the UK is a software company that has created an interactive CD-ROM business planning package further enhanced by software 'hot buttons', which take the user to an Internet site where he or she can access additional information on specific business issues. Purchasers of small business planning tools seek a high value/low price product that can be purchased without forming a relationship with the supplier. Hence the Modbury Group markets the product through its on-line shopfront.

4 Entrepreneurial–relationship: McKesson is a US pharmaceutical wholesaler that has concentrated on finding new services for pharmacies, which the company then supplies. Its first innovation was to develop the Economost system, which offered customers greatly improved order processing and stock control. The company then offered to place terminals into pharmacies to upgrade service response time. Having acquired an extensive data-set on in-store product movement McKesson has now evolved a computer-based sales analysis system that permits customers (*www.mckesson.com*) to optimize their stock management and in-store merchandising activities.

companies are best suited to manufacturing standardized goods at a competitive price. Others are extremely good at managing 'leading-edge' technology, and clearly this skill can be best exploited by adopting an entrepreneurial orientation, regularly launching new, innovative products.

If one accepts the perspective that neither transactional and relationship, nor entrepreneurial and conservative, marketing are mutually exclusive, then this permits consideration of hybrid models of how different forms of customer need provide the basis for defining alternative competitive advantage options. Acceptance of alternative views of the world permits the suggestion that all of the following types of customer orientation may exist within a market:

1. Conservative–transactional customers seeking standard specification goods or services at a competitive price.

2. Conservative–relationship customers who, although seeking standard specification goods or services, wish to work closely with suppliers, possibly to customize some aspect of the product or the purchase and delivery system.

3. Entrepreneurial–transactional customers seeking innovative products or services that can be procured without forming a close relationship with suppliers.

4. Entrepreneurial–relationship customers wanting to work in partnership with suppliers to develop innovative new products or services.

One way of presenting these alternative market positions is to assume there are two behaviour dimensions in customers, namely the degree of closeness to the supplier desired and the level of product innovation sought. By using these two dimensions, it is possible to create a matrix of the type shown in Fig. 5.2 to visualize the four alternative customer purchase styles.

The very different nature of the various customer orientations described in Fig. 5.2 suggests that, as illustrated in Fig. 5.3, the following routes to competitive advantage may be available to companies in a market:

1. Conservative–transactional competitive advantage, achieved through offering a price/quality/value standard product combination superior to that of the competition and/or superior service through excellence in production and distribution logistics.

2. Conservative–relationship competitive advantage, achieved through offering a product/service combination that delivers a superior, customer-specific solution.

3. Entrepreneurial–transactional competitive advantage, achieved through offering a new product that delivers features and performance not available from standard goods producers.

4. Entrepreneurial–relationship competitive advantage, achieved through offering a new product developed in partnership with the customer, contributing to the customer's ability also to launch new, innovative products or services.

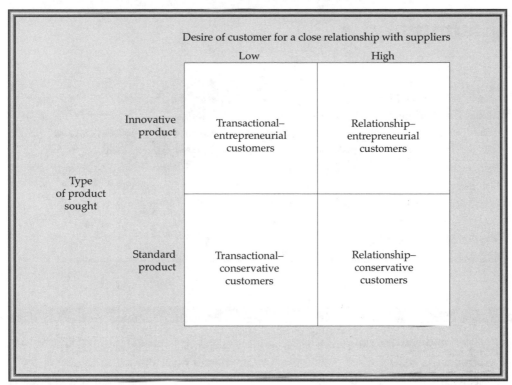

Figure 5.2 *An alternative customer need matrix*

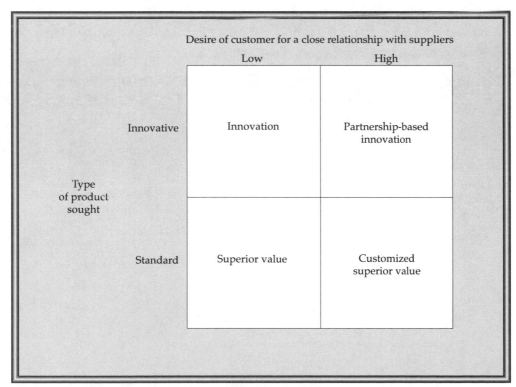

Figure 5.3 *An alternative customer-based competitive advantage matrix*

● Summary

The original marketing theories are based on the exploitation of the economies of scale —possible through mass production technology—as the basis for establishing standard formulation global brands in sectors such as cars, fast food, coffee and soft drinks. The low entry costs associated with the creation of websites in the mid-1990s caused some observers to predict that small companies using niche strategies would be prime beneficiaries of e-commerce. More recently, however, it has become apparent that large multinational brands are entering cyberspace. Additionally, the flexibility of e-commerce, along with the ever increasing ability to acquire electronic data on individual customer behaviour, is causing large companies to examine seriously the option of mass customization and one-to-one marketing strategies.

STUDY QUESTIONS

1 How could the hamburger chain McDonalds use the Internet as a mechanism to support the delivery of the company's mass marketing strategy in the fast food industry?

2 How could a bank use the concept of customer relationship management as a guiding principle in the development and operation of an on-line consumer market banking operation?

3 How might an insurance company use the Internet to develop a micro-niche approach to the provision of car insurance?

Case: *Which Way to Go in the Garden?*

Beaver Nurseries opened its first edge-of-town garden centre 15 years ago. Through a mix of both investing in new green-field sites and acquisition, the company has steadily expanded, and now operates 14 sites across the country. The founder of the business is an expert in the cultivation of plants and shrubs. Consequently, the company's core vision has always been to focus on an extensive range of plants, the sales of which are complemented by the provision of specialist guidance to the amateur gardener.

Over time, however, to accelerate revenue growth the company has diversified into a range of related products and services. These include garden furniture, a garden design service, a landscaping service, a restaurant, conservatories, storage sheds, indoor plants, plant chemicals, garden fertilizers, fencing, garden implements, building materials, barbecues, pets and pet supplies. Delivery of this diversified range is achieved by the company managing the sale of some product ranges, others being marketed by alliances with companies that operate 'shop-within-a-shop' outlets across all sites.

QUESTION

1 Beaver Nurseries has decided to establish a website capable of both promoting goods and accepting on-line orders. Prepare a report for the company reviewing the strengths and weaknesses of (1) the option of offering the entire range of products currently sold through the 14 retail outlets and (2) the option of tightly restricting the on-line marketing operation to the sale of plants and the provision of advisory services to amateur gardeners.

In undertaking this assignment you may benefit from visits to existing sites, such as
www.garden.com, www.gardenmart.com, www.gardenmakers.com,
www.baylaurelnursery.com, www.dragonagro.com *and* **www.wcfarms.com**.

search

Case: *More of the Same, or Diversification?*

Brush Ltd, a UK company, and one of the dominant suppliers of accounting software systems to small and medium-sized companies around the world. The proportion of its sales made in different world regions is: UK 50 per cent, mainland Europe 30 per cent, US 10 per cent, Australia and New Zealand 10 per cent. The company offers a broad portfolio of systems, ranging from simple one terminal book-keeping systems for very small companies through to multi-terminal complete financial management packages capable of supporting automated management accounting and manufacturing costing systems. The company markets the product range through distributors, accountancy practices and office equipment retailers, and operates training centres and an on-line customer support service operation.

Approximately a year ago, the company established a website providing information about its product range and an on-line ordering facility. The experience was useful, and the company is now considering its future on-line market positioning strategy. There are two prevailing views. One seeks to concentrate on the accounting software market and offer an in-depth relationship-oriented operation linking the on-line selling system into the company's existing tele-support department. The other view sees accounting software as too limited a market because over the longer term the company will end up competing with on-line office equipment retailers and distributors. Supporters of the latter perspective feel the company should move to a transaction orientation, and offer, on-line, office hardware, software and supplies.

QUESTIONS

1 Prepare a report reviewing the merits and drawbacks associated with each of these possible on-line market positions for Brush.

2 Use the report to formulate a reasoned argument to justify which of the two positions you think the company should adopt.

*(You may wish to visit some on-line office supply operations—**www.officedepot.com**, **www.officemax.com** and **www.staples.com**) and then contrast these with some accountancy software websites (**www.sage.com**, **www.accpac.com**, **www.bestware.com**, **www.quicken.com** and **www.peachtree.com**).*

Chapter 5 Glossary

Customer relationship management, or **CRM** (p. 101)

Using data about customers to ensure a company offers an optimal product proposition, prices the product to meet specific customer expectations, and tailors all aspects of service quality such that every point of contact from initial enquiry to post-purchase service is perceived by the customer as a trouble-free, 'seamless' service).

Data warehousing, or **data mining** (p. 99)

Using computer-based statistical analysis to identify clusters and trends in large volumes of customer purchase data.

Inventory turn (p. 100)

The speed with which inventory is acquired and then sold on to the customer.

Lean manufacturing (p. 99)

The concept of operating highly flexible production facilities using machine tools programmable for a range of tasks.

One-to-one, or **mass customized, marketing** (p. 99)

A philosophy of creating products or services designed to meet the specific needs of an individual customer.

Universal product codes, or **barcodes** (p. 99)

The numerical codes printed onto product packaging that permit automatic identification.

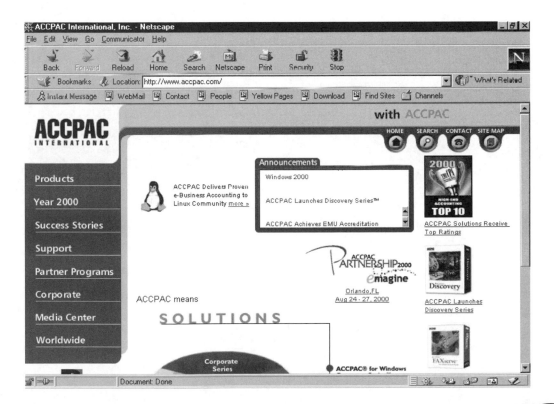

Chapter 6

SELECTING E-STRATEGIES AND CONSTRUCTING AN E-PLAN

Learning Objectives

This chapter explains

◆ The role of planning in the marketing process.

◆ The matching of organizational competence to market opportunity.

◆ The construction of a resource-based planning matrix.

◆ The selection of core competences to underpin the marketing plan.

◆ The development of the e-commerce marketing plan.

◆ The marketing of remould tyres in cyberspace.

Hamel and Prahalad (1994) suggest that 'competition for the future is competition to create and dominate emerging opportunities…to stake out new competitive space'. They further recommend that 'a firm must unlearn much about its past…recognize that it is not enough to optimally position a company within existing markets…develop foresight into the whereabouts of tomorrow's markets'.

In offering guidance on how to achieve this aim, Hamel and Prahalad rely very heavily on the concept of understanding the probable nature of future market conditions and ensuring that the organization has acquired competences appropriate to ongoing success. Their definition of a successful company is one that is able accurately to vision the future, acquire core competences ahead of competition, and thereby become the dominant player within an industrial sector.

Clearly this is a conceptual philosophy that in practical terms only a minority of firms can ever aspire to achieve. Nevertheless, the logic of the process of exploiting company capabilities as the basis for beginning to define a potential source of competitive advantage is often an appropriate starting point in the formulation of a e-commerce marketing plan.

Day (1994) develops an eloquent argument proposing that a capability-based approach to planning is more likely to be a productive source for determining competitive advantage than the competitive forces model tabled by Porter. In defining capabilities, Day suggests that capabilities are complex bundles of skills and accumulated knowledge which, when integrated with the company's organizational processes, permit the optimal utilization of assets. He illustrates this perspective by pointing to Marriott Hotels, which consistently achieve high ratings for their ability to deliver a level of service quality which sets them apart from their competitors such as Hyatt and Hilton. Day describes this superior service as the 'distinctive capability' that permits Marriott to out-compete other firms operating in its sector.

Matching Competence to Market

A similar perspective on the utilization of distinctive capability as a basis from which to evolve a marketing plan is presented by Hunt and Morgan (1995, 1996) in their resource-advantage theory of competition. As illustrated in Fig. 6.1, the internal resources of a company determine market position, and this in turn influences financial performance.

In tabling their model, Hunt and Morgan specify some observable variables that they think overcome many problems associated with applying neoclassical economic theory to an explanation of the management of the marketing process. Firstly, they suggest that customer preferences are rarely homogeneous, because customers usually choose different product features. Secondly, the imperfect information the most customers have causes variations in behaviour. Thirdly, companies, in seeking to achieve superior financial performance, do not act to maximize profit but instead use the benchmark of other firms in their market sector to define financial performance superiority. Fourthly, they see companies as having a multiplicity of competences and resources, and this results in the adoption of very different approaches to finding a route to competitive advantage in the same market sector. Fifthly, it is usually the distinctiveness with which companies use their resources and competences that results in them being able to occupy different market positions.

Hunt and Morgan propose that their model can be used to define alternative competitive positions by using the dimensions of (1) **relative resource costs** (*the degree to which a company's operating costs are higher or lower than competition*) and (2) **relative resource-produced value** (*the degree to which the company's financial performance is better or worse than competition*). Although this a very effective model, one potential risk is that the marketer using the concept as a decision model might be directed towards placing too great an emphasis on financial performance. In view of the fact that the primary

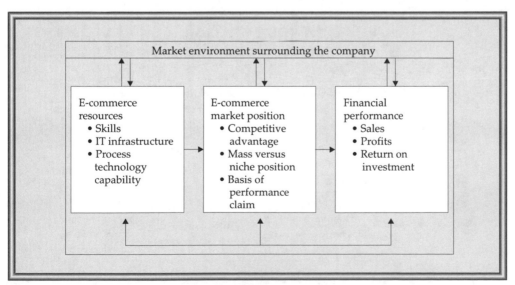

Figure 6.1 A resource-based approach to e-commerce planning

objective of the marketing process is to produce perceptions of products or services as offering the highest possible value to the customer, it seems reasonable to propose that 'perceived value to customer' is preferable in a planning model to the concept of 'relative resource-produced value'.

The start point in building a resource-advantage matrix (RAM) is to determine which factors influence the degree to which (1) a product or service is perceived as offering value to the customer and (2) current operating costs differ from those of the competition. Factors influencing relative perceived customer value will vary by both industrial sector and nature of marketing style. Examples of reasonably standard factors which might be considered in virtually any situation include:

1 The level of actual performance the product or service delivers to the customer.

2 The range of benefits offered by the product or service.

3 The level of service quality being delivered.

4 Price.

5 The effectiveness with which information is made available to the customer.

Similar to perceived value, factors influencing relative operating costs will also vary by industrial sector and marketing style of the organization. Examples of standard factors applicable in virtually any situation include:

1 The cost of producing a unit of product or service.

2 Raw material costs.

3 Employee productivity.

4 Distribution and logistics costs.

5 The cost of fixed assets per unit of output.

		Perceived value to customer		
		Low	Average	High
Relative operating costs	High	(1) Immediately withdraw form market	(2) Phase withdrawal from market over time	(3) If feasible invest in major cost reduction project
	Average	(4) Phase withdrawal from market over time	(5) Sustain market position	(6) Invest in cost reduction programme
	Low	(7) Examine how efficiency can be used to increase value	(8) Invest in market diversification	(9) Invest in retaining value and cost leadership position

Figure 6.2 A resource–advantage matrix

SELECTING E-STRATEGIES AND CONSTRUCTING AN E-PLAN

Having defined key factors, the next stage in the process is to rate these factors on some form of scale. Possibly the simplest approach is a scoring system ranging from a low of 1 through to a high of 10. Where a score approaches 10 for each dimension, this indicates (1) much higher perceived customer value than competition and (2) much lower operating costs. Having executed the scoring, the average total score is found by dividing summated total scores by the number of factors used in the analysis. This generates an overall score for perceived customer value and relative operating cost. Data can then be interpreted by entering scores on a resource-advantage matrix (RAM) of the type shown in Fig. 6.2.

As can be seen from the RAM diagram in Fig. 6.2, resultant positions in the matrix guide the organization towards the possible adoption of the following generic strategies (numbers refer to cell numbers):

1. Low perceived customer value and high operating costs suggest that the company has minimal chance of success. The company (assuming it also has operations in other, more successful, sectors) should withdraw from this market sector immediately.

2. Average perceived customer value and high operating costs suggest poor future prospects, but withdrawal should be a phased process because this will permit avoidance of major financial write-downs for redundant capital assets.

3. High perceived customer value is an opportunity that must be exploited. The company should initiate a major internal process revision project to bring about a significant reduction in operating costs. If, however, this project fails to deliver the required cost reduction, then a departure from the market sector would be the next plan.

4. As in cell 2, low perceived customer value and only average operating costs suggest poor future prospects. Again market withdrawal should be a phased process because this will permit avoidance of major financial write-downs.

5. Perceived customer value and operating costs are both at parity with other firms in the marketplace. For many organizations this type of classification applies to a core business area generating a major proportion of total revenues. The existing operation should be managed to sustain current market performance (for example, if the competitors begin to offer perceived higher value, action should be taken to match these movements). Similarly, if competitors appear to be making efficiency gains, action should be taken to ensure parity of operating costs are sustained.

6. Operating costs are only average but perceived customer value is high. The organization should initiate a cost reduction programme with the eventual aim of achieving much greater internal operating efficiencies than competition.

7. Operating costs are low, but perceived customer value is below average. The company's advantage in the area of internal operating efficiencies should be examined to determine whether this situation can provide the basis on which to offer additional customer value (for example a price reduction or the offer of additional services).

8. The company can exploit lower than an average operating costs as the basis for moving into new market sectors in which it is possible to offer average perceived customer value.

<u>9</u>   A highly attractive position for the organization: high perceived customer value and low operating costs have both been attained. This probably means that the company has already achieved a market leadership position, and this therefore mandates ongoing investment in order to protect the operation from any new competitive threats.

● Selecting Core Competences

Having matched markets to capabilities using an analysis tool such as the RAM matrix, the next issue confronting a company is to select which core competences will be the driving force upon which to build future market success. A frequently quoted example of an organization which illustrates this approach is the Japanese computer giant NEC (Kobayashi 1986). Originally a supplier of telecommunications equipment, the company realized that the communications and computer industries were on a convergent path because both exist to serve the needs of customers wishing to manage information electronically. The identified opportunity was to become a global provider of systems which simultaneously handle voice, data and image traffic. To be successful, the company recognized that excellence would be required in three areas: distributed data processing using networked computer systems, evolving electronic components from simple integrated circuits to ultra large-scale integrated circuits, and moving from mechanical to digital switching. By the internal development of resources and the formation of both technology and market access alliances the company has been able develop core competences that took revenue from $3.8 billion in 1980 to over $30 billion in the 1990s.

A useful tool for assisting the selection of core competence is Porter's (1985) 'value chain' concept. This model, as shown in Fig. 6.3, proposes that opportunity for adding value comes from (1) the five core processes of inbound logistics, process operations, outbound logistics, marketing and customer service, and (2) the four support competences of management capability, HRM practices, exploitation of technology and procurement.

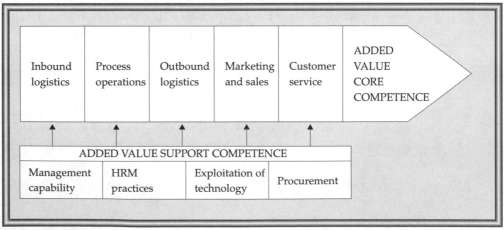

Figure 6.3 A value chain model

SELECTING E-STRATEGIES AND CONSTRUCTING AN E-PLAN

Applying the RAM Tool at Brymor Systems

Brymor Systems manufactures the component materials used by UK companies which fabricate and install new and replacement windows. The industry originally used aluminium as the standard material for window frames. The first significant technological advance was the introduction of 'double glazed' frames that offer superior heat conservation. Approximately 50 per cent of industry unit volume comes from sales in the domestic market, with the balance of sales split between industrial products (shopfronts, office buildings, etc.) and the public sector (local government and housing associations etc.).

Important trends in the domestic market were the introduction of low cost, plastic (or uPVC) frames, and for performance-oriented end-users the introduction of 'composite frames' made by coating aluminium with polyvinyl compounds. The industrial market mainly still considers aluminium the best material for durability and variety of shape.

Brymor supplies (1) bar lengths of all four product types (aluminium, thermal break aluminium, uPVC and composite) to customers who want to fabricate windows and (2) window frame kits to customers who want to install frames without any involvement in fabrication. From the company's first day, the founders recognised that because Brymor was too small to capture the economies of scale available to larger, national competitors, it recognised that it would be unable to compete on the basis of price. Consequently, it consistently operated on a market positioning of offering (1) high quality products, (2) exceptional customer service and (3) a free technical advisory service for customers confronted with a difficult or unusual window replacement contract. This strategic orientation has resulted in the company developing strong relationships with window fabricators and installers that make their purchase decision on the basis of factors such as product quality, just-in-time delivery and good technical support in the pre- and post-purchase phase. Although limited industry data prevents an accurate assessment of market share, Brymor is believed to be a market leader in the supply of premium quality, advanced design, bar lengths and kit products.

Over the years, the company has invested in new technologies to sustain quality and further enhance speed of response in order fulfilment. It was one of the first replacement window firms in the UK to invest in a computer aided design/computer integrated manufacturing system (CAD/CAM). Although the intended use for this system was to optimise manufacturing productivity, the company soon found the system useful when negotiating an order with customers needing 'one-off' designs, to overcome complex installation problems.

Three years ago, the company's problem-solving reputation led it to be approached by architects and larger building firms involved in complex renovation contracts such as the refurbishment of older hotels and office buildings. Brymor had for some years been producing a range of conservatories for domestic homes. When one of its new architect customers who was working on the renovation of 150-year-old hotel, became aware of the company's involvement in this product area, he asked if it would be possible to develop a massive customised conservatory reminiscent of the orangeries popular in the

Applying the RAM Tool at Brymor Systems CONTINUED

Victorian era. Using CAD/CAM, Brymor was able to develop, manufacture and deliver the components for the conservatory in eight weeks.

Currently the company uses a sales force to call on major customers. Meetings are strategic in nature, focusing upon customers' future needs and how Brymor can assist in the resolution of complex problems. Customers are supplied with a detailed catalogue listing Brymor's product line. Price lists which accompany this catalogue are updated on an 'as needed' basis. If a customer has a specific design need or installation problem, he or she contacts Brymor's technical department by mail, telephone or fax. Orders are placed with the sales-service department, again using mail, telephone or fax. This department also acts as a contact point, advising customers on the status of product shipments and delivery dates. Over the last three years the company has been investing time and resources in seeking to ensure that various computer systems are used within the company (for example for accounting, sales management order entry, computer-based manufacturing scheduling and CAD/CAM) are integrated to allow automated information interchange between all company databases.

During this period of investing in building a more effective management information system, the increasingly competitive nature of the replacement window industry has been putting pressure on Brymor's net profits. Hence the company decided to examine how involvement in e-commerce might generate additional sources of competitive advantage. To achieve this goal the directors implemented a strategic marketing planning exercise in which factors such as benefits offered to customers, quality of service, manufacturing

Relative Operating Costs	Perceived customer value: Low	Perceived customer value: Average	Perceived customer value: High
High	Withdraw immediately • No product	Phase withdrawal • No product	Invest in major cost reduction • No product
Average	Phase withdrawal • Aluminium products sold to price sensitive customers in industrial markets	Sustain position • Thermal break windows in both industrial and consumer markets	Reduce costs • UPVC products in both industrial and consumer markets
Low	Value through efficiency • Aluminium products supplied to small fabricators/installers in domestic markets	Diversify • Large customized conservatories in industrial market	Retain leadership • Composite products

Figure 6.4 *The Brymor RAM analysis*

costs, and distribution efficiency were used to construct a RAM matrix. As can be seen from Fig. 6.4, the company has some products which fall in the phased withdrawal categories, a core thermal break business, an area for cost reduction, an enhanced value opportunity, a market expansion opportunity and the need to retain leadership.

The directors recognise that there are few opportunities for introducing new products into the industry, or for cost reduction benefits to be gained from new production equipment or new process technologies. Their decision, therefore, is to build upon their newly integrated information management system as the basis for examining how moves into e-commerce might enhance perceived value by upgrading customer services and reducing operating costs.

The focus of their planning is to undertake a cost/benefit analysis of the following areas:

1 Establishing an on-line pricing and ordering system which would be of major benefit in decreasing operating costs across all market sectors. This system is perceived as having critical impact on the ability to pass cost-savings along to customers in (1) the aluminium product range sold to small fabricators and installers in the domestic market, and (2) the uPVC market.

2 Linking the logistics system with a national distribution company both to decrease time between order completion and delivery, and to offer customers an on-line enquiry system for tracking goods in transit.

3 Permitting major uPVC customers to interface with the production scheduling system to ensure large orders receive scheduling priority, thereby reducing the response time between order placement and shipment.

4 Providing architects and building contractors with on-line access to the company's CAD/CAM conservatory design and manufacturing software.

5 Offering an interactive on-line design and technology applications website service to assist customers for composite products to (1) exploit more effectively the structural benefits offered by this material and (2) configure product designs and purchase orders to optimise quoted prices.

Jarillo (1993) posits that analysis of the precise value chain role an organization will undertake within a market system is a crucial step in the determination of future strategy. A fundamental objective in this process is to ensure that the organization is able to maximize its contribution to value-added activities within the system. He further points out that the exact nature of opportunity may change over time. An example he uses to illustrate this point is the computer industry, which in the past offered producers of hardware the ability to enjoy a major proportion of the profits generated by value-added activities. More recently, however, as the knowledge of the technology associated with the assembly of 'boxes' has become more widely available, greater profits have begun to accrue to those who have retained a 'lock on key technologies' (for example Intel in the manufacture of microchips, or Microsoft in the area of operating systems and software applications).

Jarillo also proposes that when and if the promise about how IT advances permit firms rapidly and efficiently to exchange information, many firms should examine how their more peripheral activities might be sourced from other organizations with higher

The Virtual Drug Company

In the world of diagnostic medicine, biological research and bio-technology, one of the ways of trying to understand the complex interactions that occur within organic systems is to keep as many variables constant as possible. All three of these disciplines use animal cells, bacterial cultures and strains of viruses in their laboratories. One way they achieve constancy in their experiments is to use the same cell, bacteria and viral cultures over many years, because this then results in the production of 'pure strains' which have a known biological history.

Cell-Tec is a UK company which specializes in the supply of pure strain biological cultures. Started as a small laboratory in the 1950s supplying universities, over the years the business has expanded. The company now has customers in medical establishments, commercial research centres and university laboratories across all of Western Europe. The company operates by growing pure strain cultures, which are then frozen and stored in its warehouse. Customers are serviced through a network of local sales staff and a central tele-sales centre in the UK. Shipments are arranged by the company's distribution department which use the services of various parcel express and air freight operations. Although long since retired, the founders of the business have left an accepted view that the company's leading market position is due to its extensive pool of knowledge that is heavily relied upon by customers in the successful design and operation of experimental techniques in their laboratories.

Unfortunately, over recent years the management has found it increasingly difficult to retain effective control over the business because sales have been increasing very rapidly. Inside the company, more and more time was spent sorting out inventory problems, shipment errors and delivery mistakes. Additionally, the sales force, whose intended role is to act as technical consultants to the laboratories in their respective areas, were finding themselves spending inordinate amounts of their time 'fire fighting' shipment problems and placating angry customers.

The management were aware that the pharmaceutical industry in the US had exploited the opportunities offered by e-commerce to revise radically structures and operations with the intention of (1) permitting manufacturers to concentrate on managing the technologies associated with the development and launch of new drugs and (2) outsourcing other activities in order to improve customer service levels. A small project team was sent on a study tour with the assignment of using observations of the US scene as the basis for recommending how Cell-Tec might be restructured.

The project team's visit to the US confirmed both the logic and feasibility of outsourcing non-core business activities. The company was able to identify another company which produces and stores frozen vaccines that are distributed to a customer base very similar to Cell-Tec's. It was also apparent that distribution could best be handled through outsourcing to an international delivery operation, and in this case the US multinational Federal Express was selected. To establish an interface with the customers, a website would be constructed offering information, an order entry facility and an

The Virtual Drug Company *CONTINUED*

automated technical knowledge search system database. This latter system would be easy to evolve because for some years the company has been using Lotus Notes to accumulate internal expertise from all departments. The vaccine company already had a totally automated, computer-based scheduling and inventory management system. Hence by linking both the Cell-Tec website that provides order placement information and the Cell-Tec cell production and freezing operation into the vaccine company's automated system, Cell-Tec would be able to confirm orders placed, and by balancing available inventory on-hand against sales patterns automatically determine production schedules to ensure on-hand inventories are adequate. By providing electronic links between Federal Express, Cell-Tec, the vaccine company and customers, all parties would be able to gain immediate on-line data concerning the status of goods in transit.

Fortunately, both Cell-Tec and the vaccine company had already established internal integrated databases and intranets to manage information interchange between departments. Also Federal Express's extensive experience in IT meant that integration of their shipment management system into the Cell-Tec and vaccine company operations was a simple process. The only major investment was in the creation of the Cell-Tec website. By hiring the services of a US Internet development company with extensive experience in the pharmaceutical industry, and basing the system within a major UK Internet service provider site, it was possible to complete the development and launch of the website in less than nine months. Only six months into the new operation, inventory control and all aspects of customer service quality have improved dramatically. Even more importantly, sales and technical staff have been able to return to their primary role of using knowledge to offer superior products and advisory services to their customers across Europe.

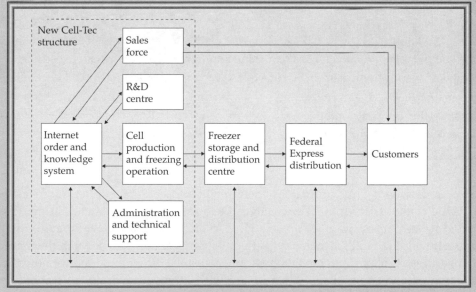

Figure 6.5 Revised Cell-Tec e-commerce operation

Planning Survival at Reuters

Founded 150 years ago, Reuters has spent most of its life as a news agency. Twenty years ago the company moved into the financial services market, supplying information to over 60 000 companies around the world. The company has retained a major market share of the $6 billion financial information market (anon. 2000). One emerging problem is that the big brokerage houses are under pressure as their profit margins fall in the face of competition from on-line brokers. Another, possibly even greater, threat is that the Internet is opening up new channels of information. In the past, sellers of real time information such as the New York Stock Exchange needed to go through an intermediary such as Reuters to reach the final buyers of information. Now information suppliers can use low cost e-commerce systems to communicate directly with end-user markets.

One possible solution is for Reuters, in the face of potential Internet disintermediation, to move from being a wholesaler to a retailer of information. In the past, the company sold information to hundreds of thousands of customers using dedicated telephone lines. The Internet offers the chance to sell to millions of potential users. Reuters.com could become a financial portal to a whole range of retail investors. Concurrently, however, the company would need to invest almost $500 million in converting its proprietary data distribution system into an operation compatible with Internet communication protocols. However, one risk facing Reuters is that a move into the retail information business may cannibalize revenues generated from the existing wholesale financial market information system.

The company plans to continue operating its very successful news agency business. In fact the Internet has opened up a new market for the supply of news services to over 900 websites around the world. In the US, sales to this customer group are now higher than revenues from supplying information to newspapers. As in the financial information market, Reuters is planning to change from wholesaler to retailer. Here again, however, the company may face sales cannibalization.

At the moment, Reuters has possibly one of the most extensive news-gathering operations in the world. In addition, unlike most Internet information retailers, the company does not just collect data. The company reports, analyses, offers real time price information and operates in 23 languages. Clearly, however, as the Internet renders obsolete the company's proprietary information distribution system, evolving a plan based upon sustaining a new, long-term competitive advantage will be no easy task.

levels of competence. Thus companies operating in transactional markets might assess their value chain to determine if any activity such as sourcing raw materials might be assigned to an outside supplier. In relationship-oriented markets, companies might examine how horizontal partnerships with other firms at the same level in the market system, and vertical partnerships with suppliers, can be utilized to identify how their specific value-added activities, when linked with others, can optimize competitive advantage.

The arrival of e-commerce technology has created a technological framework in which companies can genuinely evaluate how IT can be used to manage effectively the outsourcing of certain aspects of the value chain to lower operating costs. Alternatively, more effective IT systems might permit delivery of increased perceived customer value. Whichever route is taken, the managerial resources of the company can be released to concentrate even more attention on optimizing those core competences associated with maximizing added-value activities from activities retained within the company. Such ideas lead to the emergence of a management paradigm in which the company becomes a hub containing core competences critical to generating internal added value whilst being surrounded by a satellite of other companies performing out sourced activities. This alternative paradigm is sometimes referred to as the 'virtual organization'. The indications are that as companies become involved in e-commerce, more of them will increasingly transform themselves into a virtual entity in order to maximize competitive advantage within their supplier–customer value chain.

● Developing the E-Commerce Marketing Plan

The format and contents of marketing plans depend upon the size of the organization (most small firms, for example, produce very short plans, whereas in multinational branded goods companies the plan can approach the size of a small book), its attitude to the degree of formalization required within the annual planning cycle process and accepted sector conventions (for example consumer goods companies typically produce much more detailed plans than their counterparts in many industrial markets).

E-commerce marketing is usually based around applying established marketing management principles as the basis for defining how new technologies are to be exploited (Bradbury 1999). Additionally, in many organizations e-commerce proposals involve building upon existing off-line activities as the basis for providing new sources of information, customer–supplier interaction and/or alternative purchase transaction channels. In view of this, it seems logical to propose that an e-commerce plan will be similar in structure to that used in the conventional marketing planning process. The elements of an e-commerce plan are:

1 A situation review.

2 A strengths/weaknesses/opportunities/threats (SWOT) analysis.

3 A summary of key issues.

4 A statement of future objectives.

5 A strategy to achieve objectives.

6 A marketing mix for delivering strategy.

7 An action plan.

8 Financial forecasts.

9 Control systems.

10 Contingency plans.

Extracts from the Dragon Tyre Company E-Marketing Plan

Situation Review

The world tyre market is estimated to have an annual turnover in the region of £68–70 billion. It is a mature industry exhibiting annual growth in the region of approximately 3 per cent per year. The two largest markets are North America and Europe, and together these probably represent some 60 per cent of total world demand. Within both markets, approximately 30 per cent of sales supply newly manufactured vehicles. The balance of sales are replacement tyres. The top three manufacturers are Bridgestone, Goodyear and Michelin.

For many years, an alternative to new tyres has been remoulds. These are manufactured by bonding a new tread to a used tyre casing. When remoulds were first introduced, quality was poor, and they had a short road life, and consequently prices were much lower than for new tyres. Over the years, however, as tyre manufacturing technology has advanced, remoulds have increasingly been able to challenge new tyres for quality and durability. Despite this trend, however, most remould customers have remained extremely price sensitive.

Dragon Tyres is a UK company specializing in the provision of remoulds for lorries in both the business and public sector markets. The company has managed to create and sustain a premium quality/premium price position by:

1 Investing in ongoing R&D to support the development of remoulds with a higher durability, and therefore longer mileage life, than offerings from the leading multinational producers.

2 Offering a technical evaluation service to companies operating long-haul lorry fleets that involves analysing returned tyre casings and advising customers on how changes in aspects of lorry fleet operation (for example tyre pressures, rectifying suspension and brake system faults) can extend tyre life.

3 Developing customized designs to suite specialist usage applications (for example tyres for brewery lorries, van fleets for national and international delivery services, and off-road tyres for waste-haul fleets).

The company operates a manufacturing facility in Southern England. Using its own lorry fleet, Dragon delivers products directly to the depots of those customers that operate their own truck maintenance sites and also to national tyre distributors that fit remoulds to their customers' lorries. Dragon's primary promotional activity is the use of a national sales team to call on both primary customers and tyre distributors. The sales force and the customers place orders with Dragon's head office by telephone, fax or mail.

Over the last few years, the company has been enjoying a year-upon-year growth in sales of over 10 per cent per annum. Increasingly, however, its market success is attracting the attentions of the bigger manufacturers. These organizations, unable to match Dragon on technically advanced products or customer service quality, are approaching major Dragon clients with extremely low prices. Dragon has been forced to respond by reducing prices on standard lorry remoulds, and as a result net margins are gradually being eroded.

The other factor in need of a response is that some of Dragon's major long-haul fleet customers are moving into pan-European operations, and to simplify their procurement procedures, wish to purchase their remoulds from a single source in all countries. To date Dragon has stayed out of mainland Europe because of the perceived high costs of establishing an overseas sales force and a European product distribution system.

Key E-Commerce Issues

1 Can e-commerce provide a route to respond to price competition through enhanced customer service or reduced operating costs?

2 Can e-commerce provide a platform on which to support a move into mainland Europe?

E-Commerce Objectives

1 To assist in sustaining current net profit margins.

2 To support entry into mainland Europe and within three years generate incremental sales of at least £2 million per annum (equating to 10 per cent of current UK sales).

E-Commerce Strategy

While retaining an overall strategy of providing premium quality/premium price remould tyres, to exploit e-commerce as a route through which to (1) improve customer service and reduce operating costs in the UK market and (2) support entry into mainland Europe.

E-Commerce Marketing Mix

1 UK product: The proposal is to create a website which provides product information, a price list for standard orders, an order entry system, and a system that permits customers to track tyre shipments in transit. As different customers receive different prices depending upon both purchase volumes and other services provided by Dragon, the standard price list will have to be accompanied by confidential extranets to provide customer-specific pricing terms. Virtually all of the customers to which Dragon delivers direct have access to the Internet from their offices. National tyre distributors tend to authorize their individual outlets to order their own remould requirements and most of these companies do not provide Internet access at depot level. Hence Dragon will have to continue to service this latter customer group using the existing off-line product ordering system.

2 Pan-European product: In mainland Europe, most UK long-haul fleet operators either have their own in-country maintenance depots or authorize a major national tyre distributor in each country to provide tyre maintenance services. Initially Dragon intends to offer a website facility, similar to the UK site, to permit long-haul fleets that have their own in-country maintenance operations to order tyres on-line. This will mean that tyre delivery will be relatively simple, and the sales force will only have to be expanded to include a small team to cover these European maintenance operations. At a later date, Dragon will examine how to handle the marketing and logistics problems of servicing the needs of long-haul operators that use national tyre distributors to take care of their lorries across Europe.

3 Technology product services: The website will draw upon Dragon's years of expertise to offer generic guidance on the selection and optimal utilization of remould tyres. At the moment, the way the customer feedback tyre inspection and usage service is delivered is that casings are returned to the Dragon plant. Dragon technical staff inspect each tyre and prepare a written report. The tyres are held at the Dragon manufacturing plant until customers can visit the company, see the casings, and review the technical report with the Dragon inspectors. To

improve the effectiveness of this service, the intention is that the inspectors will video the casing to highlight areas of identified damage. These visual materials and inspectors' reports will be made available on-line through customer extranets. Customers can then download these materials in the comfort of their own offices and use e-mail to pose questions of the inspectors. It is hoped that this procedure will remove the need for customers to visit the Dragon plant. Once a reasonable video library has been accumulated, Dragon will then add these materials, suitably edited to protect customer anonymity, to enhance product information pages.

4 Pricing: Although the move to e-commerce trading is expected to reduce operating costs, Dragon will attempt to sustain the same pricing policy for both on-line and off-line customers.

5 Promotion: Dragon will continue to use traditional promotional tools, including trade exhibitions, trade advertising, press releases, a company newsletter and a sales force. It is hoped that the advent of the e-commerce facility will permit the sales staff to spend more time acting as remould advisors and less time 'fire fighting' problems of incorrect orders, invoicing errors and product shipment delays.

6 Distribution: The company will continue to use its own delivery lorries to service UK customers. Upon entry to Europe, the services of a long-haul fleet provider will be used for delivery across the continent. Selection of a fleet operator will be dependent upon the selected supplier being able to link automatically into the Dragon on-line order entry/product shipment delivery system.

E-Commerce Infrastructure

Last year Dragon completed a major upgrading of the IT operation to create an integrated ERP system that already permits real time data exchange between sales, manufacturing, production scheduling, quality control, procurement, shipping and accounting databases. This will simplify the construction of the e-commerce infrastructure, because the main elements required for the new system will be the construction of an on-line 'front end' for displaying product information, permitting on-line ordering, the downloading of specific data to key customers via extranets and provision of customer access to check on the status of tyre shipments in transit. In the case of the off-line order entry system, this will be integrated into the on-line operation by providing office sales staff with terminals and an intranet via which to enter orders received by telephone, fax or mail. Given Dragon's limited e-commerce expertise, the front end will be developed by a US software company with experience in the US tyre manufacturing industry. The actual system will be installed off-site at a major Internet service provider (ISP) based in the same town as the Dragon head office. Preliminary costings suggest the new system can be developed and implemented for a total cost of £250 000. Ongoing annual operating costs are estimated at £75 000 per annum.

Financial Forecast

Although the new system is expected to halt any further erosion in the UK operation net profit margins, this factor is not budgeted into the cost analysis. Hence the financial

Within the situation review there should coverage of the strategic situation facing the organization. This will be based on a description of e-market size, e-market growth trends, e-customer benefit requirements, the use of the marketing mix to satisfy e-customer needs, the e-commerce activity of key competitors, and the potential influence of changes in any of the variables which constitute the core and macroenvironmental elements of the e-market system. The review should include analysis of whether the company is merely going to service end-user market needs or concurrently seek to integrate e-commerce systems with those of key suppliers.

The internal e-capabilities of the organization are reviewed within the context of whether they represent strengths or weaknesses which might influence future performance. Key issues will be that of whether staff have appropriate e-commerce operational skills, and whether new staff will need to be recruited or aspects of the project outsourced to specialist e-commerce service providers. Another issue is the degree to which existing databases can be integrated into a new e-commerce system to work on either a real time or **batch processing** (*storing received data and then entering this new information into the computer regularly, such as once or twice a day*) basis.

Favourites

E-market circumstances are assessed in relation to whether these represent opportunities or threats. Consideration needs to be given to whether the move is proactive or, alternatively, a reactive response to initiatives already implemented by competition. Other issues are (1) the degree to which existing markets will be served through e-commerce and (2) whether e-commerce will be used to support entry into new markets. Combining the external and internal market analysis permits execution of the SWOT analysis. The SWOT, when linked with the situation review, provides the basis for defining which key issues will need to be managed in order to develop an effective e-commerce plan for the future.

The degree to which e-commerce marketing objectives are defined can vary tremendously. Some organizations merely restrict aims to increasing the effectiveness of their promotional activities. Others may specify overall forecasted e-sales and desired e-market share. Some organizations may extend this statement by breaking the market into specific e-market target segments and detailed aims for e-sales, e-expenditure and e-profits for each product and/or e-market sector.

The e-marketing strategy defines how, by positioning the company is a specific way, stated marketing objectives will be achieved. The marketing mix section will cover how each element within the e-commerce mix (product, price, promotion and distribution) will be used to support the specified strategy. In relation to the product, it is necessary to determine whether the e-commerce offering provides an opportunity for product enhancement. Such opportunities include improvements in customer service, expansion of product line, and reductions in delivery times. In pricing, thought must be given to whether off-line and on-line prices will be different, and to the potential implications of any price variation on existing off-line customers. The promotional mix is reviewed in relation to how the website provides information and the investment which may be needed for off-line promotion to build market awareness for the e-commerce operation. If on-line transactions are to be an offered to customers, the implications of new distribution methods need to be examined. Finally, after the marketing mix issues have been resolved, these variables provide the basis for specifying the technological infrastructure needed to support the e-commerce operation.

The action plan section provides detailed descriptions of all actions to be taken to manage the e-marketing mix, including timings and definitions of which specific individuals or departments are responsible for implementing the plan. Financial forecasts provide a detailed breakdown of e-revenue, the cost of e-goods, all e-expenditures and resultant e-profits. Many organizations will also include forecasts of fund flows and, via a balance sheet, the expected asset/liability situation.

Control systems should permit management, upon e-market plan implementation, to identify rapidly variations of actual performance from forecast, and be provided with diagnostic guidance on the cause of those variations. To achieve this aim, the control system should focus on measurement of key variables within the plan, such as targeted e-market share, e-customer attitudes, awareness objectives for e-promotion, e-market distribution targets by product, and the expected and actual behaviour of competition.

Contingency plans exist to handle the fact that events rarely happen as predicted by the original plan. If the organization has already given thought to alternative scenarios prior to the beginning of the trading year, then if actual events are at variance with the plan management is more able immediately to implement actions to overcome encountered obstacles. The usual was to achieve this goal is that during the planning cycle the marketer examines the implications of alternative outcomes (for example the impact of actual e-sales revenue being 25 per cent higher and 25 per cent lower than forecast). Having reached conclusions from this analysis, the marketer then includes alternative plans as a component of the overall package for which senior management approval is being sought.

● Planning to Go International

The Dragon plan is specifically aimed at using the Internet to expand the company's overseas operations. However, what many on-line operations need to recognise is that although their products may be aimed at a domestic market, their presence on the Internet implies that they are global businesses (Leibs 2000). For example, when the US department store Macy's went on-line, 15 per cent of enquiries came from overseas customers. The company does not operate outside the US and hence for the moment is unable to accept orders from other countries.

As well as hosting more websites than any other country, the reason that US on-line operations attract overseas customers is that list prices for retail products are often significantly lower than similar items available in those customer's own countries. Unfortunately, when the cost of air freight and import duties is added, these customers often end up paying more on-line than they would have had they purchased the goods in a local shop. For those companies that operate in business-to-business markets, overseas distribution costs are usually less of a problem. Orders tend to be larger and hence duties and shipping charges tend to be a much smaller proportion of the total cost.

This situation does mean, however, that for those companies with international aspirations, an issue raising early in the planning process is how to handle distribution effectively. For many the solution is probably to open physical distribution facilities in key markets around the world. The US clothing retailer Lands End, for example, has established such facilities in the key markets of Germany, Japan and the UK.

Forrester Company research found that probably only 10 per cent of companies are able to present themselves to their markets as truly international on-line operations. At the moment, with the US continuing to account for half of the world's e-commerce business, many of the US on-line operations can probably afford to ignore overseas market opportunities. Nevertheless, this situation is likely to change over time. Western Europe is expected to offer a total market opportunity of $430 billion by 2003. The Asia–Pacific region can also be expected to grow rapidly in size over the next few years. In this situation it is extremely likely that the companies most likely to benefit from these trends will be those which have for many years already run successful terrestrial businesses in these regions.

In cases in which markets are already global, firms going on-line have little choice but to think internationally from the start. For example when Enron Corporation (*www.enrononline.com*)—a Houston-based operation involved in electricity, natural gas and energy facilities, moved onto the Internet, it was necessary to replicate in cyberspace those activities that already occur at the company's terrestrial global trading desks. The company is the top buyer and seller of natural gas in the US, and the leading wholesaler of electricity. The website offers its global customer base the opportunity to purchase, on-line, hundreds of different products. Additionally prices are posted in real time, and the site is required to handle trades in a variety of different currencies.

Summary

Achieving and then sustaining long-term success is usually made more certain if the organization has evolved a marketing plan to guide ongoing operations. Given the highly competitive nature of most markets, success can be made more certain by the adoption of a resource-based view of the company in which core competences are matched with identified opportunities. Implementing this type of marketing philosophy can be made more certain by the construction of a resource-based planning matrix. In the context of e-commerce there are few differences between cyberspace and terrestrial marketing when it comes to the construction of a plan. A marketing plan designed to guide a remould tyre company into cyberspace is a good demonstration of these points.

STUDY QUESTIONS

1 How can a resource advantage planning matrix be used in the development of an e-commerce marketing plan?

2 Compare and contrast the value chain for (1) a manufacturer of PCs and (2) a national chain which retails PCs.

3 Describe the components which constitute an e-marketing plan. Review the purpose of each of the components within the planning document.

Case: *Brush Ltd Part 2*

Please note that work on these case materials should only be considered after completion of the case in Chapter 5, in which market position (whether focused marketing of accounting software or diversification into office equipment) was selected as the basis of Brush's future expansion of e-commerce operations.

Following the decision already made concerning Brush's selection of an on-line market positioning, the next issue raised by senior management was whether to focus efforts in a single country or seek to establish a global business. One of potential drawbacks to the latter strategy is that different languages, cultures, currencies, accounting principles and tax legislation have to be accommodated. The complexity of this proposition, linked to an analysis of current market circumstances around the world, led to the conclusion that for the foreseeable future the company should focus upon developing an e-commerce marketing plan restricting operations to the US market, this selection being based upon the fact that within the US small companies sector (comprising enterprises with less than 100 employees) use of the Internet is extremely high, whereas usage levels in, for example, the UK and Europe are very much lower.

Recent market research on the US small companies sector provides the data in the table below.

For planning purposes, the company product range can be considered to contain simple systems (average price $100 contributing 40 per cent of total sales), middle range systems (average price $300, contributing 30 per cent of total sales) and top-of- the-range systems (average price $500 also contributing 30 per cent of total sales). All products achieve an average gross profit (sales less cost of goods) of 50 per cent.

Data in '000s of companies

Company size	With Internet access	Websites with no on-line shopfront	Website with on-line shopfront
Less than 5 employees	2402	1134	677
5–9 employees	997	587	294
10–19 employees	664	451	194
20–49 employees	453	413	168
50–99 employees	169	164	67
	No Internet access	**No website**	**No on-line shopfront**
No of small companies	2999	4935	6283

Source: US Internal Revenue Service

QUESTION

1   Assume the role of Marketing Director of Brush, and prepare an e-commerce marketing plan for entry into the US market. Market positioning should be based on whichever option was selected during work on the case in Chapter 5.

Case: *Virtual Education*

A recent government report concluded that continuing economic growth would be frustrated by the fact that, with the exception of very large organizations (those with more than 250 employees), insufficient attention is given to providing secretarial, clerical and administrative staff with ongoing training in the use of IT business software. Portchester Business School has developed a university certificate in IT business systems. The course is in a modular form that requires students to complete eight modules in various aspects of IT (for example using spreadsheets, desk-top publishing, website design). Using the Internet, the course can be delivered as distance learning anywhere in the country. Students can be provided with on-line support via e-mail and groupware. Their end-of-module assignment can also be submitted and marked electronically.

The business school has decided to launch the product as a part-time, self-study module aimed at people in work. It is estimated that it will take part-time students two years to complete the programme. It is estimated that the annual total market size for this type of product is 100 000, and the business school's maximum achievable market share, given competition from traditional non-electronic providers (for example commercial training centres and local colleges), is in the region of 5 per cent. The total fee for the two years of study is £2000. The estimated direct costs of delivering the course (administration, on-line tutor support, assignment assessment, materials etc.) are £750 per student.

QUESTION

1   Assume that you have been assigned the task of developing and launching this virtual teaching product. Prepare an e-commerce marketing plan for consideration by the Dean of the business school.

Chapter 6 Glossary

Batch processing (p. 133)
   Storing received data and then entering this new information into the computer regularly, such as once or twice a day.

Relative resource costs (p. 119)
   The degree to which a company's operating costs are higher or lower than competition.

Relative resource-produced value (p. 119)
   The degree to which the company's financial performance is better or worse than competition.

Chapter 7

E-COMMERCE INNOVATION

Learning Objectives

This chapter explains

- The determination of innovation priorities.

- The evolution e-commerce beyond PC-based platforms.

- Strategic focus in the innovation process.

- The management of the new product development process.

- The management of the new product development process.

- The management of complex technology innovation.

- Market expansion in the innovation management cycle.

E-commerce innovation, whether directed towards the development of new products or the introduction of very different internal organizational processes, can be an extremely a high risk activity. Failure can be expensive in terms of both unrecovered investment and the time staff have been diverted away from mainstream activities which could have been financially more rewarding for the organization. Therefore, before embarking upon a race to develop new e-commerce products or introduce an e-based marketing operation, organizations need to assess clearly the relative merits of the medium-term alternatives of (1) focusing upon innovation to generate the most of financial performance improvement from e-commerce, and (2) focusing upon actions directed towards improving existing off-line business operations.

Another issue which should be considered is whether the organization wishes to behave in a conventional manner or adopt a more entrepreneurial orientation towards innovation. Reaching a decision requires recognition of an important point; namely that selecting an appropriate attitude to innovation should be perceived as the determining a point somewhere along a continuum. At one extreme is the decision to progress innovation through minor extensions of conventional activities (for example a cheese producer who sells products through distributors and supermarket chains might opt to create a small-scale, on-line sales outlet). The other extreme involves the organization creating a radically different, entirely unconventional approach to future operations. An example of this is UK retailer Dixons, traditionally as a multi-outlet electronic consumer goods discount operation deciding to make a

	Organizational process	
	Current	New
Current	(1) Zero risk Current marketing strategy	(2) Low risk Existing product marketed through e-commerce channels
New	(3) Average risk New e-commerce product marketed through traditional channels	(4) Above average risk New e-commerce product marketed solely through e-commerce channels

Product form (left axis); Organizational process (top axis)

Figure 7.1 An innovation e-commerce options matrix

major investment to establish the largest new e-business portal in the UK (*www. freeserve.com*)

Innovation in e-commerce can come from changes to the product form or a revision of internal organizational processes. Combining these two dimensions generates the alternative medium-term option matrix of the type illustrated in Fig. 7.1. Cell 1 is a zero risk option because it involves concentrating on continuing to exploit existing products using a conventional marketing mix. Cell 2 involves slightly more risk because the proposed action is to continue marketing an existing product, merely revising internal organizational processes to make the product available in an e-commerce form.

Cell 3 is a somewhat higher risk option. It involves a company developing a new product form, with an e-commerce application. This new product is marketed, however, using a conventional marketing mix. The highest risk option is cell 4. In this case, the company develops a product, with an e-commerce application and revises the organizational processes to support the new item in e-commerce marketing channel. Examples of the four options are provided in Fig. 7.2

The model in Fig 7.1 is posited as a dynamic process, changing over time depending upon the circumstances confronting the organization. For example, when a high risk strategy proves to be very successful, the tendency of most firms is not to seek another high risk innovation option. Typically, having validated the commercial viability of a new innovation pathway, the entrepreneurial organization tends to become somewhat

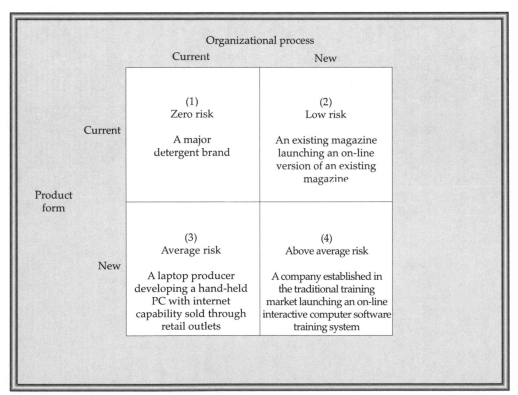

Figure 7.2 Examples of e-commerce innovation options

more conventional. The outcome is that the company seeks out new options similar in character to the initial success. One could argue, for example, this is exactly the scenario that now faces Amazon. Having established a highly entrepreneurial on-line bookselling operation, the company is now diversifying into other retail sectors, such as an on-line pharmacy.

Another way of defining risk in e-commerce innovation is in relation to the two dimensions of (1) adding e-commerce features to an existing product versus launching a new product, and (2) modifying the way an existing market is served versus entering a new market sector. Combining these two dimensions creates the product/market matrix shown in Fig 7.3.

● Confirming Strategic Focus

It was proposed in earlier chapters that most companies opt for one of four areas of possible strategic focus: product performance excellence, price performance excellence, transactional excellence or relationship excellence. Given the high risks associated with any significant form of innovation, it is probably much safer for a company to retain its existing strategic focus when considering plans for e-commerce innovation. The reason for this is that marketing effort will not have to be expended on establishing the new e-commerce activity at the same time as gaining market acceptance for a completely new strategic position.

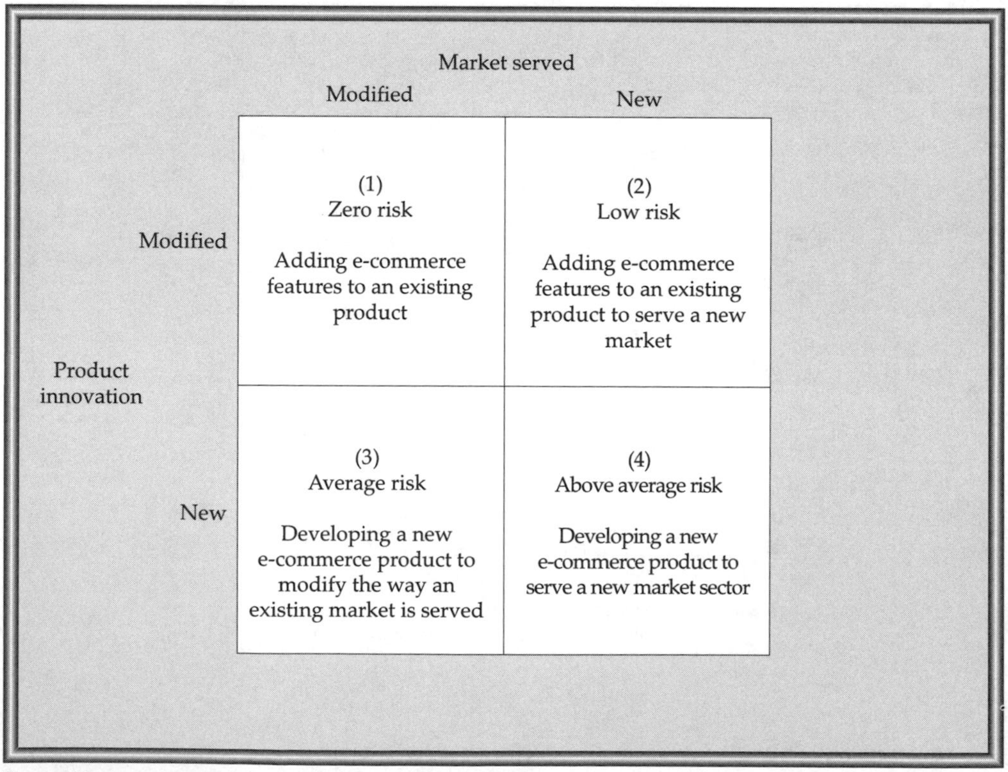

	Market served	
	Modified	**New**
Modified	(1) Zero risk Adding e-commerce features to an existing product	(2) Low risk Adding e-commerce features to an existing product to serve a new market
New	(3) Average risk Developing a new e-commerce product to modify the way an existing market is served	(4) Above average risk Developing a new e-commerce product to serve a new market sector

Product innovation (row label spanning Modified/New)

Figure 7.3 *An e-commerce product/market innovation matrix*

Regional Stockbroker

The product/market matrix model shown in Fig. 7.3 can be demonstrated by examining the application of the decisions tool to innovation planning by a regional stockbroker. In Fig. 7.4 that cell 1 is the lowest risk proposition because it merely involves adding e-commerce features to an existing product. The example in Fig. 7.4 is a small regional stockbroker which has traditionally provided a telephone share trading service to private investors. By adding an on-line facility, the company can expand market coverage to include private investors who want to trade on-line. Until now, the stockbroker has only offered services to individuals, and has avoided corporate customers. Cell 2 is the next highest risk pathway because it merely requires expanding into a new market sector with a modified existing product. In the specific case of the stockbroker, this means offering an on-line share trading service to pension managers and advisors in local companies.

A somewhat higher risk option is cell 3, which involves launching a new e-commerce product as a way of modifying how an existing market is served. For the stockbroker, this means offering private investors the opportunity to trade on-line in fixed-term bonds and currency futures. Cell 4 is the highest risk option, involving both a new e-commerce product and entry into a new market sector, in this case offering a fixed bond/currency futures on-line trading facility to pension managers and advisors.

	Market served	
	Modified	**New**
Product innovation — Modified	**(1)** Zero risk — A traditional regional stockbroker providing an on-line share trading scheme	**(2)** Low risk — A traditional regional stockbroker offering on-line share dealing facilities to pension fund managers and advisors in local companies
Product innovation — New	**(3)** Average risk — A traditional regional stockbroker offering an on-line fixed-term bonds/currency futures trading facility	**(4)** Above average risk — A traditional stockbroker offering an on-line fixed term bonds/currency futures trading facility to pension fund managers and advisors in local companies

Figure 7.4 *Examples of e-commerce innovation options*

The four strategic options are described in Fig. 7.5. Product performance excellence is represented in Fig. 7.5 by Dell which offers corporate customers the facility of designing and customising products on-line. An example of price excellence is provided by American Airlines who have decided that one way of marketing empty airline seats is to ask for bids from potential customers by featuring available flights on the on-line auction site e-Bay.

An example of excellence in transaction management is United Airlines, which has established a website for frequent fliers that not only offers flight information and a reservation service, but also provides assistance and reservations capability for ground services needed by the traveller at the destination, such as car rental, hotel accommodation and restaurant reservations. The car rental giant, Hertz, illustrates relationship excellence. In the face of increasing price competition from other car rental firms, the company has established an on-line reservations site that features 'memory' of car model rental preferences, based on booking history. Additionally these corporate clients are provided with cars with an e-commerce navigation link to assist them in a strange city.

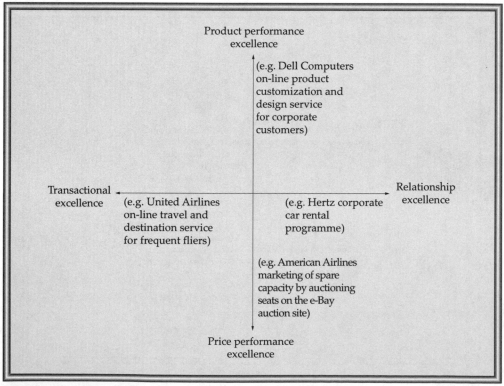

Figure 7.5 *Alternative e-commerce strategic positioning options*

E-COMMERCE INNOVATION

● Process Management

A number of authors have undertaken research to identify factors influencing the success and failure of new products. One of the most prolific writers in this area, Professor Cooper (1975, 1986, 1988, 1990), has conducted numerous cross-sectional and longitudinal studies of Canadian firms. He concludes that factors that need to be assessed in determining the probable performance of a new product are:

1   Product superiority/quality: how product features, benefits, uniqueness and/or overall quality contribute to competitive advantage.

2   Economic value: whether the product offers greater value than existing products.

3   Overall fit: whether the product development project is compatible with the organization's existing areas of production and marketing expertise.

4   Technological compatibility: how compatible the product is with the organization's existing areas of technological capability.

5   Familiarity to company: whether the company can draw upon existing expertise or will be forced to learn completely new operational skills.

6   Market opportunity: the nature of market need, the size of market and its growth trend.

7   Competitive situation: how easy it will be to penetrate the market and cope with competitive threats.

8   Defined opportunity: whether the product fits into a well defined category, as opposed to being an innovative idea providing the basis for a completely new market sector.

9   Project definition: how well the product development project is defined and understood within the organization.

Over the past 20 years, recognition of the factors influencing success, and the high financial costs associated with failure, has resulted in the development of various innovation management control systems. These systems have mainly been applied to the development of new products. However, as illustrated in Fig. 7.6, a significant proportion of their conceptual aspect is also applicable to organizational process innovation. Innovation management systems tend to be of a linear, sequential nature. The ultimate aim of a process is to launch only e-commerce products or implement e-commerce organizational processes guaranteed of success. As the organization moves through the project, at each stage the question arises of whether the product or process under development should be progressed or terminated. Development costs increase at an almost exponential rate while projects are in progress. The earlier the company reaches a termination decision, the greater the savings. The attraction of these linear models is that they are capable of identifying what might be commercially very risky ideas early in the development process prior to significant expenditure. It should be recognized, however, that they are essentially negative control systems, designed not to maximize success but to minimize the possibility of failure.

The entry point to the innovation process is idea generation. The objective of the idea generation stage is to maximize the number of ideas available for consideration.

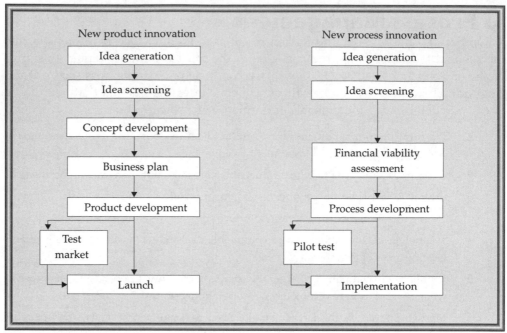

Figure 7.6 *Linear innovation management models*

Traditionally, this is achieved by involving customers, intermediaries, the sales force, employees from all areas of the organization—to identify weaknesses in competitors' products—the R&D department and suppliers. Organizations that operate in a market in which customer and/or suppliers are relationship-oriented can draw on these external sources for additional ideas. This contrasts with organizations operating in transactionally-orientated market sectors, which often are forced to develop products with little assistance from other members of their market system. Organizations may seek to extend the breadth of their search for ideas by exploiting sources such as research into markets in other countries, the forging of links with research institutions, and the monitoring of scientific breakthroughs in areas outside of the mainstream technology within their industrial sector.

It should be recognized, however, that many 'new to the world' ideas do not come as a result of carefully managed searches of many sources. A more usual scenario is that an intuitive entrepreneur suddenly perceives a new concept or starts work trying to exploit an emergent area of technology with little consideration for the scale of potential commercial opportunity that might exist. The problem is that this type of individual is often uncomfortable working in large organizations, preferring the freedom and flexibility offered by smaller companies. One outcome of this is that the source of many of the most dynamic, impactful new ideas in e-commerce are new-to-the world, start-up businesses founded by 'techies'.

The problem that large Western companies face in trying to establish more innovative, entrepreneurial internal environments has now attracted the attention of business researchers. A very common conclusion by writers such as Buzan (1993) is that a

E-COMMERCE INNOVATION

fundamental underlying cause for low creativity in large firms is the logical, positivist education traditional in Western nations. As a result of this, the majority of people emerge from education as 'left-brain' thinkers whose mind-set is biased towards conventional solutions. This type of person typically favours systematic investigation of problems and the formulation of a solution through a step-by-step analysis of a situation. It is argued that what is required within many large organizations is a higher number of intuitive or 'right brain' thinkers. Using an open-minded, exploratory approach, these individuals often generate ideas capable of challenging established conventions. One outcome of the theory concerning alternative thinking styles is the fact that over recent years an increasingly diverse range of techniques have been developed for enhancing employee creativity (for example mind mapping, lateral thinking and brain-storming).

At the idea screening stage, the objective is only to progress those ideas that appear to have genuine potential for success. Given that originators of ideas often develop an emotional attachment to their proposals that can reduce their ability to see clearly, some organizations use highly structured systems for evaluating ideas. Typically, these are based around some form of scoring system in which all ideas are rated against factors such as market size, market growth trends, impact on existing product portfolio, opportunity for market diversification, intensity of competition, ability to produce goods/services, financial resources and availability of key raw materials.

E-Commerce Life After the PC

After two decades of phenomenal sales growth, the PC industry is beginning to entertain the idea that industry annual sales may have finally peaked. In 1998, the average price of a desk-top PC fell by 17.3 per cent and the total market shrank by 3.6 per cent. During 1999, even the market stars of the hardware sector (laptops, notepads and servers), only sustained year-on-year growth because manufacturers were willing to reduce average prices by 15 per cent (anon. 1999a). The outcome of this is that the computer industry, having accepted that the PC may no longer be a growth market, is now beginning to examine how e-commerce might provide the route to regaining sustained profitability.

One possible route is to move from 'box shifters' to becoming e-commerce service providers. The scale of this alternative opportunity is illustrated by e-commerce portals such as NuAuction (***www.nuauction.com***) and DirectWeb (***www.directweb.com***) giving away PCs to consumers willing to commit to a three year Internet connection. Dell has launched Gigabuys.com, a site where consumers can choose from 30 000 products ranging from digital cameras to computer bags. IBM and Hewlett Packard have announced similar moves. In the meantime, the two computer industry supply giants, Intel and Microsoft, are seeking new ways into e-commerce (anon. 1999b). Intel is developing new chips for use in low-power products and domestic appliances. Microsoft is moving into telecommunications, car navigation systems and set-top TV boxes.

A major problem for the computer industry is that the convergence of electronic appliances, computers and telecommunications will lead to head-to-head battles between a range of global giants from all three sectors. Matsushita is investing $140 million to acquire small Californian e-commerce software companies. Nokia (***www.nokia.com***) and Motorola are developing the next generation of Internet telephones. Sony has already launched innovative products such as a digital picture frame that displays 50 different colour photographs and a smart software unit, which will recognize when people enter a room, turning on their favourite TV programme or playing their favourite CD.

Possibly the sector of e-commerce attracting the strong interest among telecommunications companies is the use of Wireless Applications Technology (WAP) to bring the Internet to the mobile phone (Reed 2000). Forrestor Research predicts that by 2004, a third of Europeans will regularly access the Internet via mobiles. The potential of WAP technology has already attracted the interest of providers of time-sensitive information such as news, share prices, sporting results and weather updates. Some airlines have entered the sector, offering journey information and electronic check-in facilities. Finnair moved into WAP in September 1999, and were followed by both Swissair and Lufthansa.

Nokia was the first mobile telephone manufacturer to offer WAP services in the UK. They were followed by Ericsson and Motorola. In November 1999, Orange launched a WAP service offering news, sport, traffic information, business directories and travel offers. The company is also working with NatWest to develop on-line banking services. BT Cellnet unveiled its mobile Internet service in January 2000. This offers users access to ***www.lastminute.com***, the BBC, Excite and ***www.european.investor.com***.

New ideas are usually framed around phrases and descriptions used by individuals within an industrial sector, many of which are not understood by the customer. Hence the first step in the concept development phase is to redefine ideas into customer-oriented benefit and product attribute statements. The resultant concept statements can then be tested on possible target audiences using techniques such as focus group meetings and one-to-one interviews. Because in many cases the product does not yet physically exist, this research is often undertaken using surrogates such as the storyboard of a possible TV campaign, the layout for a print advertisement and/or a mock-up of the product packaging. Data from focus groups and interviews permit the researcher to assess purchase probability, relative appeal of product benefit, and customer price expectations.

Purchase probability information provides the basis on which to forecast sales and to evolve a business plan for the new product. The sales forecast, when linked with estimates for costs of goods, marketing expenditure, operating overheads and fixed asset requirements, permits estimation of expected profits and return on investment for the project. These profitability figures are usually assessed against the minimum new product financial performance standards, established by the organizations. Only if the plan can demonstrate that the minimum performance standards will be exceeded should approval be given to proceed to the product development phase.

Understanding of specified customer benefits identified during the concept development stage, when linked to forecasted production costs in the business plan, permit the creation of a detailed specification for use by the R&D department during

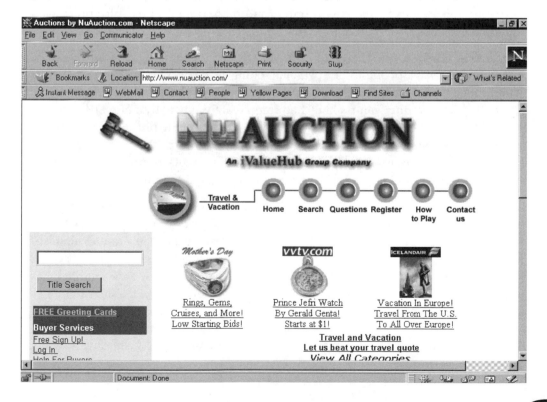

the product development phase. Once prototypes have been produced, market research to determine whether the actual product is capable of fulfilling customer needs can begin. In consumer goods markets, this research is often based on activities such as blind side-by-side comparisons and in-home placement tests. In industrial markets, companies often involve potential customers in the evaluation activity through a technique known as beta-testing. In this situation, customers are kept closely involved in all aspects of the prototype development programme, and through use of the test product in their organization can provide detailed feedback that is used to identify possible improvements. Advantages of beta-testing are that 'in-use' problems are recognized before launch, the experience offered to participants often leads them to be the first purchasers of the new product, and these organizations also often act as part-time marketers, promoting the item to contacts within their market sector.

In industrial markets, the small number of customers, the high value of purchases per customer and the use of one-to-one personal selling as the primary promotional vehicle usually means that, following successful completion of the prototype development phase, the new product can be launched immediately. Virtually none of the market research undertaken during the new product development phases will, however, answer the question of whether a new product will survive in the self-service environment characteristic of many consumer goods markets, or provide data on how the product will respond to different levels of promotional spending.

This means that before the decision to launch, many consumer goods are further evaluated through the medium of a test market. The objectives of the test market are to assess, in a geographically restricted area, the performance of the product alongside competitive offerings. During the test, research studies are undertaken to measure variables such as product awareness, trial rate, repeat purchase rate, market share attainment, level of in-store distribution, and competition behaviour. Measurement of the last of these is necessary in order to determine whether competitors are behaving normally or mounting a specific response to the test market which could not be duplicated nationally (for example doubling promotional spend or offering 'buy one, get one free' sales promotions).

In relation to customer test market response, there are four possible outcomes in trial and repeat sales rates, each of which have different implications. One outcome is high trial/high repeat sales. This usually means the test market has been successful and the product should be launched immediately. A second outcome, low trial/high repeat rate requires further investigation. Given that the repeat rate is high and product appeal was presumably positive during both concept and prototype development phase evaluations, the most likely cause of an observed low trial rate is inadequate awareness and/or poor levels of in-store distribution. Both of these matters can usually be remedied through increased consumer and trade promotional activity. Thus all that needs to be assessed is whether the increased expenditure associated with these activities would still permit the product to exceed the organization's minimum financial performance standards.

A third outcome, of high trial/low repeat, is a little more worrying because it usually implies that, having tried the product, customers remain unconvinced of its merits. Typically, further investigation of this situation reveals that due to unforeseen manufacturing problems the product evaluated at the prototype development stage is no longer the one used in the test market. Unless the manufacturing department can find a way of overcoming this problem, thereby duplicating the prototype product specification, the product will probably have to be dropped.

The worst scenario is the fourth outcome, in which both trial and repeat rates are low. Here it must be assumed that fundamental organizational problems exist, and that therefore serious questions need to be put to the project team to find exactly what has been going on at all stages of the development process. A very usual outcome is that the post-mortem will reveal the need to make major changes in either the staff and/or project management processes used by the organization.

Once a launch decision has been reached, the next question confronting the marketer is whether the product should be introduced on a national or a phased, market-by-market, basis. The financial attraction of the latter scenario is that investment in new production facilities can be spread over a longer period of time, and revenue from one market can be used to fund the introduction into the next market area. These gains have to be weighed, however, against the drawback that competitors may develop an equivalent product that can be launched into areas not yet reached. Global companies in the same situation face the even larger problem of how to fund a multi-country launch if they wish to avoid being pre-empted by competitors in key markets around the world.

In view of the pre-emption risks associated with phased launch, and the even larger financial burdens facing the global company, some organizations might decide that the safest option is (1) to wait until another company launches a new product, and enter the market with an equivalent proposition at a later date, and (2) never consider entering overseas markets when developing new products. The available research evidence tends to indicate, however, that neither of these is commercially wise. Robinson and Fornell's (1985) study of mature markets, for example, concludes that if market pioneers implement an effective marketing strategy based around a new product offering

*Innovation at Hitachi (**www.hitachi.co.jap**)*

Hitachi who are world leaders in developing the low-power chips demanded of laptops and e-commerce devices such as Internet-linked telephones and 'smart' domestic devices. To acquire core software design skills, back in the 1980s the company entered into a development alliance with Texas Instruments. It then applied its competence in electron beam lithography to test manufacture the world's first low-power 64 megabyte memory chip. Experience then permitted it to move onto making 256 megabyte, 1024 megabyte and 4000 megabyte chips. Underlying this rapid innovation pace is a philosophy based around (1) investing in the acquisition of technological intelligence from outside the company, (2) very rapid internal organizational learning, (3) the ability of the workforce to assimilate new technologies (4) using alliances to enhance core competences, and (5) exploiting concurrent engineering to minimize product development time.

genuine customer benefit, then they will usually achieve a market share higher than that of competitors that enter the market at a later date. Cooper and Kleinschmidt (1990) compared the implications in industrial markets of designing new products solely for domestic market use with an innovation orientation seeking to use the new product to enter overseas markets. They found that products designed for international markets tended to be significantly more successful both at home and abroad. The conclusion of this study is that an international new product orientation results in a company taking much more care to avoid mistakes in the product development process and sets much higher standards in relation to design, selection of raw materials, specification of product benefit, marketing planning and market research.

The Changing World Of Photography

A market sector in which the Internet has stimulated innovation is photography. Numerous new companies are emerging enabling customers to store, print and share photographs via the Internet (Shaffer 2000). A major catalyst has been that these companies have the knowledge and equipment to generate high quality prints.

The sites **www.photo.access.com** and **www.shutterfly.com** have plants equipped with high capacity machines for processing and printing prints taken using digital cameras. Going even further is **www.zing.com**. Customers can create free on-line ZingAlbums, meet other people with similar hobby interests or store pictures of items they are selling via on-line auctions. The site also offers photography tips and tools for viewing, searching, printing and enhancing pictures.

● Managing Complex Innovation

E-commerce innovation, especially if concerned with revising internal organizational processes, is not a simple task. Firstly, the developers are dependent upon compatibility in the software systems operated by the company, suppliers and customers. Most e-commerce software developers can tell stories of the months spent achieving software compatibility between standard platforms and specialist architectures (for example linking brand name word processing and graphic software to an automated document imaging system), only to find that a supplier or the customer's IT department innocently installs an upgraded version of a standard software platform with the immediate effect of crashing the entire system.

The second complexity in the innovation management process is the need for e-commerce systems to (1) be linked into every database within the organization and (2) run data interchange on a real time basis. This goal demands that all departments are oriented towards giving priority not to their own information needs but the effective operation of the organization's e-commerce system. Even in off-line companies, efficient inter-departmental communication during execution of an innovation project is rarely an easily achieved goal. Once the communication requirements are for real time data interchange, seeking to establish effective communication flows usually becomes many more times more difficult.

The third complexity within e-commerce innovation is that in many cases the developers will need to draw upon new technologies from a very diverse range of sources, such as computing, telecommunications and optoelectronics. Although the Japanese have yet to emerge as dominant players in the e-commerce industry, their achievements as leading innovators in other high-tec industries does suggest that their new product and process management techniques can provide some useful lessons. Bowonder and Miyake (1992), in their research on Japanese innovation management, use a number of sources to evolve a model in which the following factors are perceived as critical in achieving success:

1   Clarity of purpose in focusing on fusing together a broad range of different technologies.

2   A willingness among companies to collaborate with each other to gain access to critical core competences.

3   The use of multiple source of technology to lower the risk of failure through one single technology frustrating progress for other elements within the project.

4   The use of concurrent engineering to exploit the interaction that can come from parallel activities and offer the potential to drastically reduce development cycles.

5   An emphasis on involving the entire workforce in organizational learning to ensure new ideas and skills are spread throughout the operation.

6   An emphasis on continuous technological innovation to ensure the latest scientific thinking is incorporated into the organization's core competences.

Other researchers have examined the influence of organizational structure on effective innovation management. In a seminal review of this extremely diverse area of the academic literature, Nanata and Sivakumar (1996) examine the degree to which an orientation towards individualism or collectivism within a national culture can influence successful innovation activities. They conclude that, especially in high technology industries, outstanding new ideas tend to come from companies in which individualism is both valued and nurtured. It appears that this type of orientation provides innovators with sufficient freedom and autonomy to permit them to evolve totally new visions for products and organizational processes. The potential problem with this orientation is that, although it can be the source of outstanding new ideas, it may not be favourable for managing the latter stages of new product development. For in this subsequent phase it is necessary to bring together the contributive but diverse interests of all of the departments in the organization with a role in the latter stages of product development, prototyping, scaling up manufacturing systems and product launch. Nanaka and Sivakumar conclude that during the latter stages of an innovation project reduction of development times and overall scale of success is likely to be higher in organizations oriented towards collectivism.

It would, therefore, appear to be the case that there are two phases in the optimal management of an e-commerce innovation project. During the idea search and identification stage, developers should be granted extensive freedom to maximize the number and range of approaches to be considered. Once, however, a specific idea has been selected as offering the best way forward, the implementation stage is more likely to be successful if there is a shift to a team-based approach based around close co-operation, cohesion of effort and single-minded purpose.

> ## A Diverse Approach to Innovation
>
> In 1998, after 10 years of over 30 per cent compound annual growth, Intel, the world's leading chip manufacturer, found that industry consolidation and increased competition resulted in revenue growth slowing to 5 per cent per annum (anon. 2000b). In response to this situation, Intel's Chief Executive, Craig Barrett, sought to implement a diverse range of innovation activities to move Intel towards heavy involvement in the Internet.
>
> In order to win acceptance of a very different strategy, Intel faced the need to persuade staff to drop their 'not invented here' attitude to innovation. To assist this process, in 1999 the company spent $6 billion acquiring 12 companies already operating in the Internet sector. The company also expanded its venture capital operation, Intel Capital, and in 1999 invested approximately $1.2 billion in more than 350 software and Internet companies. This strategy quickly scored some notable hits, and soon these investments were valued at more than $8.2 billion.
>
> Internally, the company has sought to evolve a more entrepreneurial spirit among employees by offering funds to support new start-up ideas proposed by employees. These range from a scheme to equip doctors with secure IDs, in order to encourage on-line medicine, through to installing information terminals in the backs of seats in Madison Square Garden. One idea which emerged was to move the company into the Web-hosting business, and in 1999 the company's first Net centre was established in Santa Clara, California. Early success has caused Intel to plan more computer centres around the world to host e-commerce operating services for other companies. At the same time, the company is not seeking to leave the world of microchip manufacturing. What is happening, however, is that the company is investing heavily in new generations of chips for use in the networking, telecommunications and information appliance markets.

Another obstacle confronting e-commerce innovation, especially if the project involves a complete reorganization of internal processes, is the need to ensure that there is a culture fit between the innovation developers and the innovation users (Klein and Sorra 1996). These authors illustrate the importance of culture compatibility by describing the example of a company that decided to move to an automated computerized production scheduling and inventory control system. The objective of the developers was to use integrated information systems to build an organization that (1) provided customers with an ability to respond flexibly and rapidly to changing market trends, and (2) significantly improved profitability. Unfortunately, those on the shop floor believed that they were already able to respond to sudden changes in customer orders through working practices developed over the years. Their approach was based around workers applying an unstructured and fluid response to how best, and when, to handle customer orders. As the new automated system demanded a much more disciplined culture, with decisions vested centrally, it is not unsurprising that the new computer system was met with severe resistant on the shop floor, with the result that project implementation took too long.

The workers' perceptions over their level of flexibility were correct, but their chaotic approach to production scheduling, managing flow of work in progress through the plant, and fluctuations of finished goods levels were also the reason for the poor financial performance of the company. What the developers failed to recognize was that before their new automated system was brought on-line, there was a need to change attitudes, and develop among shop floor staff (1) an understanding of the financial implications of current work practices and (2) the new skills required in an environment driven by real time computer-based production and inventory control.

● Product Adoption Behaviour

A common practice among mass marketing companies is to gain rapid widespread distribution for a new product and to underpin the launch with heavy promotional spending. This approach has a fundamental flaw, in that it assumes all customers are willing to change their product usage patterns immediately and switch to the new offering. Yet as Rogers (1983) posits, there exists an 'innovation diffusion process' in which there are five adopter groups exhibiting the following very different purchase behaviour:

1   Innovators, who are venturesome individuals so willing to try new ideas that they are often prepared to accept that such a new product may perform less than perfectly.

2   Early adopters, who are opinion leaders within their industrial and/or personal social groups, willing to try new ideas ahead of others, but carefully assess potential risk before placing an order.

3   Early majority, those who try new ideas ahead of the majority but typically delay initial purchase until information from early adopters indicates the new product is meeting claims made by the supplier.

4   Late majority, those who tend to be sceptical about new ideas and avoid purchase until there is clear evidence that the new product is successful.

5   Laggards, who are traditionalists suspicious of change and who will delay purchase until the new product has been in the market for a significant period of time.

The speed with which a new product gains market acceptance and is adopted by the five different customer types on the diffusion curve is influenced by a whole range of factors which the e-commerce marketer needs to understand in designing a successful market launch. These include such factors as the relative advantage, compatibility and complexity of the new product, the level of **divisibility** (*the degree to which the product can be tried on a limited basis*) and **communicability** (*the degree to which the benefit claims can be easily described to potential users*) (Gatignon and Robertson 1985). In reviewing these issues, Moore (1991) concludes that companies marketing high-technology goods are often confronted by a 'chasm' between each of the five customer groups. The reason for this is that each customer group requires significantly different benefits. This means that the new product must be repositioned upon arriving at the next chasm in order to offer the desired product benefits to the next type of customer. Moore's concept of 'crossing the chasm' in the marketing of high-technology products and services is reflected in

Fig. 7.7. This diagram proposes that very different marketing strategies will be required to satisfy the very major differences in buyer behaviour between the various customer groups on the innovation diffusion curve (Chaston 1999).

With high-technology goods, the earliest adopters are often 'techies' whose interest is more in the ownership of the latest technology, often without giving consideration of practical purpose. This type of market is usually best served by entrepreneurial–transactional firms (see Chapter 4) which tend to draw upon the latest technological breakthroughs in their sector as the basis for developing new-to-the-world propositions. The majority of their customers are researchers working in scientific institutions, R&D laboratories or quality control departments of manufacturing firms who are also fascinated by the exploitation of the latest technology. Like the developer, their primary interest, moving forward the frontiers of knowledge, often outweighs considerations of reliability and practicality. In many cases the management of the marketing process is undertaken by the supplier's researchers, who operate in a world in which customers find out about new product expertise through word-of-mouth recommendations within the same sector of industry or academia.

For a new idea based upon the latest technology to sell to a broader market the customer will often have to help in development. Management of this phase of a new product's evolution is often most effectively managed by entrepreneurial-relationship firms who are able to form innovation partnerships with like-minded customers in order that together, they can develop a new product offering genuinely superior performance.

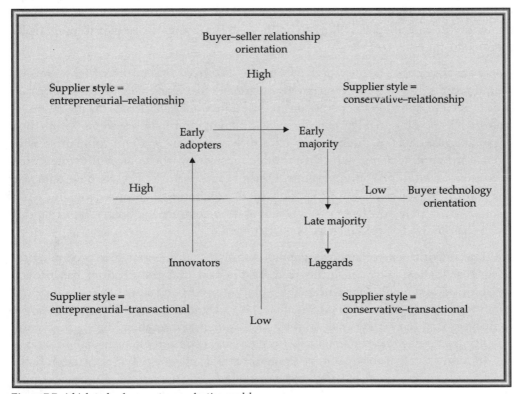

Figure 7.7 *A high-technology customer adoption model*

The marketing process of the entrepreneurial–relationship company is one which relies heavily upon word-of-mouth recommendations. The company must also have a clear idea of which customer groups are early adopters willing to take risks in the process of identifying new, often radical, solutions to existing problems. An early example of this scenario in the e-commerce market was the launch of the first groupware system, which has subsequently evolved into one of the leading platforms for supporting intranets. The developers, Lotus, persuaded the accounting and consultancy giant Price Waterhouse to enter the era of the 'electronic office' by purchasing 10 000 copies of the then unproven Lotus Notes (*www.ibm.com*).

Once the market begins to recognize widespread use of a new product by early adopters, the early majority will begin to become interested in the benefits. Unlike innovators or early adopters, the early majority take a much more pragmatic attitude to new products. Proven, superior benefits to the user are significantly more important that the nature of the enabling technology. At this stage in the life of the product, the supplier needs to use the more traditional marketing tools of identifying customer targets, formulating promotional campaigns to communicate new benefits, and be prepared to commence the battle to convince the market that the new product is capable of outperforming existing products. Market expansion is made significantly easier if the supplier has an in-depth knowledge of the customer. This fact is why, unless entrepreneurial–relationship companies are willing to change marketing orientation, their role in the life of the product often passes into the hands of conservative–relationship companies. These are often larger, and have typically monitored the progress of any innovations ready to enter the market when they think a majority of customers is willing to adopt it, offering a realistically priced, carefully targeted, competitive offering.

An example of this is provided by Oracle (*www.oracle.com*) which carefully monitored the growing concerns among customers that many new database software products were designed to operate on specific hardware platforms. This meant that it was often impossible to integrate effectively different information systems within their organizations. Oracle's solution was to launch a database system, compatible with most hardware systems, which permitted customers to create fully integrated computer-based information systems. Oracle's ability to deliver genuine database integration was a critical contribution to the technology required by the early e-commerce system developers. As a result, as the e-commerce industry has expanded Oracle has enjoyed a rapid increase in sales revenue.

The late majority customers are usually completely uninterested in technological advances. Instead they are influenced by the fact that the product has proven capabilities, is widely used within their market sector and is competitively priced relative to existing products. Servicing this type of customer is best undertaken by larger companies that can exploit scale in their manufacturing operation, have a marketing operation capable of implementing large scale promotional campaigns, and a distribution operation able to service a range of market channels. Typically these are the skills found within conservative–transactional marketing operations. A recent example of how a company with a dominant marketing position is most likely to exploit this type of opportunity is provided by Microsoft and its Internet Explorer's overwhelming attack on the leading browser supplier, Netscape (*www.netscape.com*).

Laggard customers are only really interested in proven solutions at low prices. The strong price orientation means that market needs are best served by very large, conservative–transactional firms specializing in producing and distributing large volumes of goods at highly competitive prices. Similar to recent trends in the VCR market, it is likely that in the digital TV sector, when most of the market has accepted this technology, volume producers from countries such as Korea or mainland China will come to dominate.

Major new-to-the world innovation typically occurs because a highly entrepreneurial individual or organization decides to break free from existing customer satisfaction conventions and offer a radically new solution. This type of innovation has become very common in e-commerce, where many of the technologies fundamental to success have first been developed by small companies based in California. A key reason smaller organizations tend to dominate the early phase of the technology innovation cycle is that most large firms are oriented towards discovering new ways of improving the quality/value mix for existing products through investing in projects offering a steady improvement in product performance.

One way to visualising the changing role of firms during an innovation cycle is an innovation ownership matrix in Fig. 7.8 (Chaston, 1999). He proposes that once a new-to-the world concept is launched there are two possible life cycle pathways. Which of these dominates within an industrial sector will be determined by two factors: ease of access to the new product technology and market penetration. In those cases where the ease of access to new and complex technology is relatively high (for example there are a high number of companies that would have few problems adding an Internet connection to a mobile telephone or a digital TV), as the product is accepted in a market the originating entrepreneurial–transactional company usually faces two choices: firstly it can move to retain ownership through the late growth/maturity stages of the product life cycle by revising corporate operational style, or it can accept that, over time, product ownership will shift into the hands of conservative–transactional companies more competent at producing standardized products offering a superior price/quality/value combination. Whether the new product originator changes style or ownership moves to other firms, the focus of innovation within the market sector will tend to shift away from product performance towards a focus on using upgraded process technologies to further enhance product value. Examples are: exploiting economies of scale to drive down prices; simplifying manufacturing processes to reduce costs; offering customers greater choice by expanding the breadth of the product line.

In many sectors of e-commerce, once a breakthrough has been made the complexity of technology usually means that successful commercialization will depend on the entrepreneurial originator forming partnerships with other organizations. This brings access to additional expertise required to create a product that offers genuine

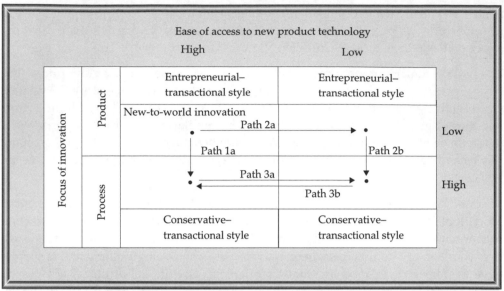

Figure 7.8 *An innovation ownership matrix*

performance benefits. This was a feature of the global expansion of the Internet. Originally created as a data interchange system for US scientists, the Web only became a truly commercial proposition following collaborative R&D by specialist software firms in Silicon Valley. Here again, however—as demonstrated by Microsoft's growing dominance of the Internet software market—once a new product begins to achieve high market penetration the entrepreneurial–relationship developers had to change style or accept loss of ownership to larger firms more able to deliver standardized, low cost products.

Once a product has entered the late growth/maturity phase of the life cycle, as shown in Fig. 7.8, effective process innovation may involve switching between transactional and relationship marketing styles. It is posited that path 3a may occur because members of a supply chain recognize that to exploit new technologies it is necessary to work in much closer partnership with others. IBM, for example, in seeking to improve further the performance of its e-commerce products and systems, has demonstrated the benefits of forming R&D partnerships with software tool developers and specialist component suppliers in the server sector of its industry.

It is also suggested by path 3b in Fig. 7.8, that once a technology is widely understood, and price becomes the dominant influence on the purchase decision, firms that are extremely competent at conservative–transactional process innovation will become the major players in a market sector. It is for this reason that, over time, one can expect more Pacific rim companies to enter e-commerce, offering, for example, electronic consumer goods with Internet portals, and cars with diagnostic links, so that dealers can offer consumers an early warning system.

● Summary

Given the high commercial risks associated with innovation, organizations need to determine carefully which aspect of new product development is best able to support and enhance a company's existing marketing strategy. One of the ways technology is influencing e-commerce innovation is in the rapid development of products based around interactive TVs and mobile communications equipment. Over time, these developments can be expected to replace the PC as the primary platform for Internet access. Having determined the company's strategic focus of innovation, the minimizing of market failure can usually be achieved by adopting some form of linear, phased action control system. E-commerce innovation often involves complex technology. Hence many firms are now turning to inter-organizational alliances to accelerate the effective creation of new products. Speed of market development is also influenced by customer adoption behaviour. Implementation of a new product market expansion plan is usually dependent upon recognition of the need to revise strategic positioning to reflect evolving customer usage.

STUDY QUESTIONS

1 Review the factors likely to influence the success or failure of a new product.

2 Describe a management control model designed to ensure that only good new product ideas are ever progressed through to market launch.

3 Why should high-technology firms need to be aware of the role of customer behaviour in influencing the market acceptance rate for a new product? What strategies can these firms use to maximize the speed with which their products achieve a high level of market penetration?

Case: *Natural Eating*

Natural Eating Ltd is a company that was originally founded as a traditional retailer. The company operates a chain of 20 stores in metropolitan areas selling up-market, premium-priced, non-perishable, organic health food products (for example coffee, flour, preserves, breakfast cereals) and a diverse range of health food supplements. Two years ago the company reviewed plans for the next 5–10 years. It decided that both rising labour costs and retail outlet rents would be a major obstacle for any plan based around expanding their terrestrial retailing operation. Instead, the company launched an on-line store. Its marketing position, based on exploiting its existing distribution infrastructure and the savings possible through giving up retail outlets, was to pass along savings by offering products at lower prices to e-customers.

The entry into e-commerce has been very successful, contributing almost 20 per cent of the company's annual sales revenue. Management is keenly aware that they can expect increased competition in cyberspace both from other health food companies and health food manufacturers. Hence it sees a need to identify new product opportunities that can be exploited by the on-line store.

QUESTION

1 **Assume the role of Natural Eating's Director of On-Line New Product Development and develop one or more new product ideas that can be submitted in a report to the board.**

   *In developing your report you may find it useful to visit one or more terrestrial health food stores and use a search engine such as **www.yahoo.com** to research the on-line sector of the health food business. You may also find it beneficial to know that the typical Natural Eating customer is (1) an owner of one or more pets, (2) interested in homeopathic medicine, (3) participates in various forms of exercise in an attempt to remain healthy, and (4) committed to protecting the environment.*

Case: *Down Farm Music*

Greg Grumble was a pop star in the 1970s. At the end of a brief but lucrative career, he moved to the country and bought a dairy farm. Having settled in his new community, he became concerned about high unemployment amongst young people. His solution was to start Down Farm Music Ltd. The company provides potential young musicians with training, gets them onto the touring circuit, and provides access to a fully equipped rehearsal and recording studio on Greg's farm.

One of the obstacles facing new bands is that the music business is dominated by the big multinational recording companies, and at a retail level by a small number of multi-outlet music stores. Greg was therefore fascinated to read an article on the new Internet technology, MP3. This is a summary of the article that first sparked Greg's interest.

Traditionally, storing audio files on a PC meant that even a few minutes of material occupied a vast quantity of hard disk space. The Moving Pictures Expert Group (MPEG) was formed in 1988. Over the years, researchers at MPEG have been experimenting with ways to compress audio data. The latest invention, Moving Pictures Experts Group 1 Layer 3 (or MP3 for short) permits 30–40 megabytes of file to be shrunk down to 3 or 4 megabytes. This means that individuals or companies can put music onto the Internet and, if you have MP3 software CD-quality recordings can be downloaded at the click of a button. The implications for the music industry are fascinating, because it means that virtually anybody can create recordings, put them on either on their own site or a multi-artist one (for example *www.songs.com*). This means that access to the music business without the co-operation of a big record label and a major chain of music stores.

Source: Fisher (2000)

QUESTION

1   **Assume you are acting as a marketing consultant to Greg Grumble. Prepare a report describing how he might use MP3 as the basis for greater innovation.**

*In preparing your report you might find it beneficial to visit some MP3 information sites (for example **www.mp3site.com**, **www.mpeg.org/MPEG/mp3.html**, **www.bigg.net** and **www.apple.com/publishing/music/mps/**) and sites which offer free music downloads (for example **www.mp3now.com**, **www.listen.com**, **www.emusic.com** and **www.riffage.com**).*

Chapter 7 Glossary

Communicability (p. 158)

The degree to which the benefit claims can be easily described to potential users.

Divisibility (p. 158)

The degree to which the product can be tried on a limited basis.

Chapter 8

E-PROMOTION

This chapter explains

- *The role of promotion in the marketing mix.*

- *The contribution the Internet can make to the promotional mix.*

- *The changing role of the Internet in the promotional process.*

- *The assessment of the promotional effectiveness of websites.*

- *Emerging trends in Internet promotion.*

- *The development of e-based promotional plans.*

The traditional view of promotion is that it comprises all activities associated with communicating information about a product or service. The aim of these activities is to cause the customer to purchase the organization's output. Marketers have a variety of information delivery systems available to them, and these can be used to construct an appropriate 'promotional mix strategy'. This portfolio of delivery mechanisms include (Kotler 1997):

1 Advertising, which permits the delivery of a non-personal message in rented time and/or space within an advertising channel (for example radio, TV, cinema, newspapers, magazines, Internet service provider [ISP] websites and billboards).

2 Collateral promotion, which covers a variety of message delivery approaches, including brochures, packaging, merchandising materials, logos and company information on delivery vehicles, layout of office areas in which service providers have contact with the customer, and the corporate clothing worn by company personnel.

3 Direct marketing, which exploits advances in technology to create an ever increasing portfolio of techniques to interact with the customer (for example mail-shots, telemarketing, e-mail, Internet, fax and voice-mail).

4 Personal selling, which involves one-to-one interaction between the customer and the producer's sales force (and/or the sales staff of intermediaries) within the marketing channel.

5 Public relations and publicity, which is constituted of a broad range of activities designed to promote the organization and/or the organization's products (for example an article about the organization in a trade magazine, or sponsorship of a popular sporting event, such as a round-the-world yacht race).

6 Sales promotions, which involve activities that offer the customer some form of temporary increased value (for example a coupon good for a next purchase, or participation in a competition offering the chance to win an overseas holiday).

Promotion and the Product Life Cycle

The nature of customer behaviour in relation to (1) the diffusion of innovation curve and (2) the growing importance of price as customers gain knowledge through usage of the product over time does mean that the role of promotion should be expected to change depending upon the product's position on the product life cycle (PLC) curve (Wasson 1978). The implications of this situation are summarized in Table 8.1. from which it can be seen that in the early stages of the P.L.C., generic promotional activity is directed at educating the customer about the new product and seeking to build market awareness. As the product enters the growth phase, promotional activity, although still aimed at generating trial among the early majority type of customer, now also has a role in stimulating repeat purchase. Maturity is typically the most competitive period during the life of the product, and promotion activity is very much concerned with defending the product against competition. Typically this will require a promotional strategy stressing the nature of the benefit superiority offered to the customer. Once the product enters the decline phase, price usually becomes the dominant factor influencing demand, and therefore, promotional activity is drastically reduced.

Sales promotion is an activity designed to offer higher temporary value to the customer. Examples of sales promotions include price packs, free product, money-off coupons and competitions. As such, therefore, sales promotion management is as much concerned with providing a tool to supplement the product pricing strategy, as it

Table 8.1 The marketing mix and the product life cycle (source Chaston 1999)

	Introduction	Growth	Maturity	Decline
Sales	Low	Rising	Maximum	Falling
Marketing objectives	Trial and awareness	Ongoing trial and initiation of repeat purchase behaviour	Maximization of sales by defending market share	Sustaining of required sales volume
Product strategy	Basic product proposition	Increasing of variety by product line expansion	Maximization of choice of product types	Scaling down of breadth of product line
Pricing strategy	Pricing to meet innovator value expectations	Pricing to increase market penetration	Pricing to support chosen product positioning	Reduction of price to sustain sales
Generic promotion strategy	Education of potential customers and building of market awareness	Expansion of awareness and stimulation of repeat purchase	Communication of product benefit superiority claim	Reduction to minimum level to sustain loyalty
Sales promotion strategy	Stimulation of trial	Stimulation of repeat purchase	Defence against competitor activities and price competition	Alternative to price reduction
Distribution strategy	Selective, restricted to full service intermediary outlets	Entry into new outlets to expand market coverage	Minimization of market coverage	Return to selective distribution

E-Couponing

For many years, major brands and many retailers have made use of 'money-off' coupons to stimulate customer purchase rates. Coupons can be delivered by mail or placed in newspapers and magazines or on the packs of products. Very early in the new age of on-line shopping a number of entrepreneurs realized that offering coupons via the Internet could open up an exciting new era in sales promotion delivery systems (Lindsay 2000, Wolf 2000).

At Value-Mail (*www.value-mail.com*), you register your address and the company mails you a selection of 30–40 coupons. At Salesmountain (*www.salesmountain.com*), he or she can select coupons (if necessary using the on-line genie that focuses on stores within 10 miles of his or her home) and then download and print off the coupons of interest. Some sites offer the alternative approach of revealing codes that can earn discounts when entered into a sales order system at e-retailer sites (for example *www.ecoupons.com*). Additionally there are sites that display deals discovered by their on-line customers (for example *www.dotdeal.com*).

The Internet provides a much larger universe for the distribution of coupons than the mere offer of such savings via an advertisement in a local newspaper. This means that the volume of coupons that may be redeemed can create huge liabilities for the company offering the deal. There is also the added problem that on-line users may gain repeated access to available discounts through the simple process of registering multiple names on the e-coupon site. At the moment, most e-firms seem tolerant of this practice because thousands of first-time customers are being attracted to their websites. Over time, however, some companies, having established high site visitor levels will begin to introduce technology to reduce the level of coupon abuse currently prevalent in many sectors of the on-line universe.

is a mechanism for communicating information to customers. In most cases price becomes a more dominant influencer of customer purchase behaviour the further one progresses through the PLC. Consequently, as shown in Table 8.1, sales promotion only begins to really dominate the promotional mix during the late maturity and decline phases of the PLC.

● The Promotional Mix and Market Structure

Promotion can be considered as a process whereby information about the organization's product or service is encoded into a promotional message for delivery to the customer (Ray 1982; Crowley and Hoyer, 1994). Following message delivery, there are two possible feedback responses that may be initiated by the customer. In those cases where reaching the product purchase decision and/or subsequent usage of the product requires a high level of knowledge, it is very probable that the customer will seek more information from the supplier. As dialogue is possibly the most effective form of communication, it is likely that up until recently the supplier would have relied heavily upon the use of a sales force to deliver much of the promotional message.

Unfortunately, personal selling is possibly the most expensive method per customer contact to deliver information to the market (Anderson 1994). Hence although all companies would probably like to include a large sales force in their promotional portfolio, it only becomes cost-effective where the average purchase per customer is very high. Consequently, personal selling dominates the promotional mix in industrial markets, and is replaced with lower cost per customer delivery systems such as advertising (1) in industrial markets where the value of the purchase per customer is quite low (for example office supplies such as staples or paper clips) and (2) in the majority of consumer goods markets. Even in industrial markets organizations are continually striving to find new ways of minimizing the costs associated with the delivery of information to the customer. Thus promotional planning must be perceived as a dynamic process that is continually being adapted to suite identified changing circumstances in the external market environment.

The Hewlett Packard case (see box) is no longer a rare example of promotional practices within the world of e-marketing . Many other organizations now use similar 'real time' communications systems for monitoring the enhancing promotional activity and using the knowledge gained from on-line communication to evolve new forms of competitive advantage. By tracking customer order patterns and collecting data on which promotional device prompted customer response, these companies are in a position to assess rapidly the effectiveness of the various promotional activities in relation to specific customer target groups. This then assists in the forecasting of future near-term demand patterns for each product (Nash 1995).

Stauffer (1999) posits that e-promotion means that companies need to re-examine carefully the aims of the sales force strategy, implementing revisions where these are required. He suggests that e-commerce is causing the emergence of two product categories, the first category 1 being commodity sales. Products and services within this group are virtually identical, which means that purchase decisions will be based mainly on price. If customers for this category of items are using the Internet to acquire pricing information, Stauffer believes that companies really have little need to use a sales force as a channel through which to deliver promotional information.

The second category of products or services are those of sufficient complexity that the customer will often require access to a one-to-one interactive discussion to reach a purchase decision (for example advanced machine tools or complex investment portfolios). Customers will also be using the Internet to acquire comparative information. Hence they no longer require the services of a sales person to provide basic information about the relative merits of alternative propositions. Instead, the role of the sales force becomes consultant, assisting and guiding the customer to make the optimal purchase decision most suited to their specific needs. Stauffer sees this new selling orientation as requiring (1) a sales force with in-depth product knowledge, (2) that all members of the selling organization be able to contribute to offering consultancy advice to the client, and (3) a workforce totally proficient in the use of multi-media channels.

*Hewlett-Packard (**www.hp.com**)*

Hewlett-Packard, even before the advent of the Internet as a medium through which to deliver information, had identified ways in which advances in electronic technologies could be exploited in the effective management of promotional processes. In the mid-1990s the company found that it was encountering problems caused by slowing industry growth, increasing competition, and the fact that complex products are harder to sell, and rising promotional costs per order generated. As part of the solution to these problems the company reviewed how IT might assist in improving promotional activities. It upgraded its direct marketing operation by creating a computer-based customer database that linked enquiries from mailings, advertising and other awareness-building activities directly with its sales order entry and product shipping systems. The sales force could now use its laptop computers from anywhere in the world to gain access to the company's centralized database for information on potential or existing customers and to communicate with employees elsewhere. The marketing department could also utilize the customer database to analyse markets, determine why orders were won or lost, evaluate the effectiveness of promotions and generate revised sales forecasts.

The impact of this integrated electronic promotional system is demonstrated by the fact that Hewlett Packard achieved the following outcomes:

1 Overall direct marketing costs were reduced by 10 per cent.

2 Sales staff now discard only 15 per cent of generated leads, compared to the previous 75 per.

3 Sales volumes dealt with by the tele-sales operation rose by 15 per cent.

4 Knowledge of customers increased by 100 per cent.

5 Promotional costs per customer order decreased by 10 per cent.

● The Internet and the Communications Mix

The advent of the Internet has added various new dimensions to the promotional management process. One dimension is that the Internet is a medium that combines the features of both broadcasting and publishing to facilitate two-way communication. Berthon (1996) suggests that the Internet might be considered a cross between an electronic trade show and a community flea market. As such, it faces the same dilemma as conventional trade shows or a flea markets, namely how to convert website visitors from browsers into purchasers.

A somewhat different perspective is provided by Leong et al. (1998), who used mail surveys followed by cluster analysis to obtain the views of Australian marketing practitioners about where the Internet fits within other media. They concluded that most practitioners consider the Internet similar to direct mail because many websites in their early stages of development are used to offer what essentially are on-line catalogues. Like direct mail, the Internet has the ability to precipitate a purchase. Perceived advantages over direct mail are that the costs of reaching target markets are much lower on the Web.

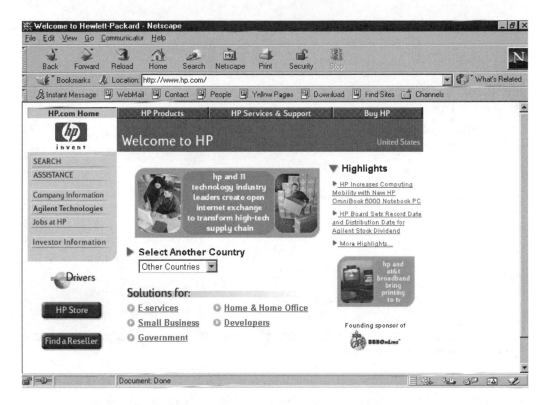

Importantly, most marketing practitioners do not see the Internet as replacing other media. Instead most see it as complementary to other media channels such as TV or magazine advertising. Furthermore, most respondents have adopted the approach of adding the Internet to the range of channel options being considered during the process of deciding which media mix offers the most cost-effective approach for achieving the aims specified for a promotional campaign.

Berthon (1996) provides an alternative perspective of the Internet as a mix of personal selling and broadcast advertising. He suggests it can be used to generate awareness, passively to provide information, to demonstrate the product, and, if required by the customer, to support interactive dialogue. Acceptance of this perspective permits the evolution of a customer purchase behaviour model in which the Internet can be used to move customers through the phases of the buying decision process. This phased movement begins with attracting website visitors. Making contact with interested individuals, converting some visitors into customers, and then supporting the purchase and post-purchase phase of the supplier–customer relationship follows this. As illustrated in Fig. 8.1, as individuals progress through each stage phase of the buying process it is theoretically possible to assess the effectiveness of the website. Application of the measurement tools posited in Fig. 8.1 assumes that a website is capable of recording all hits and that data can be acquired about the nature of these hits. Unfortunately, as will be discussed later in this chapter, the technology has yet be evolved to the point that this is a completely viable proposition.

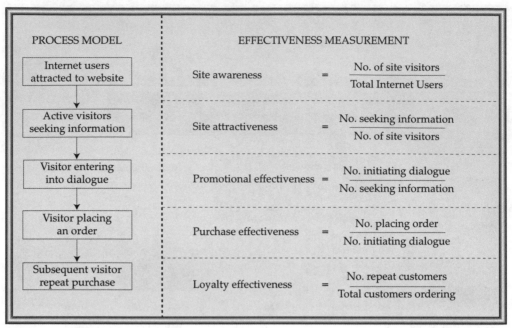

Figure 8.1 *An Internet process model and assessment tools*

● The Changing Face of the Internet

When the Internet first became available, some academics perceived that the medium would introduce a new level of promotional democracy into world markets. Berthon (1996) proposes that the medium offered these unique characteristics:

1 The customer has to find the product or service to a greater extent than with other media.

2 Creating a presence on the medium is relatively easy and inexpensive.

3 Compared to other media, access opportunities are the same for all firms, no matter what size.

4 The size of each company's voice is uniform; no company can drown out the others.

5 Initial set-up costs mean that there are virtually no barriers to entry.

Even today, a small potter in Nowheresville, Anywhere can use readily available design software to build a low cost website. Having registered a domain name, customers out there in cyberspace with a high interest in craft goods can be expected to search out the website, and sales revenue will flow. Unfortunately, however, as large companies have come to understand the potential offered by the Internet they have acted to ensure that they, not small companies, can dominate cyberspace markets. The first important event was the realization by the major portals that their visitors were a valuable asset for which they could charge money, and along with this realization came the 'banner advertisement'. These Internet advertisements, the first of which was sold by HotWired Inc. in 1994, usually take the form of a small insertion on a website, communicating a brand name, a simple benefit message and/or web address.

In 1997, Briggs and Hollis published one of the earliest research studies aimed at gaining an understanding of how banner advertisements impact the consumer. They adapted the research company Millward Brown's proprietary measurement system to assess awareness and reaction to banner advertisements (*www.mbinteractive.com*). The conclusion reached from their experiment is that banner advertisements can contribute both to increasing brand awareness and strengthening brand loyalty. Using Millward Brown's force model, which permits evaluation of alternative media forms, Briggs and Hollis found that for creating brand awareness banners compare favourably with both TV and magazines. On the basis of their analysis, these authors posit that an influencing factor is the nature of advertising message in terms of (1) its immediate relevance to the audience and (2) the degree of involvement or intrigue it creates. They also conclude that response to banner advertisements is strongly influenced by the predisposition of the viewing audience. These audience-related factors include:

search

1   Any innate tendency to click on banners.

2   The immediate relevance of the product to the audience.

3   Any pre-existing appeal of the brand or company name.

In 1995, only $312 million was expended on on-line advertising. By 1997, this had risen to $906.5 million and was forecasted to exceed $4.0 billion by 2000 by Drez and Zufryden in 1998. A Forrestor research study estimates that by 2004 Internet advertising expenditure will rise to $33 billion, 33 per cent of which will be outside the US. The reason for this situation is that long established brands, such as Ford and IBM,

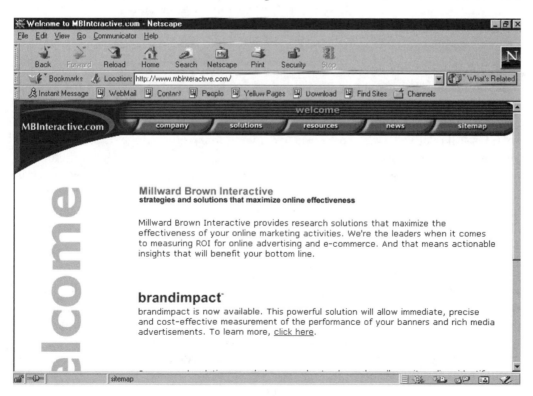

Mass Market Brands and Internet Promotions

Unilever in the US has created a site for Dove soap which offers on-line health and beauty advice, customized to suit visitors' skin types (*www.dovespa.com*). To increase site visitor levels, the company purchased a banner campaign on *www.women.com*, a US site offering guidance to women on a broad range of fashion and beauty issues. In Europe, the company launched a site for Bird's Eye Fish Fingers aimed at generating visitors from the 9–11 age group who are the prime consumption target for this product (*www.birdseye.com*). The site offers cartoons featuring the exploits of Captain Bird's Eye and his crew. Site visitors are attracted via banner advertisements in the children's section of America Online and the Disney website. (*www.disney.com*)

Proctor & Gamble has adopted a similar philosophy (*www.procterandgamble.com*). For its disposable nappy product, Pampers, it has developed a site offering baby advice health issues for parents. It features information on infant feeding and nutrition, plus an e-mail newsletter giving specific advice based on the age of the child. The company is also beginning to forge new partnerships. One of these is with *www.reflect.com*, which offers a range of over 50 000 cosmetics and beauty products on-line. Proctor & Gamble sees an on-line make-up site as an additional channel through which to reach consumers seeking up-market, premium quality health and beauty aids.

and newly established e-commerce companies are both committing large budgets to on-line advertising. One example of the latter group is Amazon.com which signed a $19 million contract to rent banner advertising space for three years on America Online's home page (*www.aol.com*).

Even companies which market low interest consumer goods such as detergents and food, and which have traditionally relied upon mass marketing linked to distribution through mass market outlets such as supermarkets, also perceive the Internet as offering new opportunities for further reinforcing brand awareness. Their level of e-commerce spend is still relatively small compared to conventional media. In the second quarter of 1998, for example, Procter & Gamble's Internet spend in the US was only $3 million out of a total advertising expenditure of $3 billion (Rosier 1999). As the fast moving consumer goods (f.m.c.g.) companies gain on-line experience, however, they are recognising that the Internet is a powerful vehicle to provide information that cannot be effectively communicated through traditional channels such as a 30-second TV spot.

A critical advantage enjoyed by large companies is that most Internet visitors are not interested in spending hours searching out unusual, lesser known products located on very small websites around the world. The two reasons for this are that the average customer is (1) too busy to spend time running on-line searches and (2) unwilling to risk the probability of purchase dissatisfaction, and tends to opt for leading brand names. Customer awareness of national brands is, of course, continuously being impacted by off-line exposure to advertise via conventional media channels and in-store product encounters.

Another factor that is reducing the ability of small firms to generate a high number of website visitors is that larger e-commerce companies are now expending vast sums of money on building awareness of site addresses using conventional media channels. The scale of this type of promotional spending is currently greatest among e-commerce companies in the US. For example, in 1999 E*Trade (*www.etrade.com*), an on-line discount stockbroker, spent $200 million communicating its website address. CNet, (*www.cnet.com*), an on-line publisher, has spent $100 million, and the toymaker Mattel $90 million. The outcome of this spending spiral is that over the period between 1997 and 1999 the off-line cost of establishing an e-commerce brand is estimated to have risen from $5–10 million to somewhere in the region of $50–100 million (Alexander 1999). As this trend is expected to continue, it will become increasingly difficult for small companies to establish viable new on-line businesses.

McLuhan (2000) feels that even now many advertisers are still struggling to learn how to use the Internet as an effective element in their marketing mix. Because many brands have not evolved Internet strategies capable of differentiating their offering from competition or building long-term on-line relationships, many consumers are just switching between websites looking for the lowest possible price. Already in the US almost 80 per cent of on-line shoppers admit that price is the main motivator in causing them to revisit a website.

To overcome this problem, McLuhan believes advertisers must develop on-line offerings that are more personalized and of real interest to their customers. This can sometimes be achieved by using the Internet to offer specialist knowledge to specific customer groups (for example the establishing by tyre company BF Goodrich of a tactical microsite, *www.discoverthegrip.co.uk*, targeted at male car enthusiasts). An alternative approach is to offer entertainment to the site visitor, such as the table football game provided by the J&B whisky's site, *www.j&b.com*. Similarly, the retailer Top Shop recently presented website visitors with a list of 100 dance tracks and encouraged them to select their own top ten tunes. Within 48 hours, the site visitor received a CD carrying his or her music selection. To stimulate site usage, the campaign was backed by in-store couponing and press advertisements in the London Evening Standard.

Another approach to offering added value to attract site visitors was recently used to launch the British Telecom comparative shopping portal *www.btspree.com*. This portal is designed to assist visitors to locate the best on-line offers from 21 participating traders, including Tower Records, Value Direct and Shopsmart. The site's initial objective was to build a customer base of at least 50 000 users within three months. To encourage a high number of on-line visitors, new site users were sent an electronic booklet of vouchers, worth a total of £200, offering discounts on products ranging from cinema tickets to skiing holidays. Supplementary off-line promotional activity included national radio and press advertising.

● Internet Measurement Issues

Website servers have an amazing ability to collect data about visitor numbers, time spent on-site, and information reviewed by the visitor. Hence for the company which operates a site, or rents space from a service provider, these data can be used to gain greater understanding of site visitor behaviour and demographics. For both the advertisers buying banner space and the site owner offering to sell such space, assessing the cost-effectiveness of on-line promotion is somewhat more complicated.

This is not a new problem. Every time a new advertising medium is launched, sellers and buyers of space need to reach agreement on how best to assess the merits of the new medium against other alternatives. In the case of magazine advertising, media analysts have access to data which include audited paid circulation figures, surveys to establish readership socio-demographics, and 'reading and noting' studies to assess the impact of specific insertions. For TV advertising, through techniques such as meters on TV sets in panels of households, analysts are provided with data on **reach** (*the proportion of the viewing population exposed to the advertisement*) and **frequency** (*how many times the average viewer sees the advertisement in a specified time period*). These two data are used to calculate gross rating points (GRPs) using the formula GRP = reach x frequency.

Website servers do have the ability to measure the number of pages requested, how much time is spent in each web-page and what types of computers made the page requests. Some companies have attempted to use these statistics to provide reach and frequency measures in an effort to provide comparability with other media. However, the accuracy of such measurements is questionable due to the problems of identifying site visitors and the way the visitor's PC stores (or 'caches') data locally (Drez and Zufryden 1998).

In the traditional media, surveys and panel studies permit the unique identification of customer by name, telephone number or address. On the Internet, the tendency of many service providers is to avoid investing in expensive audits to track customer behaviour. Instead they use the visitors' Internet Protocol (IP) addresses to build files which measure visitor traffic and site usage patterns. Unfortunately, these IP addresses may not be unique to a specific provider. Several users may be assigned the same IP in multi-user systems such as America Online. Additionally, visitors using a service provider operating a dynamic IP allocation system may have different IPs assigned to them each time they connect with the ISP. If this were not a sufficiently large problem, if the ISP is using a 'multiple proxy server' system, site visitors can be assigned multiple addresses even during a single session.

An important variable in the assessment of banner advertising effectiveness is the number of pages requested by the site visitor. If a visitor requests a page, the displayed page will have links to both other pages and the banner advertisement. Should the visitor, having requested a second page, then use the 'back button' to return to the first page carrying the advertisement, the website will not record the second exposure to the banner advertisement. The reason for this is that the user's PC caches the first page on its local hard drive and retrieves it from there rather than returning to the website. Under these circumstances the website statistics will underestimate exposure frequency for the banner advertisement.

Another issue in the reliability of reported measures is whether the requested page is actually received by the reader, and if received actually read. For example, the user may place a request, decide it is taking too long to download, and terminate the session. The issue of whether the downloaded page is actually read is no different that the problems faced by the traditional media, however. People may have their TV on, but there is no guarantee that anyone is watching. Similarly, a person may buy a magazine but only look at certain pages.

To overcome these problems, some websites are beginning to invest in market research based around panels of PC users. This approach, known as a user-centric approach (as opposed to website statistics, which are based upon a site-centric approach), uses customers who have agreed to their PC being connected to a meter. The meter generates data on the length of time surfing, the movement between pages (including pages cached locally) and time spent reviewing each page. Additionally, the panel structure means data can also be acquired on how usage patterns may differ in relation to user socio-demographics (Wood 1998). Over time it can be expected that additional audit tools will be developed for measuring audience size and user behaviour on the Internet. Until then, however, most advertisers will remain reliant upon the server statistics generated by the Internet site carrying their banner advertisements.

To determine whether these site statistics provide a meaningful assessment of whether data on **page impressions** (*the number of times a page carrying a banner advertisement is visited*) can be utilized to evolve measurements of reach and frequency, researchers such as Leckenby and Hong (1998) have run comparative studies in which they have monitored both user-centric and site-centric data. They conclude that it is feasible to used conventional media planning equations to generate reasonably accurate reach and frequency data for web sites.

A similar study by Wood (1998) also concludes that reach and frequency data can be generated from website statistics. In his research, he concluded that the Internet provides a very high level of reach. Wood believes that this is explained by the fact that Internet usage is still rising, which in turn provides an ever expanding source of on-line visitors. His study also reveals that reach varies by type of site. Game and sports sites tend to exhibit relatively low reach, but high frequency levels, reflecting the fact that most visitors are regular, repeat users. This contrasts with search engines sites and sites offering services for which users have a limited need (for example travel), where reach is much higher but frequency levels are relatively low.

At the moment it would appear that most major advertisers are content for the Internet to offer a media vehicle for reaching high numbers of people. They are willing to accept the traditional approach to media planning, in which the purchase decision is based on some form of cost per thousand (CPM) pricing model. With this pricing system the advertiser pays for the **number of impressions** (*the total number of times a page is visited*)

Favourites

Favourites

for a defined period. Hence for the near-term, the standard way that websites charge advertisers for space will continue to be based on some form of rate card related to site CPM data. Over time, however, as measurability and metering technology improves this type of pricing can be expected to become more sophisticated, with advertisers demanding to purchase guaranteed levels of impressions for specific customer target groups.

Some advertisers have already concluded that number of impressions is far too crude a pricing tool. They also believe that it ignores the Internet's unique feature, interactivity: site visitors click onto a banner advertisement to receive more information (known as 'click-through' in the industry). As servers are capable of measuring click-through rates, these data provide a better measurement of whether visitors noted an advertisement than relying upon a measurement based upon the total number of impressions. Some leading advertisers, led by Procter & Gamble, are now insisting that the prices charged for Internet advertising must be based upon click-throughs to their sites, not page impressions.

In the case of some sites, the visitor is able to exploit interactivity by actually downloading data or software products. To be able to do this they are required to provide demographic information, such as e-mail address, postal code, occupation etc. These data provide the site publisher with knowledge of visitors that then provides the basis for constructing a rate card demanding a premium from advertisers seeking to target a very specific on-line audience group. A further premium can be demanded because this type of site visitor is identified as exhibiting willingness to download information. This means that they are a prime prospect in terms of their interest in purchasing other services via the Internet. Linked to this type of pricing model is a tiered one in which the advertiser is charged for each phase in the site visitor's level of interactivity. Advertisers on Fleetsearch, a UK on-line magazine for the fleet car industry, pay £1 for every click-through, £5 for each click-through that becomes a new sales lead (Woolgar 1998).

● Internet Trends

When any new form of media is established, it will take time for operating experience to permit advertisers to gain a detailed understanding of how to obtain optimal benefits from the new channel. Such is the case with the Internet. There is growing evidence, for example, that as people become experienced in using the Internet they are increasingly unlikely to click on standard banner advertisements (anon. 1999b). One outcome of this situation is that advertisers have found that for banner advertisements to remain effective content must be revised very frequently if click-though rates are to be sustained. Alternative ways are being found to make banners more interesting.

When Gillette launched its Mach 3 razor in the UK in 1998, the banner campaign broke on the Internet three weeks before the conventional TV advertising campaign (*www.gillette.com*). The Internet campaign was directed at 18–34 year old males who are known to be early adopters of new technology. To gain their interest, the banner offered viewers the opportunity to enter a sweepstake being run on the US Mach 3 website.

Until recently, the narrow bandwidth of the Internet also meant that banner advertisements had to restricted to very simple text and graphics. Advances are now being made in 'rich-media technology'. This permits the advertiser to incorporate high-grade graphics with audio and interactive capabilities (Reed 1999). This approach to upgrading website technology has permitted customers interested in the Toyota Lexus, for example, to be provided with video clips of various models. Similarly, Sony Pictures has promoted its new film *Muppets from Space* using a banner that allows users to download a free Muppet screensaver, shows previews, and offers access to an on-line computer game (***www.spe.sony.com***)

With some advertisers beginning to question the cost-effectiveness of banner advertising, some companies are experimenting with alternative approaches. Some are establishing editorial advertising campaigns based around pages containing detailed information about product usage. At the site operated by the retailer Gap, visitors can try out mixing and matching clothes on-line (***www.gapinc.com***). The Sharp website offers access to the Zaurus personal digital assistant, which permits them to input calendar and address information, thereby trying out the features of the product prior to purchase (***www.sharp-world.com***).

Another increasingly popular trend is for major advertisers to enter into sponsorship agreements whereby their brands become a permanent feature on Internet sites. For example, a US women's site, ***www.ivillage.com***, has a section in which Ford asks visitors to design their dream car (anon. 1999b). By sponsoring a site that consumers value, the advertiser hopes to build positive associations for their brand. Inclusion of materials on the site by the sponsoring brand overcomes the communication limitations of banner advertisements. Thus, because of the greater breadth of information available to the site visitor, stronger brand imagery can be communicated. It is interesting to note that this approach represents reversion of a promotional model extremely popular in the early days of TV advertising.

Over time it can be expected that ongoing improvements in technology will permit advances in both the content and sophistication of Internet advertising. Virtual reality technology will permit the site visitor to totally 'experience' the brand before purchase. Advertisers will also be able to customize advertisements to meet the needs of individual customers. The Ultramatch technology launched by Infoseek already makes it possible to target those Internet users most likely to respond to a certain advertisement. The system uses **fuzzy logic** (*a type of software that analyses data, drawing conclusions and thereby 'learning' is a way similar to the processes found within the human mind*) to observe users' on-line behaviour when they seek out information on the Internet. Ultramatch ascertains which individuals are responding to which advertisements, thereby permitting advertisers to select Internet users who have been pre-screened as a suitable target group (Cartellieri et al. 1997).

Favourites

Another area in which the Internet is having an impact is on the structure and role of advertising agencies. The traditional structure of an advertising agency involves the high fixed costs of a large creative team being covered by the commission earned from media buying. Even by the 1980s some large advertisers had questioned this concept, and insisted on moving to a retainer and fee-per-project model. This trend forced many agencies to re-examine their operating structures.

An implication of the Internet is that clients increasingly require that their agencies be much faster and produce more creatively. Additionally, the agencies are unable to generate significant revenue from banner advertisements, and so are under increasing pressure to find new ways of optimizing internal organizational processes. The agencies also have to ensure their staff have the necessary skills to manage the development and execution of Internet promotional campaigns. Creative teams, who in the past have focused on using 30-second TV spots to communicate brand values, need to acquire the skills to orientate their output towards prompting target audiences to respond to on-line campaigns. Media buyers will have to use new models to build plans that incorporate a mix of websites that can deliver cost-effective reach and coverage targets. Account managers must become proficient in advising the client on how best to use the Internet as a component in an overall brand promotional strategy. Only time will tell whether these new demands will result in (1) the established, global agencies continuing to thrive and grow in this new world or (2) the Internet proving a catalyst that leads to a complete restructuring of the agency business.

● Promotional Planning

The various stages associated with the promotional planning process are summarized in Fig. 8.2. The usual starting point in the process is to review the market situation to determine the effectiveness of the current promotional activities relative to both the organization's marketing objectives and the promotional activities of competition. As the purpose of promotion is to communicate information about the organization's product or service portfolio, it is critical that the situation review be accompanied by an assessment of computability between the organization's overall marketing plan and the current promotional strategy.

Issues covered in the determination of future aims and objectives typically include quantitative specifications for customer awareness, product trial/repeat purchase rates, product distribution targets and definitions of cost of information delivery per customer for each area of promotional activity. These aims and objectives can then be used in the preparation of future promotional budgets using techniques such as task quantification (for example calculation of the optimal size for the sales force through analysis of data on the number of customers, required call frequency per customer and known acceptable workload per sales person) or the construction of multivariate equations which express sales as a function of customer usage rates, promotional activity, pricing and distribution.

It is frequently the case that early budget calculations generate expenditure levels incompatible with overall financial performance forecasts. This will often cause the marketer to re-examine promotional targets and/or proposed promotional processes for delivering information to customers. The advent of e-commerce has provided a range of new options through which to evolve more cost-effective information delivery techniques. For example, large firms seeking to reach small or medium-sized businesses have often found that the revenue generated per customer is smaller than the cost of allocating sales staff to make calls in this sector of the market. Firms such as IBM, however, are now using conventional TV and print advertising to promote awareness for the IBM website address, and find it affordable. The site provides potential customers with advice on how to select appropriate hardware and software

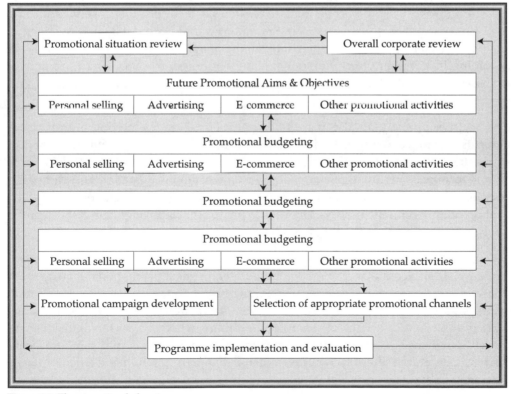

Figure 8.2 *The promotional planning process*

The Internet is also already providing a new platform through which to undertake market research. London International, the manufacturers of the Durex condom, has used its website to test the appeal of different advertising concepts. By monitoring page selection, click-throughs and response rates, the company has been able to determine which concept provided the basis for the most effective major new TV advertising campaign. Other companies are using the Internet as a replacement for toll-free telephone numbers as a way to obtain customer feedback. Major market research companies are implementing on-line surveys and hosting on-line focus groups as a way to acquire in-depth customer viewpoints. The latter activity appears popular with participants because, unlike off-line events, the anonymity of an on-line environment permits people to express views without worrying what others in the group might think of them. The added bonus of on-line focus groups is that a widely dispersed membership can be assembled at the fraction of the cost of organizing an off-line event.

for building an e-commerce operation that they can either order on-line or through their nearest IBM distributor.

Direct marketing organizations are now moving to complement their use of direct mail as a primary marketing platform with a mix of (1) TV advertising to communicate the website address and (2) faxes or e-mails to communicate the product or service offering to potential customers. Large retailers that have accumulated detailed knowledge of customer buying behaviour through data mining of information from loyalty cards are becoming involved in direct marketing, using both mailshots and e-mails to deliver information about customized sales promotions such as money-off coupons and special in-store offers.

The Internet option may also permit companies to consider moving into overseas markets without having to find funds to support the establishment of an export marketing operation. The UK media agency Razorfish, for example, created 20 or 30 rich media pop-ups for Beefeater Gin, an Allied Domecq brand. The campaign positions Beefeater as a cutting edge brand in overseas markets. The pop-up, which contains animation and audio, generated a 15 per cent click-through rate on Beefeater's London Radio Site, thereby doubling the level of traffic on Allied Domecq's stable of websites (Reed 1999).

Having determined the overall marketing budget, the next promotional management phases are the concurrent activities of planning promotional campaigns and selecting appropriate channels through which to deliver information to the market. Some of this work may be done in-house (for example determining whether sales force effectiveness might be enhanced by equipping sales personnel with laptops that can be used to develop customized offerings while on a customer's premises). Other elements may be delegated to specialist external suppliers, such as the company's advertising agency.

New Players

Already organizations are emerging that specialize in providing Internet promotion management services. One of the first, founded by Kevin O'Connor, was DoubleClick (*www.doubleclick.net*) (Brown 1999). This company's operations are composed of two elements, selling advertising space and 'ad serving'. The former is a simple idea. The company acts as an agent selling advertising space on behalf of over 1500 websites. Its commission is high, in some cases approaching 50 per cent. The company's success is that DoubleClick creates a media package consisting of numerous second-tier websites. The advertiser, by making a single purchase with DoubleClick, gains access to a diverse range of target audiences. Conversely, the small websites represented by DoubleClick gain access to blue chip clients to whom it would be impossible to sell direct.

An understanding of the ad serving side of the business requires an explanation of Internet technology. When a website is visited, the page that appears is composed of information that may have come from a number of sources, for example content from one, background look from another, frames and borders from a third and banner advertising from a fourth. Bringing together material from this range of sources is known as ad serving. The company has added further value to this service by creating DART (dynamic advertising, reporting and targeting). This software, by reading the visitor's PC, captures data such as the IP address of website users. This knowledge can then be used by DoubleClick to offer a media planning formula that advertisers can use to select an appropriate website mix to give them the target audience that they want to reach via the Internet.

These organizations will then embark on assessing how a specified target audience can be reached, and required customer awareness levels achieved. The advent of e-commerce is resulting in agencies evolving new media campaigns in which the new technologies have an integral part. Ford has recently decided to reduce drastically its level of magazine advertising in favour of switching moneys to Web-based marketing campaigns (Campbell 1999). This move represents a shift of approximately $100 million from print to Internet advertising. The reason for the move quoted is that the company wants to develop more effective ways of communicating with the consumer on a one-to-one basis.

● Summary

The role of promotion within the marketing mix is to provide information to bring customers through the purchase decision process. The marketer has access to a wide range of alternative promotional platforms and communications channels for the delivery of information. Both market structure and the position of the product on the product life cycle curve influence the selection of an appropriate promotional mix. In the early years of e-commerce, websites were mainly perceived as a medium for the display of what were essentially on-line brochures. As both technology and marketers' understanding of the Internet have progressed, organizations are now perceiving e-promotion as a core element in their marketing mix. With all promotional channels there is a need to measure effectiveness. Only in the last few years have tools become available to help the marketer evaluate the effectiveness of on-line advertising. Access to such knowledge is greatly assisting marketers in developing cost-effective promotional plans that incorporate heavy utilization of the Internet as a mainstream promotional platform.

STUDY QUESTIONS

1 Compare and contrast a website as an advertising vehicle with (1) an advertisement in a magazine and (2) a TV commercial.

2 How can the concept of the product life cycle be used in the effective management of the marketing mix?

3 How might the Internet be used by small firms to enhance the promotional dimension of their marketing activities?

Case: *Sports Portal*

Broadband communications, delivered via cable, modem, telephone or satellite, offers lightning fast connection to the Internet and permits users to download huge files at speed 50 times faster than a 56K modem. Broadband will enable e-retailers almost to put sales assistants into the shopper's home using real time videoconferencing. Any website will be able to become a broadcaster delivering audio and video materials to remote users via their PC, TV or mobile phone. The major sports clubs in football, American football, baseball and basketball have already recognized the benefits of the Internet as a means to communicate with fans around the world. Their sites provide information and the ability to purchase club-related products such as team strips and collectables carrying the club logo.

Source: James (2000)

QUESTION

1 The major sports clubs in football, American football, baseball and basketball have already recognized the benefits of the Internet to communicate with their fans around the world. Their sites offer both information and the sales of club-related products, team strips and memorabilia. Given the huge number of fans that follow clubs (for example Manchester United's estimated 24 million fans around the world), these club sites offer major branded goods companies extremely exciting opportunities to reach very specific customer groups. By exploiting broadband technology, these sites can become 'mini-TV' stations with a global reach.

Assume you are the Marketing Director of a sports club portal that will be exploiting broadband technology. Develop a presentation demonstrating why your site should be the place where major brands should wish to promote their products. In developing this presentation you may find benefit in visiting some of the existing websites of leading major sports clubs. These can be found by running a search using an engine such as *www.yahoo.com*.

Case: *Launching the Portchester Certificate Programme*

As first mentioned in Chapter 6, Portchester Business School has developed a University Certificate in IT Business Systems. Using the Internet, the scheme can be delivered as an electronic distance learning product anywhere in the country. Students can be provided with on-line support via e-mail and groupware. The Business School will launch the product as a part-time, self-study module aimed at people in work, such as secretaries and office administrators.

QUESTION

1 As Director of the project, develop the promotional plan for launching the new scheme. It is advisable to use a mix of both off-line and on-line promotional tools to reach this audience. In preparing this report you may find benefit in reviewing the off-line promotional materials used by universities and through a search engine such as *www.yahoo.com*, visit some on-line college websites to see how education is becoming involved in electronic promotion.

Chapter 8 Glossary

Frequency (p. 178)

How many times the average viewer sees the advertisement in a specified time period.

Fuzzy logic (p. 182)

A type of software that analyses data, drawing conclusions and thereby 'learning' in a way similar to the processes found within the human mind.

Number of impressions (p. 179)

The total number of times a page is visited.

Page impressions (p. 179)

The number of times a page carrying a banner advertisement is visited.

Reach (p. 178)

The proportion of the viewing population exposed to the advertisement.

Chapter 9

E-PRICING AND DISTRIBUTION

Learning Objectives

This chapter explains

◆ Conventions underlying pricing strategies and policies.

◆ Pricing strategies in e-commerce.

◆ The emerging role of on-line auctions.

◆ Price wars in e-commerce markets.

◆ Distribution channel management.

◆ The impact of e-commerce on distribution strategies and policies.

Pricing is an area of the marketing process in which there are a number of clearly identifiable rules and conventions, that governs its effectiveness as a means to optimizing organizational performance. One of the most fundamental rules is that customers, not suppliers, determine prices in a market sector. The implication of this rule is that if a company decides to ignore the price preference of the majority of customers and, on the basis of internal operating costs and/or profit margin aspirations, sets a price significantly higher or much lower than that expected by customers, then the company should not be surprised to find that pricing decision adversely impacting overall sales volumes. Price expectations within most markets emerge through a convergence between what customers are willing pay and the price at which suppliers are willing to offer goods or services. In making products available that fulfil customer price expectations, the aim of the supplier is to manage production and other operational cost to allow an adequate profit margin.

Key factors influencing customer price expectations are prevailing economic circumstances and product usage experience. If customers feel economically insecure due to circumstances such as rising unemployment rates, then typically this will be reflected by a desire to pay a lower price. The reverse is also true: rising optimism among customers is usually reflected a willingness to pay a higher price. In relation to usage experience, product life cycle (PLC) theory contends that prices tend to fall as the market approaches maturity (Day 1981).

An underlying force affecting this situation is that as the product enters the maturity phase on the product life cycle curve, customer learning, derived through usage, is reflected in an expectation that generic category prices will decline. Companies trying to sustain a high price during maturity, will typically only be able to achieve this if customers perceive that through improvements in product and/or product services they are being offered greater value than is available from the products that constitute the generic market sector.

An important convention which influences purchase decisions are what economists refer to as 'demand curves'. These curves posit that for most goods and services demand is 'elastic'. This means that as prices decline customers can be expected to purchase more goods, and that conversely as prices rise customers can be expected to purchase less. There also exists what is known as 'cross elasticity', that is where the price is increased for an item in a group of goods which are perceived as similar, customers will switch their loyalty to alternative goods. For example, if hotel prices in Spain start to rise, then many customers will probably holiday in another country, such as Greece.

Another convention is that most people expect to pay a higher price for goods or services that deliver higher perceived value. The implication of this convention is that, as shown in Fig. 9.1, depending upon the perceived value of goods being offered, suppliers face a number of different pricing scenarios. Organizations positioned on the basis of offering superior product value have three alternative pricing strategies to consider. Premium pricing involves charging a high price to support the claim that the customer is being offered the highest possible product value. Companies wishing rapidly to build market share through aggressive pricing use penetration pricing. Successful application of this strategy usually involves being able to offer the customer an explanation for the price being below that normally quoted for this quantity of product. Typically this is achieved through the economies of scale that a large market share offers. Offering a low price on a superior product usually involves the risk that the customer, applying the adage 'you get what you pay for', is suspicious about the validity of the value claim. This pricing strategy only tends to be successful, therefore, when the supplier makes claims.

A skimming strategy involves the customer deciding there is benefit in paying a high price for what he or she clearly recognizes to be only average value goods. Average pricing is used by companies which service the needs of most customers, who are seeking an average value from products purchased. Sale pricing involves lowering the price on average value goods. To retain customer confidence over the value claim, sale pricing is usually a temporary phenomenon used by companies to stimulate a short-term increase in sales.

A policy of low value and high price is rarely able to sustain long-term customer loyalty. Those organizations that use this strategy can usually only survive if new buyers entering the market segment easily replace customers lost after a single purchase. Similarly, organisations using a low value/average price strategy can only survive in markets in which customers who change their loyalty after two or three purchases are regularly replaced by an influx of new, less informed, customers. Economy pricing involves offering low, but acceptable, value at highly competitive

		Price		
		High	Average	Low
Product value	High	Premium pricing	Penetration pricing	Trusted supplier value pricing
	Average	Skimmimg	Average pricing	Sale pricing
	Low	Zero loyalty pricing	Limited loyalty pricing	Economy pricing

Figure 9.1 *A price/value option matrix*

prices to customers whose price sensitivity is usually a reflection of limited financial means. It can be an extremely successful market position, but the low margin per unit of sale does mean that the supplier has to sustain a very high level of customer transaction in order to sustain an adequate level of profit.

SouthWest Airlines (*www.iflyswa.com*)

An example of the exploitation of e-commerce to sustain an economy positioning is provided by SouthWest, a US airline. At the time SouthWest was established, industry conventions were based upon (1) the high fixed costs associated with operating a large fleet of aircraft to provide national route coverage (2) delivering a reasonably high level of in-flight services, and (3) a 'hub and spoke' configuration in which airlines fly passengers to a central hub to be transferred to their ongoing destination.

Herb Kelleher of SouthWest started an operation based in Houston which adopted a business model aimed at delivering a 'no frills', low price service positioning. Specific attention was given to minimizing operating costs through using non-union labour. This permitted the introduction of unconventional, far more flexible working conditions. The company was not willing to pay the annual fees demanded of national reservation systems used by travel agents. Customers have to buy tickets from the airline. Customers also carry their own bags, and if they want to eat need to bring their own food with them. Furthermore, because the company avoids operating out of congested airport hubs, planes can be turned round in 20 minutes, allowing the company to offer more flights per day between cities than their competitors.

In 1995 the company moved to offer ticketless travel. Passengers calling the airline receive a confirmation number instead of a ticket. Initially, if passengers required a receipt this was faxed, mailed or held for collection at the airport (Berry and Yadav 1996). The company has now moved to offer customers the option of using an on-line booking system. As a result of this move, despite the continual striving of major carriers to match SouthWest's highly efficient operation, the airline still enjoy an average seat per mile operating cost 2–4 cents lower than competition.

● E-Commerce Pricing Strategies

Price is a variable that should not be considered in isolation. As shown in Fig. 9.2, the interaction between all four elements of the marketing mix together determine customer perception of the organization's market position. Over time customers develop an expectation that a specific level of delivered value for a product will be made available at a specific price. Typically, the greater the perceived value of a product the higher will be the price that customers expect to pay. The relationship between price and value can be illustrated by plotting price expectation against perceived value. As shown in Fig. 9.3, as one moves from price point P1 through to price point P3 customer expectations are that perceived value also rises.

Should events lead to a shift in the price/value relationship curve, then customers would expect (1) if value is unchanged, for prices to fall (in Fig. 9.3 to the new price points NP1, NP2 and NP3, or (2) if prices remain unchanged, perceived value to increase. The reason for presenting this price/value relationship concept is that in market sectors in which e-commerce has been widely adopted, many firms are finding that as they move to exploit the efficiencies provided in the delivery of information to customers and/or the purchase transaction process there is a shift in the new price/value curve. This means that, as illustrated in Fig. 9.4, the advent of e-commerce presents organizations with four alternative policy options: (1) make no change, (2) increase value, (3) lower price (4) increase value and lower price. Most companies have invested huge sums of money over the years evolving the most effective combination of product, promotion, price and distribution to establish a clearly perceived market

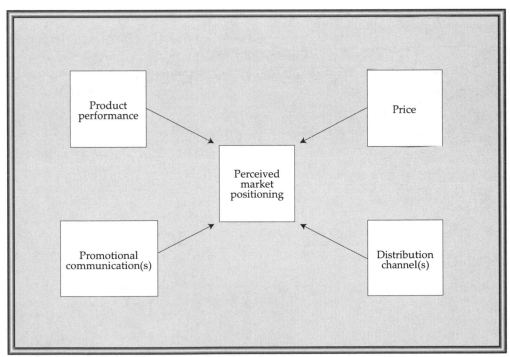

Figure 9.2 *The interaction of market mix on perceived positioning*

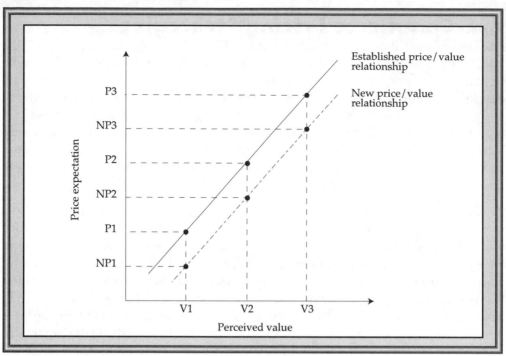

Figure 9.3 *Price/value relationships*

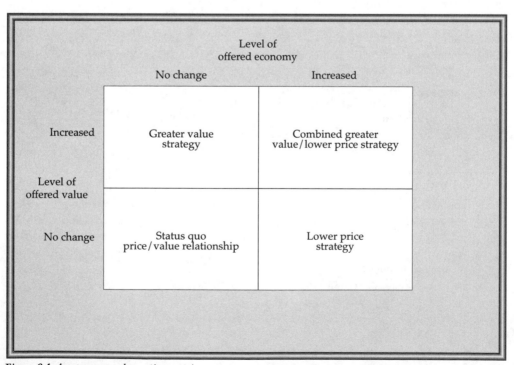

Figure 9.4 *An economy value option matrix*

E-PRICING AND DISTRIBUTION

position. Hence the usual strategic response to a shift in price/value relationships is to exploit e-commerce as a path through which to further underpin existing, established market position.

On-Line Auctions

In the mid-1990s, Pierre Omidyar decided to try the Internet as way of finding a market for his girlfriend's Pez-dispenser collection. His experience made him realize that the Internet offers a new way of creating markets, namely by establishing an on-line auction site where buyers and sellers can negotiate transactions. His business model was highly profitable from the start because his operation, eBay, does not incur the costs associated with handling inventory or distributing goods. All it (*www.ebay.com*) does is to take a commission on sales (anon. 1999).

The appeal of cyber-auctions is demonstrated by the fact that in 1999 it was estimated that on-line auctions accounted for the majority of goods being traded on-line. Currently the top-selling auction category is computers, but it is expected that in a few years this volume of trade will be matched by other categories such as airline tickets, hotel rooms, cars and clothing. To attract participants to a cyber-auction, most sites

---

E-Pricing in Computing

The computer company Dell provides an example of exploiting e-commerce technology to further enhance perceived value. From the company's first day of business it recognized that direct marketing requires an overwhelming commitment to maximizing the effectiveness of the interface between company and customer. The company was one of the first organizations to recognize how efficiencies offered by Internet trading could contribute towards the enhancing of customer value (Thurm 1998). Over time, Dell has evolved a website that does much more than just take orders. Customers can access thousands of pages of information, tap into the technical guides used by Dell technicians, and also use the site to track the progress of their order from submission through to shipment. The company has found that these types of service actually improve their selling efficiency. For example, the traditional purchaser makes five telephone calls before buying ,whereas users of the website browse and then place their order during their first telephone call. Additionally, Dell sales staff can interrogate the site to determine whether there is a need to follow up a customer's search activities with a one-to-one telephone conversation.

For corporate clients the company has now developed Premier Pages. This permits customers to specify the creation of confidential home pages to which they can direct their employees seeking information on the product specifications that their employers are willing to buy them. Premium Pages also enables the client to access databases showing what type of computers have been purchased and who within their organization has placed the order.

Charles Schwab

An example of a company that has exploited e-commerce to sustain a strategy of greater value and lower price is the brokerage firm Charles Schwab. In the late 1980s, the company realized that as individuals gained experience in investing in the stock market they had less and less need for the services available from conventional stockbroking firms. Schwab's solution was that by offering market access without providing any investment counselling support it could charge a much lower commission on trades (Business Week 1994). Within only a few years, however, other brokerage houses recognized that the Schwab philosophy was the way ahead, and redesigned their operations to reflect this market change. In response, Schwab sought to find new ways of using electronic technology to deliver increased trading functionality to individual investors. In 1989, for example, it introduced automated telephone touch-pad trading, and in 1993 launched StreetSmart for Windows, a software package allowing customers to trade via a modem. Custom Broker, a telephone, fax and paging service for active traders followed in 1994. These entrepreneurial ideas were accompanied by the launch of OneSource, which gave investors direct access to many hundreds of no-load funds run by top US money managers (Wayne 1994). Following this success, Schwab entered the world of on-line trading in which the consumer, sitting comfortably at home, can use the Internet to buy and sell shares at a cost over 60 per cent lower than that charged by a traditional brokerage house. Not only is e.Schwab currently the market leader in the provision of an Internet share trading service, some observers are suggesting that this move may eventually totally revolutionize the stockbroking business.

have followed the eBay model. The visitor fills out a registration form. Access is then granted to a list of available items and information is provided on the highest previous bid. Some auctions also make available data on bidding history, number of bids, bid amounts and the cyber-names of the bidders. One of the early problems to emerge from cyber-auctions was the protection of sellers and buyers against fraud. One form of protection offered by eBay is that a user can gain access to comments about a seller's or bidder's previous behaviour. The company also posts a star next to high reputation sellers, and visitors who are mentioned in numerous site user complaints are banned (Pitta 1998).

A major appeal of the Internet as an auction vehicle is the size of the potential audience. Cyber-auctions may eventually come to represent a major threat to the traditional auction industry. In the case of fine arts and antiques, the auction business has been dominated for over 300 years by Christie's and Sotheby's. It is estimated that these two firms control 39 per cent of a $2 billion annual market. Hundred of second-tier houses fight over the balance of the available market. Entrepreneurs James Corsellis and Simon Montford reasoned that if a significant number of second-tier houses could be persuaded to become involved in on-line auctions the new entity would have sufficient critical mass to challenge the market domination of Christie's and Sotheby's (Plotkin

1998). The new website, Auctions On-Line, rapidly recruited 150 art auction houses, permitting the company to offer access to almost 4000 catalogues. These catalogues contain information on over $400 million worth of appraised art, antiques and collectables.

Although consumer-to-consumer cyber-auctions were the first to gain popularity on the Internet, they were soon followed by the creation of business-to-business sites. Many of these sites have followed the eBay model, with the site owners taking a commission on

Pricing a Problem in Global E-Trading?

One of the aspects of traditional, off-line global marketing is that companies have to create different marketing strategies and market management systems to suit variations in buyer behaviour and market structures across the world. In some markets, for example, the company may own the distribution system, and in others it may make greater sense to employ the services of an intermediary. This can lead to major variations in manufacturing and logistics costs that need to be reflected in price variations between markets. Once a company begins to consider going on-line, the issue arises of how it copes with customers becoming aware of these price variations?

A company that has confronted this dilemma is Millipore Corporation (*www.millipore.com*) based in Bedford, Massachusetts. The company, which has annual sales of $600 million, makes filtration products for applications such as the purification of water for laboratories and the detection of contaminants in the gases used to manufacture semiconductors. Customers in the US include firms such as Eli Lilly, Genetech, Intel and Motorola. The company has a similar list of 'blue chip' corporations in virtually every other developed economy around the world. Given the global nature of the company's sales base, the Internet clearly offers an effective medium through which both to communicate information and support the customer purchase process.

The speed with which Millipore was able to achieve its Internet ambitions was affected by a series of unforeseen complications. One problem was how to integrate the company's existing Oracle-based internal databases with the Internet system. Some of the company's distributors were unable to offer secure sites, or had problems rapidly updating the price bulletins issued by Millipore. The biggest complication facing the company, however, was that it charges higher prices overseas than it does in the US. This is necessary in order to cover the additional costs of support services in overseas markets (Cronin 1997).

If Millipore created a website with an on-line purchase facility, there was the risk that overseas customers would want to cut out the local in-market distributor, place orders electronically and demand the same prices as those offered to US customers. Having examined the potential dilemmas associated with inter-country pricing differentials, Millipore has decided to postpone the decision of whether to offer an on-line ordering facility, and restricts its website to providing information associated with supporting pre- and post-purchase service activities.

search

sales. Gerry Haller, the founder of FastParts (*www.century.fastparts.com*), for example, became aware that electronics companies frequently face the problem of having too many or too few spare parts, but are unwilling to trade with other companies perceived as rivals. FastParts offers the opportunity for the anonymous auctioning of parts via a trusted intermediary. Over 2500 electronics companies now use the site's thrice-weekly auctions as a mechanism for improving stock levels (anon. 1997).

In the financial services sector, suppliers are also using cyber-auctions to attract buyers. At the IMX Mortgage Exchange (*www.imx-exchange.com*), an on-line home loan market, brokers post homebuyers' requests for mortgages, and potential lenders bid on them. The brokers then select for their clients what they see as the best lending proposition on offer. Another service example is provided by *www.adauction.com*. This cyber-auction site started by displaying and soliciting bids for unsold advertising space. The success of this first venture has caused the company to move into offering unsold print advertising space, and its eventual aim is also to offer a similar service for the broadcast media (anon. 1999).

Some business-to-business sites have adopted the model of purchasing other firms' excess inventories and offering them for sale at auction. An examples of this approach is provided by QXL (*www.qxl.com*) in the UK (Wilson 1999). This is a much higher risk model than the eBay one because the cyber-auctioneer is taking ownership of the product, and gambles that received bids will exceed purchase costs. To a certain degree, success is influenced by the volume of active bidders using the site. Hence a major

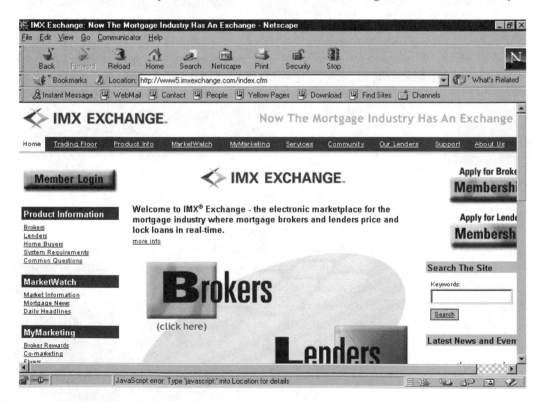

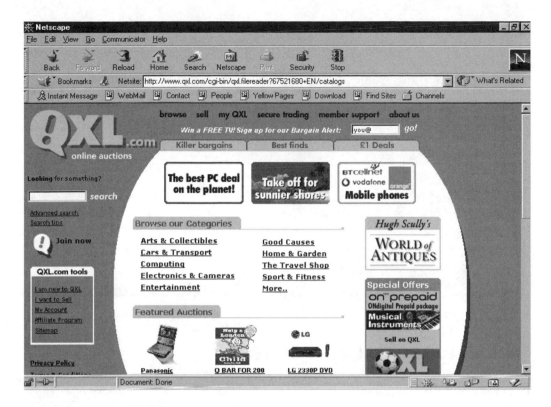

front-end cost for this type of website is promotional expenditure to build rapidly a large, loyal customer base.

Some futurists are predicting that as consumers become familiar with bidding for product instead of accepting a supplier's list price on-line shopping may lead to the elimination of whole tiers of distribution and create a highly efficient, price-sensitive global market (anon. 1998). To-date, however, such trends have yet to emerge. In part this is due to the fact by the time the on-line customer pays the shipping and handling costs the final delivered price may be higher than that charged at a local, traditional discount retailer. Hence at the moment it would appear that although auction sites are offering the world a new type of purchase experience, for the majority of people the real benefit of the Internet is that it provides round-the-clock access to an incredibly diverse range of goods. Additionally, once the cyberspace shopper has determined his or her purchase preference, there is now access to a number of sites providing comparative data on prices quoted by a number of suppliers. Examples of this type of comparative pricing service are WebMarket (*www.webmarket.com*) and Jango (*www.jango.com*). Visitors to these sites can input brand names or model numbers to receive a list of suppliers and published prices. Jango also allows searches beyond listed suppliers to seek out products available on on-line auction sites and on-line classified advertising sites.

● Cyberspace Price Wars

The conventional theory of price war in off-line markets is that these tend to break out in mature and declining markets where (1) suppliers have excess capacity relative to market demand and (2) customers perceive little difference between the performance claims being made by different suppliers (Garda and Marn 1993). In most off-line price wars, the usual outcome is that any price advantage is short-lived because competitors rapidly move to either match or beat the newly announced price reduction. Price wars can also lead to a permanent distortion in customer price expectations. An implication of this latter outcome is that if supply and demand subsequently become more balanced (for example due to plant closures or major suppliers leaving the market), a return to historic pricing levels is impossible because customer expectations cause them to resist upward price moves.

The phenomenon of price wars only tending to occur late in the PLC in tangible goods markets, when firms are forced to sustain output to cover the fixed costs of large manufacturing facilities, does not apply in information-based markets, a fundamental characteristic of which is that once the investment in producing the first item has been made, ongoing production costs are minimal. The concept has been known in the book industry for centuries. The first copy of a new book is expensive, but the cost of subsequent units reduce with quantity. A variation of this principle applies in the world of computer software. Once the development investment has been made in a new product, ongoing production costs are virtually zero because new copies of the software can infinitely loaded onto disc or CD-ROM (Shapiro and Varian 1999). The possibility of price wars occurring much earlier in the PLC has led to the emergence of new pricing models in e-commerce markets. This is because when minimal production costs combine with the ease of electronic distribution, companies seeking to achieve market leadership may buy market share by giving away free copies of their product.

An example of the way Internet price wars can emerge over time is provided by the case of the company Netscape. This company achieved domination of the world Internet browser market but then faced intense competition from Microsoft. The developer of the Netscape browser was Marc Andreessen (Tetzeli and Puri 1996). Only four years out of college he and Eddy Bina wrote the first version of Mosaic, the browser that made the World Wide Web accessible. After this first success he went into partnership with Jim Clarke to found Netscape. Like many technology entrepreneurs, Andreessen's role in Netscape is to act as a catalyst stimulating employees to develop and implement new ideas. Although he can rightfully be seen as the founder of the business, he reports to the CEO Jim Barksdale. This latter individual concentrates on guiding the business financially, leaving Andreessen free for the role of entrepreneurial visionary. The entrepreneurial act that made this new company so successful was simplicity itself. The company gave away free copies of their easy-to-use net browser, Netscape Navigator and as a result the software rapidly found a home on 45 million computers around the world. A key reason for Netscape's success was that it broke with sector convention by developing a browser that would run on any operating system.

Another characteristic of information-based markets is that minimal production costs also mean that firms are more likely to consider price wars as a route to market share. Such was the case in the ongoing story of Netscape. Apparently the company's success

Building On-Line Brands

IT companies such as Microsoft, Intel and Sun Microsystems have long recognized the benefits of establishing strong brand identities in an e-commerce world. Nakache (1998) proposes that there are four basics steps in a move from unknown to household name in a short period of time. The first, and possibly most important, is to find ways of giving the product away to as many people as possible. America Online is the giant in the give-away business, appearing in places such breakfast cereals, in-flight meal trays and on music CDs.

The second step is to conduct an aggressive public relations war against potential competitors. Sun has used this approach to build a global awareness for its flagship software platform Java. In many cases it has exploited the strange aversion among 'techies' to Microsoft products to suggest a move to Java as a way to avoid Microsoft domination of cyberspace.

The third step is to exploit the Internet to build a strong relationship with the customer. Amazon is a master of this technique, using tools such as BookMatcher to keep customers automatically updated on new titles of interest to them. Complementing this approach, the fourth step is to communicate that the company is an organization full of fun-loving people who want their customers to share in their approach to life. The Java team at Sun is a leader in this approach, as illustrated by their creation of Duke, the Java mascot that is part penguin, part tooth, 'battling to keep the Internet safe for everyone'. Another positive image of the fun to be had in cyberspace is that of Yahoo's dynamic founding duo Jerry Yang and David Filo.

deeply disturbed the senior management at Microsoft. A probable reason for this was that if software developers began to write applications compatible with Navigator, the browser would become a universal platform, potentially leading to a situation in which the characteristics of any propriety operating system such Windows would become irrelevant (Eddy 1999). To further fuel the fire, Microsoft was preparing to launch the latest version of its operating system, Windows 95.

The scene was now set for a major battle between two organizations each seeking to dominate the technological conventions underpinning the e-commerce industry. The events which followed were a component in the evidence used in the US Department of Justice's anti-trust suit against Microsoft in late 1999, in which the company was judged to have used its market dominance to stifle competition in the US software market. On 7 December 1995 Microsoft announced that it had developed its own browser, Internet Explorer which would be given away to customers. Even though Explorer was free while Navigator was then $39, most users appeared to perceive the latter as significantly superior. Additionally, at this time the majority of Internet service providers were using Netscape software. The exception was America Online (AOL) which had its own proprietary product and was seeking to purchase a better one. While Netscape sought to sell its browser to AOL, Microsoft's counter-offer was to supply Explorer free. Furthermore, in return for signing an exclusive deal, AOL would be given space on the Windows 95 product. It is alleged that Microsoft's next move was to approach other Internet service providers offering packages that went well beyond just offering a free browser.

Then, in 1998, Microsoft announced its next unconventional move, namely integrating Explorer 4 into the Windows operating system in preparation for the launch of Windows 98. Microsoft offered large discounts on licensing fees to computer manufacturers to encourage them to bundle together the two programmes. This appears to have been the last straw for Netscape. The company announced the very unorthodox strategy of not just giving away the browser, but also releasing the 'source code' that is the key to the software's inner workings (Stross 1998). The hope was that this move would cause thousands of software developers around the world to use the source code to develop new software based upon Netscape technology. Such widespread use of the technology, it was hoped, would expand market opportunity for the company's two remaining revenue streams, namely the supply of high-end, high-margin customized e-commerce software and the sale of space on the company's website, Netcenter.

● Cost Transparency

Sinha (2000) presents an excellent review of the potential impact of the Internet on the future price levels. He points out that it is in the seller's best interest to keep costs opaque, because this permits companies to claim unique benefits for their brands and thereby command premium prices. Prior to the arrival of the Internet, sellers were assisted in this because it was difficult for consumers to acquire detailed information on competitive offerings prior to reaching a purchase decision.

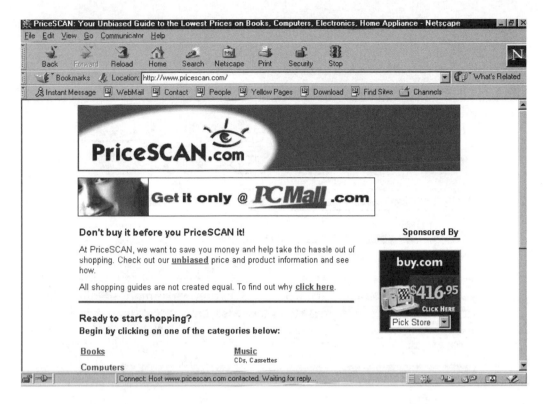

The advent of the Internet means that consumers can use sites such as *www.pricescan.com* and on-line shopping agents such as *www.bottomdollar.com* to compare rapidly prices and features on thousands of products. They can also visit sites such as *www.epinions.com* to read about the purchasing experience of others, and through sites such as *www.travelocity.com* gain access to information once only accessible to travel agents. Similar scenarios are also emerging in business-to-business markets. For example, textile manufacturers can visit the site *www.alibaba.com* to gain free access a directory of over 35 000 companies.

As an outcome of this in both consumer and industrial markets, sellers are finding that their pricing strategies are becoming much more transparent to potential customers. This reduces a seller's ability to command a premium price (as in the case of the long-distance telephone market now being highly price-sensitive), tends to turn branded goods into commodities, and weakens customer loyalty. In order to avoid being forced into cutting prices, and thereby reducing profit margins, Sinha proposes that there are a number of strategic options available to organizations. One is to seek to offer improved benefits and services, superior to those available from competition. Another approach is to bundle products together such that it is more difficult for buyers to determine the costs of any single item. Gateway, for example, bundle Internet services with their computers as a way to avoid some of the more dramatic price declines in the PC market recently. A third approach is to invest in innovation that leads to the launch of new and distinctive products. AOL, for example, as well as bundling products offers innovative services such as instant messaging, proprietary e-mail and chat-rooms,

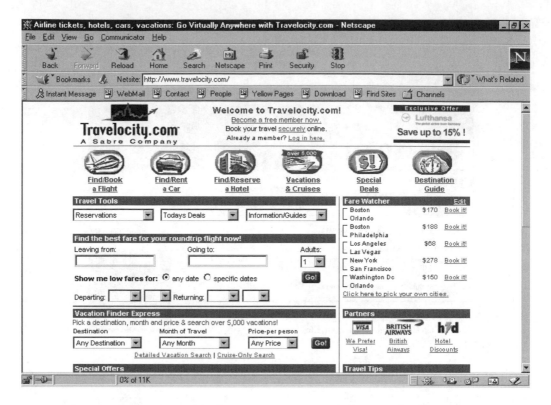

parental control over childrens' Internet access, and photograph sharing technology. Additionally, AOL will be offering users of the 3Com PalmPilot the ability to read their AOL e-mails on their hand-held sets.

● Distribution Management

Distribution of products usually involves some form of vertical system in which transaction and logistic responsibilities are transferred through a number of levels (for example fresh fish are landed at a port, sold through auction to port wholesalers, sold on, and transported by truck to inland wholesalers, who in turn sell and deliver the product to local restaurants). In terms of distribution management, Stern and El-Ansary (1988) propose that the following factors will need to be considered in the selection of an appropriate system:

1. The capability of intermediaries in the logistics role of sorting goods, aggregating products from a variety of sources and breaking down bulk shipments into saleable lot sizes.

2. The capability of intermediaries in routinizing transactions to minimize costs (for example a store selling a variety of shoe designs).

3. The capability of intermediaries in minimizing customer search costs (for example a computer store having available information and demonstration models from a range of different suppliers).

Compaq Headache (*www.compaq.com*)

Compaq was the company that initially achieved global status by developing and marketing low cost IBM PC 'clones'. Since that time the company has evolved into a manufacturer of a diverse range of computer hardware. A cornerstone in achieving widespread market penetration was the creation of a global network of distributors and value-added resellers to link the company to the IT end-user market. Dell's business model, direct marketing use of the Internet as the primary distribution channel, has severely affected Compaq's performance in recent years (Kirkpatrick 2000).

Compaq's response has been to attempt to build a system which continues to market products through terrestrial intermediaries while also building an on-line trading operation. At the moment, 80 per cent of Compaq's shipments still go through middlemen. The current CEO, Michael Capellas, is trying to accelerate the building of an effective on-line distribution operation. A major obstacle, however, is that the company is unable to match the huge expertise in Internet operations already embedded into the Dell operation. In an attempt to move more rapidly up the learning curve, Compaq has recently acquired Inacom as a fast track route to expertise for the operation in the key areas of on-line order tracking, production scheduling and distribution management.

In relation to these three factors, direct supplier–customer distribution systems tend to occur in those market systems in which certain conditions prevail: each end-user purchases a large proportion of total output, or goods are highly perishable, or the complex nature of the goods requires a close working relationship between supplier and final customer. This scenario will be encountered, for example, in many large capital goods markets such as the office block and petrochemical plant construction industries. In markets in which an indirect distribution system is perceived as being more cost-effective, the usual convention is that one or more distributors become involved in the distribution process. These distributors typically receive a truckload-sized shipment that is then broken down into smaller lot sizes. These are sold to an end-user outlet with responsibility for managing both the final customer purchase transaction and any post-purchase service needs (for example cash-and-carry-warehouses supplying branded food products to small local grocery stores.)

A common convention in Western economies during the twentieth century was that retailers perceived scale benefits in purchasing directly from suppliers, 'cutting out the middleman' and establishing vertically integrated procurement, warehousing, distribution and retailing operations. Exploitation of this ahead of competition provided the basis for the establishment of what are now considered highly conventional trading dynasties such as Sears Roebuck in the US and Marks & Spencer in the UK.

After decades of being virtually ignored as an important aspect of the marketing management process, in the mid-1980s organizations began to realize that effective management of distribution channels can actually provide additional opportunities to gain advantage over competition. A number of factors contributed to this situation.

On-Line or Off-Line?

Many of the early dot-com entrepreneurs were companies that moved an off-line operation onto the Web as a mechanism for expanding market reach and offering 24-hour customer service. Some have been so impressed by the power of the Internet that they have subsequently closed their terrestrial, or 'bricks-and-mortar' operation (McGarvey 2000). One such company is Pom Express, a Massachusetts company specializing in supplying products for those involved in cheerleading. Two years ago the company closed its retail operation, and conducts all trading activity through **www.pomexpress.com**.

Similarly, Nancy Zebrick operated a traditional travel agency in New Jersey, and moved into the Internet as a parallel operation in 1995. She soon found that although the profit margin per sale is lower on the Web, this is more than compensated for by increased volumes. In 1988, the company merged with an on-line travel superstore (**www.onetravel.com**) and left, forever, the world of terrestrial trading. A similar story can be found at **www. egghead.com**. A major leader in the retailing of software in the 1980s, this company's reaction to increasing competitive pressures in the 1990s has been to close its stores and concentrate on Internet sales.

Some industry observers are cautioning those who believe that stories of successful e-trading operations mean that all companies should close terrestrial operations. Certainly when one observes the large companies in sectors such as retailing and banking it is becoming clear that a dual strategy in both a bricks-and-mortar and on-line may be a more appropriate strategy through which to satisfy the differing customer needs. Many customers still want the level of personal interaction that at the moment can only be delivered through a traditional retail outlet. This is especially true, for example, in markets such as women's fashions, in which most shoppers want to try on the clothing before they buy. Some small businesses are also beginning to believe that a dual strategy is a more sensible option for the foreseeable future. Certainly this is the view at Star Children's Wear Inc., a children's clothing company in Washington that operates both a retail outlet and a website (**www.shopstars.com**). Similarly, in Winter Park, Florida, Wine Country Inc. has a retail outlet and also offers an on-line facility at **www.winecountryonline.com**.

Possibly two of the more important have been (1) the impact of new or improved technology in the reduction of transportation costs and/or delivery times (for example the construction of motorway networks in Europe that have made it feasible for a manufacturer based one country to service effectively from one single plant the needs of customers in all other European countries) and (2) exponentially declining prices for IT systems across all facets of the distribution process (for example the linking of supermarket computers with the production scheduling systems of key suppliers, to manage more effectively the process of matching production to demand).

Rangan et al. (1993), in reviewing the future strategic implications of new approaches to channel management, suggest that managers must now view the flow of goods and

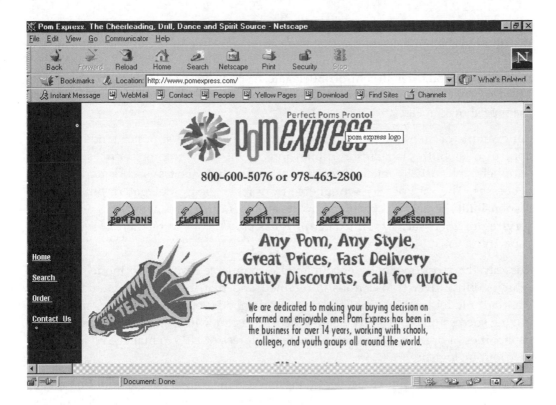

services in relation to the questions of whether exploitation of alternative channels can serve to create competitive entry barriers, enhance product differentiation and enable greater customer intimacy. These authors' proposal is that it is now necessary to 'unbundle' the channel functions of information provision, order generation, physical distribution and after sales service. The next step is to then determine how customer needs can best be met by channel members working together as a team of channel partners each performing those tasks in which they excel.

● E-Commerce Distribution

The advent of e-commerce is causing many companies to re-assess their approach to using distribution systems to acquire and sustain competitive advantage. Even prior to the arrival of the Internet, Moriaty and Moran (1990) refer to the exploitation of new electronic technologies as an opportunity for building 'hybrid marketing systems'. They perceive these technology-based systems as offering new, more customer-oriented, entrepreneurial approaches to channel management. They present the example of IBM, which over the years has moved from a single channel based around its own sales force, to being a hybrid operation involving dealers, value-added resellers, a catalogue selling operation, direct mail and tele-marketing. In the last ten years this has resulted in a doubling of the size of its own sales force and the opening of 18 new channels to serve the highly diverse nature of customer need.

One approach to determining an optimal strategy for selecting an optimal e-commerce distribution channel is to assume that there are two critical dimensions influencing the decision; namely whether to retain control or delegate responsibility for transaction management and to retain control or delegate, responsibility for logistics management. This concept can be visualized in the form of an e-commerce channel option matrix of the type shown in Fig. 9.5.

An example of an e-commerce market sector in which the supplier tends to retain control over both distribution dimensions is on-line banking services, because supplier banks usually retain absolute control over both the transaction and delivery processes. The case of the e-commerce transaction being delegated, but delivery responsibility retained, is provided by the airline industry. Many airlines use on-line service providers such as *www.cheapflights.co.uk* to act as retailers of unsold seat capacity.

Possibly the most frequently encountered e-commerce distribution model is one in which control over transactions is retained and distribution delegated. It is the standard model used by most on-line tangible goods retailers. These organizations, having successfully sold a product to a website visitor, will use the global distribution capabilities of organizations such as Federal Express or UPS to manage all aspects of distribution logistics.

In the majority of off-line consumer goods markets the commonest distribution model is one in which both transaction and logistics processes are delegated (for example major brands such as Coca-Cola being marketed via supermarket chains). This can be

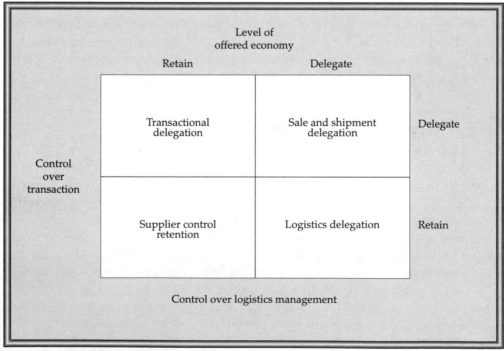

Figure 9.5 *An e-commerce distribution option matrix*

E-PRICING AND DISTRIBUTION

contrasted with the on-line world, in which absolute delegation of all processes is still a somewhat rarer event. The reason for this is that many companies, having decided that e-commerce offers an opportunity for revising distribution management practices, perceive cyberspace as a way to regain control over transactions by cutting out intermediaries and selling direct to the end-user customers. As already mentioned, the process by which traditional intermediaries are squeezed out of channels is usually referred to as 'disintermediation'.

It must be recognized, however, that delegation of transactions and logistics may offer ways to improve market service provision, through the exploitation of opportunities made available through 're-intermediation' (Pitt et al. 1999). An example of this dual delegation of channel responsibility is provided by the digital music standard MP3, which provides a solution for recording companies that have for many years faced the problem of being unable to persuade off-line retailers to stock recordings by newly signed artists or groups.

Pitt et al. (1999) propose that in assessing e-commerce distribution strategies there is the need to recognize that the technology has the following implications:

1 Distance ceases to be a cost influencer because on-line delivery of information is substantially the same no matter the destination of the delivery.

2 Business location becomes an irrelevance because the e-commerce enterprise can be based anywhere in the world.

3 The technology permits continuous trading, 24-hours-a-day, 365-days-a-year.

	Technology implications		
	Minimal delivery cost	Location irrelevance	Continuous operation
Minimizing customer search	On-line airline reservation systems	On-line insurance companies	On-line employment recruitment agencies
Transaction routinazation	On-line cross-border banking	On-line OEM procurement networks	On-line catalogue companies
Assortment management	On-line music stores offering customised CD-ROMs	On-line manufacturers of customised PCs	On-line educational institutions

Figure 9.6 An e-commerce strategic distribution option matrix (modified from Pitt et al 1999)

By combining these implications with the basic roles of intermediaries (assortment management, transaction routinization and the reduction of customer search activities), Pitt et al. have evolved an e-commerce strategic distribution option matrix of the type shown in Fig. 9.6. The authors recommend that marketers use this type of matrix to identify potential competitive threats caused by other actors within a market system exploiting e-commerce technology to enhance the distribution process. They also propose that in the future, because of the interactivity of e-commerce, marketers will begin to replace the phrase 'distribution channel' with a new term, 'distribution medium'.

A characteristic of off-line distribution channels is the difficulty that smaller firms face in persuading intermediaries (for example supermarket chains) to stock their goods. This scenario is less applicable in the world of e-commerce. Companies of any size face a relatively easy task establishing an on-line presence. Market coverage can then be extended by developing trading alliances based upon commission payments to other on-line traders which attract new customers to the company's website. This ease of entry reduces the incidence of firms' marketing efforts being frustrated because they are unable to gain the support of intermediaries in traditional distribution channels. Eventually e-commerce may lead to a major increase in the total number of companies offering products and services across world markets. As this occurs, markets will become more efficient, and many products will be perceived as commodities, with a consequent decline in average prices.

● Summary

The basic principles of the influence of supply and demand on market price have been the cornerstone of economic theory ever since Adam Smith published The Wealth Of Nations. Management of pricing strategies and policies in the real world, however, are often complicated by factors such as the position of a product on the PLC curve and the intensity of competition within a market sector. Pricing is also affected by the degree to which customers can gain access to information on alternative offerings within a market sector. The Internet has greatly expanded access to information, with the result that the advent of e-commerce has driven down average prices in many market sectors. The Internet made it possible for customers to purchase a wide range of products and services by registering their bid via an on-line auction site. In any market a critical aspect of the marketing process is the linking of company with end-user through effective management of available distribution channels. A key aspect of the Internet is that the technology permits many companies that previously used intermediaries to form direct links with their end-user market. Hence an important new dimension of the marketing management role in today's organizations is to determine how best to structure the company's distribution channels in an e-trading world.

1 How can price be utilized to support a company's market positioning strategy?

2 What are the potential risks faced by people who purchase goods via an on-line auction site. What actions can the operators of on-line auction sites take to minimize these risks?

3 What impact is the Internet likely to have on the future role of traditional 'bricks-and-mortar' retailers as market intermediaries?

Case: *The Rebirth of Pitney Bowes*

The US corporation Pitney Bowes has been the leading producer of postal franking machines for many years. In recognition of the growing potential threat of firms like Federal Express competing with the Post Office, and e-mails and fax technology reducing the demand for 'snail mail', the company has moved to ensure its survival. A cornerstone of its new strategy is to position the company as the technological resource for postal administration processes in small firms.

Launched under the brand name of Pitney Works, the range offers software support tools. ClickStamp Online and ClickStamp Plus allow users to generate addresses and print postage stamps using a standard office printer. ValueShip assists the user to select the most cost-effective route for a letter or parcel. Personal Post is a digital meter for postage stamp 'refills' from the Post Office. DirectNET is a software tool to help users design mailshots. These can then be sent to Pitney Bowes, which handle mailing list development, envelope addressing and mailing. TargetProspects is a Web-based service offering access to a database containing addresses of 11 million US businesses and 95 million consumer names and addresses. Pitney Works Business Rewards Visa Card allows the user access to a $25 000 line of credit to support business purchasing activities.

Source: anon. (2000)

QUESTION

1 Assume that you have appointed the new Marketing Director for the Pitney Works product range. Develop a report demonstrating how, by exploiting the four concepts proposed earlier in this chapter for building on-line brands, Pitney Bowes can become a household e-commerce brand name around the world.

Case: *Where is the Car Business Going?*

The huge world market that exists for cars means that the sector has rapidly attracted e-entrepreneurs seeking to change the face of car marketing forever. If you want information this is available through sites such as *www.autoadvice.com* and *www.carbuyingtips.com*. Similarly, when it comes to buying, sites such as *www.autobytel.com* take you electronically through the steps of finding a car, selling a car, and arranging finance and insurance.

Interestingly, the car industry has attracted the attentions of the software giant Microsoft.

Via *www.carpoint.com* the user is told about new and used cars from different manufacturers, and the site lists used cars available for sale and offers the facility to bid electronically on new cars available at car dealers near to the customer's home address. Initially the growing importance of the Internet was ignored by the big car makers. Things are changing. In October 1999, for example, General Motors launched a website that enables customers to purchase new cars over the Net (*www.bmbuypower.com*).

Source: Glasser (2000); Kirkpatrick (1998)

QUESTION

1 Tron Motors is a main dealer for a major car manufacturer. The company operates five new car outlets on the edge of major metropolitan areas. Each outlet sells new cars and used cars taken as trade-ins, and has a fully equipped repair and servicing department. At the moment, the company is a purely off-line retailing operation. Assume you have just been appointed as Tron's Marketing Director. The Board has requested that you prepare a report on how the company should become involved in using the Internet as an alternative distribution channel for existing and/or new products and services.

Chapter 10

THE EVOLUTION OF E-MANAGEMENT SYSTEMS

Learning Objectives

This chapter explains

◆ The role of market information systems in decision-making.

◆ The impact of 'just-in-time' (JIT) management process models.

◆ The role of process re-engineering in enhancing business processes.

◆ The influence of JIT on supply chain management.

◆ The impact of the Internet on supply chain management models.

◆ The use of extranets to link suppliers and customers.

◆ The design of effective on-line supply chain systems.

Marketers have always accepted that fulfilment of their role is critically influenced by the acquisition and use of information to support the delivery of customer satisfaction. For many years, most standard marketing texts have contained a section on the need for the organization to establish a computer-based marketing information system (MIS) that can act as a core resource to be exploited in analysis, planning, plan implementation and control. To further reinforce the importance of such systems, these texts often present a MIS model of the type shown in Fig. 10.1.

The consequence of such texts is that many graduates leave universities expecting to encounter effective MIS operations in real world organizations. Exposure to the information decision processes used by actual firms soon causes graduates to realize that a significant gap exists between marketing theory and practice. The reasons for the existence of this gap include:

1   The total lack of compatibility between the data systems in different departments which means that attempts at on-line access to inter-departmental information on production schedules, inventory levels or average age of account receivables are very likely to fail.

2   The fact that many computer systems only process data on a batch updating basis, not real time, in a format in which any attempt at on-line analysis is extremely difficult.

3   The fact that most market research studies are implemented on an infrequent basis with the results often only stored in an off-line format.

4   The tendency for market intelligence acquired by sales or marketing staff to be treated as informal knowledge, exchanged on a person-to-person basis without any real attempt to store it in a central database.

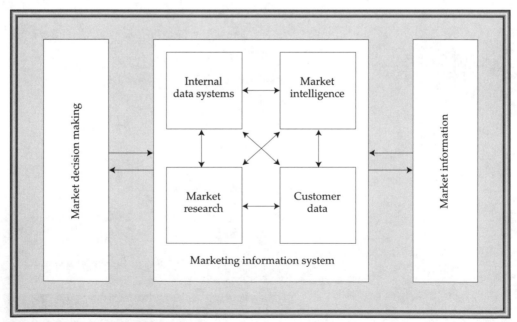

Figure 10.1   *An example of an MIS model*

THE EVOLUTION OF E-MANAGEMENT SYSTEMS

In addition to failures to build integrated systems for managing databases across the organization, by the mid-1980s Western marketers realized that their frighteningly aggressive counterparts from the Pacific rim had managed radically to reduce the time taken to complete standard manufacturing processes. Leaders in this were the Japanese, who questioned the convention that to minimize costs companies (1) should schedule long runs of a single product and (2) use economic order quantity (EOQ) models to ensure sufficient buffer stocks to handle unexpected order surges from customers. The Japanese perspective was that although this manufacturing industry convention could theoretically optimize production costs, any savings are more than offset by the concurrent massive investment in working capital required to fund cash outflows for raw materials on hand, work in progress and inventoried finished goods. Their ultimate solution was to reject the concept of long runs of individual products based upon specified EOQs and to investigate the potential for only scheduling production to match on-hand orders from customers. Their outstanding success has become better known as a just-in-time (JIT) manufacturing philosophy.

By the 1990s JIT manufacturing principles had become the new convention for any company wishing to be considered a 'world class' organization. As many Western companies have discovered, to be effective, JIT demands a commitment to (Storey 1994):

1 Careful monitoring of customer order patterns.

2 Suppliers which can respond very rapidly and have the ability cost-effectively only to deliver sufficient raw materials for the next scheduled production run.

3 Manufacturing operations in which machine tool set-up time is minimized.

4 A highly proactive, responsive workforce.

5 Logistics systems capable of economically delivering smaller order quantities to customers.

6 'Real time' information capture systems capable of immediately diagnosing the cause of any emerging procurement, production scheduling or delivery problems.

Initially some JIT practitioners perceived this philosophy as a mechanism to enhance financial performance. Within a short period of time, however, marketers realized that JIT had massive implications in the areas of delivering customer satisfaction and the development of new products. One of the first management theorists to recognize that JIT required the adoption of a new orientation to time and process management was Davis (1987). He points out that in the world of business the concept of time is undergoing a radical transition. In the industrial age, the established convention was a 9-to-5 day, whereas in a post-industrial society the customer is seeking 24-hour, 365 days-a-year service.

Davis believes that this change in customer demand necessitates that the marketer must carefully study every aspect of internal operations from product conceptualization through to customer post-purchase consumption. He reports that marginal reductions in time (of 10–20 per cent) can be accomplished by simply improving efficiency. However, a major reduction (of 50–100 per cent) usually requires a willingness to challenge every convention across the entire procurement, production, distribution and delivery cycle. He proposes, therefore, that firms should adopt the vision of zero-based time, which has the ultimate goal of never keeping the customer waiting.

Tucker (1991) also expresses similar views. He also believes that the number one driving force through which to challenge market conventions is the revision of organizational processes to accelerate the speed with which the organization can respond to customer needs. He suggests there are the following eight steps that permit exploitation of the 'speed imperative':

1   Assessing the importance of speed to the customer.

2   Challenging every time-based convention that exists within the organization.

3   Involving the customer in both identifying their waiting time dissatisfaction and generating ideas to reduce response times.

4   Continuously monitoring time savings achieved as new initiatives are implemented with the goal of eventually identifying new, incremental actions further to reduce response times.

5   Clearly promoting the nature of the company's speed imperative philosophy to the market.

6   Reflecting the costs of outstanding speed in the pricing of products and services.

7   Rewarding employees for finding new, entrepreneurial ways of saving time.

8   Having achieved high speed response, building this achievement into a customer guarantee system.

Writings on the strategic implications of time and process revision soon made the smarter marketers realize that many of the opportunities for delivering greater customer satisfaction could only be achieved by the entire organization focusing upon new ways to influence factors such as build quality, delivery time and lower prices. Unfortunately, even by the mid-1990s the more enlightened marketers were still finding that their organizations had still not been successful in creating the fully integrated, computer-based information system needed to co-ordinate time and process improvement initiatives. The outcome was that employees remained unable rapidly to gain access to information about activities in other departments that critically impacted on their work.

The Process-Engineering Solution

Two US management consultants who have championed the critical need to find new ways to break with current time and process management conventions in Western industry are Hammer and Champy (1993). From the experience gained from working with many large, highly conventional organizations, they have coined the phrase 're-engineering the corporation'. The philosophy 'means tossing aside old systems and starting over. It involves going back to the beginning and inventing a better way to do work.' The underlying principle of undertaking a searching review of operations during which no activity is sacred is further emphasized in their definition that 're-engineering is the fundamental rethinking and radical redesign of business processes to achieve dramatic improvements in critical contemporary measures of performance, such as cost, quality, service and speed'.

Hammer and Champy's opinion is that the prevailing Western world industrial model rests on the basic premise that workers have few skills and little time or capacity for training. As industrial processes have become more complex during the twentieth century, however, it has been necessary to develop sophisticated information and decision-making processes to weld together the multitude of jobs within large organizations associated with order generation and delivery of large volumes of output.

The conventional industrial model that has existed for the majority of the twentieth century, one that has until very recently had huge rewards for both nations and shareholders, is mass production. Proponents of re-engineering argue that mass production models have now evolved to the point at which they do not permit organizations to respond to the contemporary market demands for quality, service, flexibility and low costs. Hammer (1995) has gained extensive experience of facilitating major re-engineering projects across a range of industrial sectors. He concludes that there are a number of recurring themes and characteristics that can be expected to be encountered while implementing the process. These include:

1 The convention that jobs should be undertaken by various specialists within the organization is the most cost-effective approach.

2 The convention that the most effective structures are those based around vertical hierarchies in which workers 'work' but decisions pass upwards to managers because only they have the necessary breadth of knowledge to make them.

3 The convention that actions must be taken in a natural, logical order.

4 The convention that to maximize profitability by exploiting economies of scale the market should be offered a single, standard product or service.

5 The convention that specialists must be based in centralized departments.

By the mid-1990s, re-engineering had become very popular with Western companies in both the manufacturing and service sectors. Nevertheless, observations of the process in practice raise questions about whether the concept has the ability to improve time massively and process management practices in most organizations. A large proportion of the available case materials seem to imply that many companies tend to adopt a temporary operating philosophy to re-engineering projects. This lead them to identify a problem, form a project team and implement a solution that usually represents a break with long-standing internal conventions. In many cases, however, the project (1) is confined to only a small number of departments, and (2) an apparent 'Chinese Wall' is created to ensure that the activities do not spill over into those parts of the organization not directly affected by the identified problem.

In view of these observations, the attributes of re-engineering are usually that:

1   The process can be expected to be encountered within conventional organizations facing a problem that cannot be resolved by applying standard solutions.

2   The scale of the activity may involve the entire organization, but in many cases will be confined to a specific area of organizational activity.

3   Once the re-engineering team has completed its task, the team is dissolved and returns to its permanent job assignments.

4   If the new solution is publicized, other conventional companies recognize the merits of the approach and move to initiate similar changes in their operation. Thus the re-engineered operating philosophy soon becomes the new convention within an industrial sector.

● Supply Chain Management

Once Western companies began to implement JIT operating philosophies they soon discovered a lesson that had already been learned by their Pacific rim competitors: that to be effective, JIT needs to be extended outside the company to encompass all of the components that constitute a supply chain within an industrial sector. The critical need to examine the entire supply chain is illustrated by an example of a project undertaken by Cardiff Business School to examine the constituent elements for delivering cola drinks to a supermarket chain. The researchers started at the entry point of the chain, a bauxite mine in Australia. By tracking the process through the smelting and rolling associated with can manufacture, label printing, can filling and delivery to the supermarket shelf, they found the entire process takes 319 days. Even more worrying was their conclusion that only three hours are actually spent doing something that adds value. The rest of the time is taken up in transportation and storage activities. This is because organizations within this supply chain are primarily oriented towards capturing economies of scale, and do not recognize the waste involved in handling and storage (anon. 1998).

Since the late 1980s, the growing awareness of the waste within many supply chains has caused different industries to revisit the basic conventions that have determined supplier–customer relationships for most of the twentieth century. Recognition gradually dawned amongst the players that there was a need for all parties to begin to move away from traditional, adversarial relationships to a philosophy based upon co-operative partnerships with the aim of finding new ways of building more efficient supply chain systems (Buzzell and Ortmeyer 1995). The incentive that drove many

Western companies to adopt a more co-operative orientation was the recognition that without such change costs would continue to rise, and the ability to respond rapidly to changing market circumstances would become increasingly inadequate. In the retail sector, stores such as Wal-Mart and KMart moved to build closer relationships with their major suppliers. Across many areas of manufacturing, large OEMs such as General Electric, Ford, DuPont, General Motors and IBM sought to exploit the concept of working in partnership with their component suppliers.

What sales staff from suppliers and customer company procurement personnel soon discovered, however, was that without effective information management systems hopes of optimizing supply chain performance would rarely be fulfilled. They shared with the marketers seeking to exploit JIT the problem that unless ways could be found to improve the speed and accuracy of data interchange, neither JIT nor supply chain initiatives would be able to deliver the time and process management efficiency improvements sought. This caused attention to be focused upon the promise that the computer industry had been making since the 1950s, namely that electronic data exchange could revolutionize the ways companies manage both their internal operations and their interactions with other organizations within their market system.

The difference between the 1950s world of expensive mainframes and the 1990s is that hardware and software costs have fallen to the point at which smart machines have become affordable at every key point in the organization where real time data needs to be collected. Additionally, technology such as bar coding and electronic data interchange now permits real time electronic exchange of data between customer and supplier. Having adopted EDI as the medium for communication, supplier and customer are then in a position to be able to examine opportunities for the reduction of administrative burdens through such measures as reductions in purchase ordering, inventory holding, credit notes, invoices, delivery documentation and returned goods (McGrath 1996).

To demonstrate the radical changes that occur when suppliers and customers adopt a co-operative electronic data exchange philosophy, Buzzell and Ortmeyer (1995) analysed the flow of goods in the US clothing industry. As shown in Fig. 10.2, stock management in the days before electronic systems was triggered by staff at each store manually analysing individual sales tickets. This information was consolidated at head office, where manual calculations were made of replacement stock requirements, and the paperwork initiated to place an order with the manufacturer. Upon receipt of these paper-based orders, production was scheduled by the supplier and output shipped back to the retailer's central warehouse. Use of standard carriers usually meant that stock could not be tracked between departure from the manufacturer and arrival at the customer's warehouse. At the retailer's central warehouse, inbound goods were checked against orders and delivery notes prior to re-assortment for shipment to individual stores. Upon receipt of goods at store level, stock was priced and displayed.

Fig. 10.3 provides a comparison flow-chart of what can occur when a closer supplier–customer relationship is formed and data interchange is automated. At store level, the till automatically records the barcode information on sales tickets at the time

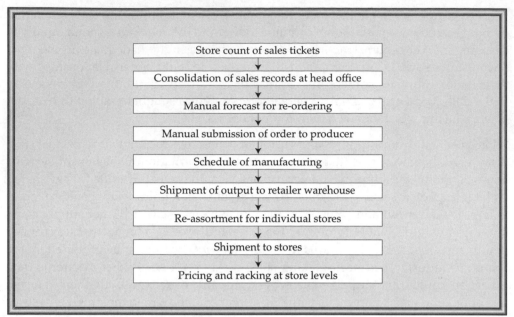

Figure 10.2 A transactional manual order placement/delivery system

of sale and these data are automatically forwarded to the head office computer. This computer system evaluates movement against a computer-based forecasting model, and where necessary an order is placed with the supplier using an automated EDI communication channel. The manufacturer is provided with data on individual store needs and product line pricing information. These data permit output to be pre-priced and the shipments sent directly to individual stores. Scaleable shipping permits real time tracking of goods throughout all phases of the delivery cycle. Because all aspects of the order replenishment/manufacturing/delivery cycle are electronically recorded, many retailers have now also moved to automatic payment for shipments from suppliers. This process is achieved by scanning the container label at the store to capture product delivery information, thereby dispensing with the need for a paper-based accounts payable accounting system.

For many manufacturing companies, a necessary antecedent to becoming involved in flexible, faster response supply chains was the total redesign of internal production processes. Here again, electronic technology has played a critically important role.

One important step forward has been the move to **flexible manufacturing systems**, or **FMS** (*a combination of engineering design and production flexibility made possible by equipment such as robots, flexible machining centres and automated assembly machines*) (Goldhar and Lei 1995). Material flows and selection of tooling changes use on-line, real time data management software to track in-process production and finished goods inventory levels. This combination of technologies is usually known as computer integrated manufacturing (CIM).

Traditional mass production factories are based around exploiting economies of scale to optimize productivity. Having adopted a CIM philosophy, firms are able to shift to

THE EVOLUTION OF E-MANAGEMENT SYSTEMS

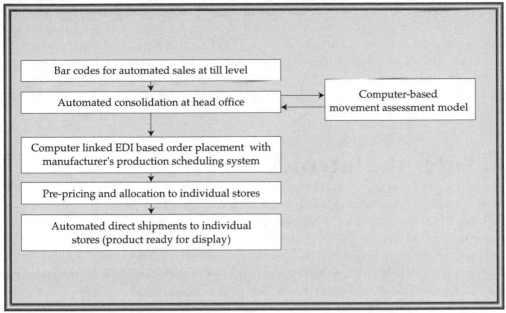

Figure 10.3 An automated supply chain system

much lower unit production runs. It then becomes cost-effective to offer both a more diverse range of products and respond rapidly to fluctuations in market demand. Having completed the computer-based integration of internal processes, organizations can begin to consider building automated response systems to link electronically the company to customers. An example of this philosophy is provided by Motorola's business pager business. Customized orders for pagers are entered on-line by field sales staff. Specifications for colour, size, transmission frequency and order quantities are directed to the factory in Boynton Beach Florida and the time between order receipt and delivery is only four days.

By the early 1990s, very large companies—such as manufacturers with highly diversified product ranges, or retailers stocking a vast selection of goods seeking both to improve flexibility and reduce inventories—found that their aims were often frustrated by an inability to keep track of **cross-functional communication** (*information flows between different departments*), ensure data was fully shared between departments, ensuring optimal use of all internal resources (Zuckerman 1999). In many cases this was because the organization was operating a number of incompatible hardware and software systems. To overcome this major problem, companies such as SAP, PeopleSoft (*www.peoplesoft.com*) and Oracle (*www.oracle.com*) developed fully integrated software known generically as **enterprise resource planning** or **ERP** systems (*software that links together all databases from marketing, logistics, manufacturing, procurement, accounting etc. to permit real time analysis of activities in progress across the organization*).

Initially these systems were perceived as providing the route to optimizing usage of resources within organizations. Over time, however, the systems have been extended outwards as a way of more closely linking together companies across entire supply chains. Colgate-Palmolive, for example, used a SAP-based ERP system to link together all elements of its global operation to halve order-to-shipment times and dramatically reduce finished goods inventory levels. They have now provided their suppliers with access to ERP information so that they can take over responsibility for managing raw material inventories (Moad 1999). Coca-Cola has extended its ERP system to the desktops of some 75 000 employees in their bottlers' operations with the expectation that this move will increase revenues and optimize delivery cycles (Oliver 1999).

● Enter the Internet

The two sectors that pioneered the use of EDI in the automation of supply chains were banking and large OEMs. Their perspective was that EDI permitted fast, secure delivery of information. Nevertheless, many organizations remained less than totally committed to the technology because of the high operating costs. EDI systems typically run proprietary software offered by operators of value-added networks (VANs). These VAN suppliers usually charge a very high up-front connection fee, and the users face heavy ongoing costs based upon the volume of data transmitted.

The Internet, using the TCP/IP protocol, offered open, non-proprietary data exchange. The initial reaction among firms with well developed EDI systems was that the Internet was unreliable and open to the risk that databases could be accessed by hackers. In these types of organization, the initial reaction to proposals to move to an Internet-based supply chain system ranged from (1) the belief that the technology was totally unsuitable for commercial operations to (2) an acceptance of the Internet as a possible communications system, though the core of the supply chain management would continue to be based around EDI because this was the only way effectively and reliably to handle the volume of transactions (Dyck 1997).

Other organizations, however, saw the Internet as a low cost platform, which meant that even the smallest of firms within a supply chain could now afford to become involved in computer-based data interchange. In response to concerns over security, software developers began to evolve virtual private networks (VPNs) that could operate over the Internet but only permit access to approved users. The usual form of VPN adopted by most organizations has been extranets, a system which runs across the Internet with limited user access. At the same time, software developers created intranets. These are computer systems for use within companies to permit rapid electronic communication between all employees. Because extranets and intranets operate on a common platform, moving to permit secure electronic communication with individuals outside the organization is technically a relatively simple task (Urbaczewski et al. 1998).

An example of an early adopter of the new technology is Countrywide Home Loans in the US. The company has an intranet application for managing back office functions such as mortgage origination and administration. This system is linked to an extranet that permits secure communication between both the company's branch network and financial brokers seeking funding for clients. These brokers can use the extranet to access information on issues such as account status, transaction status and the status of loan applications in progress, and the system has subsequently been expanded to permit estate agents to make applications for mortgage funding on behalf of their house buying clients.

With the advent of e-commerce and the move away from EDI to more open systems, a major project for many manufacturing firms has been to build e-commerce capability into their ERP systems. Cummins Engines, a Columbus, Indiana manufacturer of automotive parts (Moad 1999) has an Oracle ERP system, and it has built the Cummins OnanOnline (COoL) Web-based product configuration and quoting system. This allows both dealers and suppliers to assemble virtually a collection of parts and obtain a price quote and an inventory availability assessment.

Although the business press contains case materials on the success of ERP-enabled e-commerce systems, it is also necessary to recognize that major names such as Hershey Foods and Whirlpool, having spent millions establishing their systems, were less than happy with the outcome (Blyinsky 1999). In recognition of this, a number of new players have entered the ERP market offering lower cost, modular systems that are seen as offering a more flexible, simplified approach to data management than the very large systems marketed by firms such as SAP, Baan and J.D. Edwards. One of the new firms is Pivotpoint (*www.pivotpoint.co.uk*), which points out that unlike the founders of SAP, who were financial software experts, their company is staffed with people with extensive manufacturing experience. This expertise, it is claimed, allows the company to develop more flexible, lower cost ERP systems that the customer can adopt without having to reconfigure totally its operations to suit the new software. Another new company is America Disc, which is apparently finding many customers interested in switching allegiance from SAP and Bann systems. Possibly the key factor in this situation is the potential to make significant time and cost-savings. For example, America Disc took only 22 days to bring its system on-line at Nexion, a telecommunications switch producer, at a cost of $250 000. This compared with the quote from SAP to undertake the same contract at a price of $1.5 million.

Having observed how small firms are challenging the top ERP suppliers, other software developers are now moving into the customer relationship management (CRM) market offering systems that can operate without the need for the customer to have previously installed an ERP platform. An early example of the impact of CRM is provided by Pitney-Bowes, the $4.2 billion manufacturer of postage meters, which used this type of software to reduce delivery times by 45 per cent and achieve a 27 per cent reduction in order cancellations due to shipment errors.

● Assembling Successful Systems

Managers seeking information on the design and operation of e-commerce systems will soon find that the same case examples seem to be featured in every business magazine article and book. Repeated mention of the same company examples is no coincidence. It is a reflection of the fact that to date very few organizations have been successful in

Extranet Examples

One of the first major companies to exploit extranets was the General Electric Corporation (GE) in Fairfield, Connecticut. Its system, Trading Process Network (TPN), was adopted internally by GE Lighting to purchase parts and GE Capital Services (*www.gecsn.com*) to purchase computer equipment. Other divisions quickly recognized the benefits of using TPN to seek bids from component suppliers. The system now has tools to permit interactive on-line negotiations, and in one year handled $1 billion in transactions. The system also permits buyers to browse an electronic catalogue, TPN Mart, generate electronic purchase orders, and make payments electronically (Hasek 1997). Through the GE Information Services unit, the company has now offered TPN to other manufacturing companies wanting an on-line procurement system. The benefits marketed by GE are increased procurement productivity, extending procurement on a global scale, and decreasing costs for supplier sales forces.

Paccar (*www.paccar.com*) is an $8 billion heavy truck manufacturer. In 1997, the company decided that it needed to provide leadership in persuading its industry to exploit the benefits of on-line procurement. Its first move was to become the first truck company to join the Automotive Network Exchange (ANX), a pioneering VPN that links car makers and their suppliers into one global network. Paccar perceived that membership would permit the company's engineers at different sites to collaborate electronically with other engineers, both inside and outside the company, in the design of new vehicles (Vaas 1999). By using Microsoft Exchange the company has also created an intranet to link electronically the company's 23 000 employees based around the world. Successful implementation of the link to ANX required a complete overhaul of the company's internal computer infrastructure. Knowledge gained from this process was then exploited to build a high speed wide area network (WAN) to communicate with truck dealers around the world. Dealers without their own internal network can gain access to the Paccar architecture for a small monthly fee. Using the system, dealers can use Prospector, Paccar's proprietary truck configuration system, to place customized vehicle orders.

Boise Cascade Office Products Corporation (*www.bcop.com*) is a $2 billion operation based in Itasca, Illinois. The company acts as a hub in a supply chain comprising 1200 suppliers and 17 000 customers. For some years the company has been using EDI to manage transactions with its larger suppliers and larger customers. They recognized, however, that the cost of installing and operating EDI systems was perceived as prohibitively expensive by smaller companies within the supply chain (Aragon 1997). The company used e-commerce software developed in-house, linked to ECXpert, an integrator package supplied by Actra Business Systems of California. ECXpert permits the company to translate Internet order information into an EDI protocol understood by the company's mainframe. This approach is known as electronic data interchange internet (EDIINT) and permits transmission of data across the Internet with the same security that was previously only available through an EDI VAN system. The overwhelming advantage of EDIINT is that data transmission costs have been reduced by 20 per cent and users do not need to invest in specialist computer equipment in order to use it. Customers access the system via Boise's public homepage, and enter the order site using a user ID. They can peruse an on-line catalogue containing over 10 000 products. 'Easy order forms' assist in the ordering process, and payments can be made using standard credit cards. In the first year of operation, Boise saved over $1 million by reducing the time customer service representatives spent taking orders by telephone. On the supplier side, the company is exploiting the Internet to reduce paperwork, improve warehouse receiving procedures, and reduce inventory management activities.

creating effective, totally integrated, automated systems. One of the reasons for this is that even before considering a move into e-commerce companies must:

1   Be customer driven
    When using an automated information provision and purchasing system, frustrated customers can move to an alternative supplier 'at the click of a button'. Creating a customer-friendly interface between the market and the organization can only be achieved if the company has already developed a total commitment to delivering customer satisfaction. For it is only by being highly market oriented that an organization can acquire the in-depth understanding of customer needs that provides the template around which the e-commerce system can be constructed.

    The requirement to be customer driven is a key reason why American Airlines (***www.americanair.com***) gained an early market leadership position in the use of e-commerce to build an interactive website to enhance the company's frequent flyer programme, Aadvantage. In designing the system, the development team drew upon the organization's extensive understanding of customer behaviour to create a website capable of providing answers to questions concerning issues such as airline schedules of both American and the competition, flight arrival times, gate departure numbers and fare information.

2   Have a long established commitment to JIT and TQM
    In both off-line and on-line markets, the primary focus of marketing effort should be the retention of existing customers. The pragmatic reason for this philosophy is that the cost of acquiring a new customer is at least 10 times higher than generating additional sales from an existing customer. Loyal customers introduced to the idea of using e-commerce to communicate with suppliers expect that the on-line process will happen more rapidly than its off-line equivalent. This can only happen if the supplier is already committed to using just-in-time management (JIT) to minimize order-to-delivery times. E-commerce systems usually involve the company in the automation of every aspect of the purchase process, from information provision through to successful, on-time delivery of the ordered product. This type of e-commerce system will contain an almost infinite number of interlinked, interdependent activities, none of which can be permitted to fail if the process is to be successful. Achieving the

objective of operating a complex, zero error, operating system is only feasible in those organizations that for many years have been totally committed to a total quality management (TQM) philosophy in every area.

<u>3</u>   Have expertise in IT-based supply chain management
E-commerce systems can only deliver their promise of an interactive, rapid response to customer demands if every element of the supply chain has been integrated and there is a seamless flow of data within the organization and between all members of the market system. Achieving this objective can only occur where participants have extensive prior experience of developing effective IT-based data interchange and decision support systems. A common characteristic of companies quoted as exemplars of integration in e-commerce systems is that they have always led their respective market sectors in the incorporation of the latest advances in computing and telecommunications technology into all aspects of operations (for example Cisco in electronic switching and routers, Dell in computing, General Motors in the car industry, Motorola in telecommunications products).

In 1998 Seybold and Marshak undertook the demanding task of drawing upon their company's extensive consulting experience as the basis for formulating a set of guiding principles that must be considered when seeking to establish an effective on-line business operation. Fig. 10.4 is a summary of the elements that these two authors posit, in their book *Customers.com* as critical in the successful design and operation of an e-commerce system. The start point in system design is the requirement that the entire process be driven by the articulated needs of the customer. These can include pre-purchase information, the range of products they wish to purchase, provision of design support for customers seeking customized products, the ability for orders to be placed

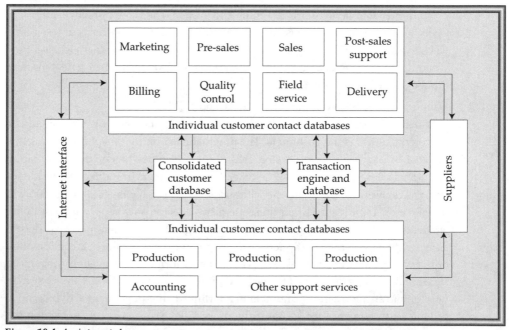

Figure 10.4 *An integrated e-commerce management system*

THE EVOLUTION OF E-MANAGEMENT SYSTEMS

on-line, electronic payment facilities and the ability for enquiries into order status at any time from point of purchase to the final delivery.

What must be recognized is that in most markets customer needs are rarely homogeneous. Seybold and Marshak's advice is that the early focus in the development of an e-commerce system be those customers that represent the most important source of profitable revenue. Only after the on-line requirements of this customer group have been fulfilled should the organization examine how to apply the technology to other, less profitable market sectors.

Moving the customer through all phases of the process, from receiving information to receipt of ordered goods, requires the involvement of a number of different groups within the supplier organization. It is critical, therefore, that data from all aspects of the customer service provision process can be consolidated into a single customer database. Only if this goal is achieved can the organization remain confident that the e-commerce system is successfully fulfilling customer service quality requirements. As proposed in Fig. 10.4, key components of the e-commerce system are the real time integration of (1) customer databases from sources such as the sales department, accounting services and field service staff, and (2) internal functional activities of various departments, such as production, procurement and warehousing. This same demand for integration of databases is also applicable in the operation of the transaction engine, the organization's central core in the management of on-line services to customers during order placement and product delivery.

To Control or Not to Control

As companies evolve their on-line systems, it is apparent that different models are beginning to emerge (Pender and Madden 2000). Some executives think that in the case of procurement or sales website companies should be hub sites retaining control over all aspects of the electronic trading process. Teradyne Inc., a Boston-based maker of telecommunications testing equipment prefers to have absolute control over customer buying activities. DuPont Corporation sees sales sites as ideally offering variety and vendor neutrality, and it has a preference for participation in sites operated by independent entities such as intermediaries. Eastman Chemicals have decided that both models offer opportunities. In one case they run an on-line procurement system constructed for them by Commerce One. The company also, however, uses sites operated by intermediaries as another element in the company's e-commerce strategy. Dow Chemicals takes the view that in determining the best way to link into e-commerce systems the focus should be on optimizing customer relations. In its view the best model is one in which suppliers and their customers are most able rapidly to gain access to data critical to ordering and inventory control processes.

The Delivery Systems Battle

Long before the Internet opened up major new opportunities in the on-time package delivery business, the two top players, United Parcel Service (UPS) and Federal Express (FedEx), were battling for market share (O'Reilly 2000). The former currently has a 55 per cent share of the US market, the latter 25 per cent.

FedEx led the way in the use of a hub sorting system next to an airport to build a strong reputation for reliable overnight delivery. It was followed by UPS, which had the added advantage of already having 150 000 trucks and drivers involved in ground-based shipment to virtually any address in the US. In an apparent response to this situation, FedEx in 1999 purchased Caliber Systems, a Pittsburgh-based trucking company. This was followed by the announcement that the company intends to create a new home delivery system based around hiring independent contractors to serve specified geographical areas.

Both companies are clearly fighting to dominate the new delivery opportunities available following the emergence of the Internet as a purchasing system in both consumer and business-to-business markets. In 1999, UPS delivered approximately 55 per cent of all of home delivery items ordered on the Internet during the Christmas period. The US Postal Service handled 30 per cent of this market, FedEx only 10 per cent. The value of the Internet delivery market was estimated at $20 billion for 1999, but in the US alone is expected to grow to $180 billion by 2004.

Both FedEx and UPS recognize that their warehouse operations and tracking systems have to exploit the latest available JIT supply chain management technology. These companies are also very willing to develop customized software to suit the specific needs of business-to-business customers shipping both components and finished products into global markets. Such projects are not cheap. It is estimated that FedEx will spend $100 million on its development of a customized system for Cisco Systems.

● New Distribution Models

Marcos Barbalho, of the consultancy firm PriceWaterhouseCoopers, believes that over the next few years e-commerce will have a major impact on supply chain effectiveness (Schwartz 2000). He is clearly critical of many earlier attempts to apply process re-engineering to supply chain processes. He notes that 'Twenty years ago, when companies talked about re-engineering, it meant eliminating non-value-added activities. It quickly became a head-chopping exercise. We didn't re-engineer a lot of things.'

Barbalho perceives the e-commerce revolution as a real opportunity to implement truly effective re-engineering projects in the area of distribution system management. He identifies the following four areas where logistics can be enhanced:

1   Dematerialization, a reduction of stock holding and warehousing that occurs because more effective systems reduce the need for investment in warehouses and manufacturing plants.

2   Disintermediation, a reduction in the number of participants in the supply chain. The Internet permits compression of supply chains by eliminating some of the steps in the movement of goods between producer and end-user.

3   Deverticalization, the process by which an enterprise undertakes more than one role in the supply chain. The Internet permits the growth of extended enterprises based around virtual networks that can span an entire industrial sector.

4   Service Development. The Internet permits supply chain members to evolve new service offerings and the ability to extend their services further 'downstream' along the supply chain.

This philosophy is exemplified in a new e-commerce hub called NonstopRx.com, created for the US pharmaceutical industry by two solution providers, Nonstop Solutions and Supply Chain Solutions. The industry is highly fragmented, with suppliers attempting to service numerous end-user sites across the country. The new website seeks to enhance supply chain operations by addressing the inefficiencies of:

1   Large volumes of product and price change information being faxed to wholesalers from numerous suppliers.

2   Highly complex pricing and distribution contracts that currently involve the time of numerous administrative staff and finance personnel.

3   Poor management of product flows, resulting in excess inventories and failures to make on-time deliveries.

4   Rebates and charge-backs, which create another massive administrative burden for wholesalers.

The objective of the new hub service is to develop and operate e-commerce supply chain models that use client data to develop delivery systems that can optimize deliveries by determining how best to manage transportation, product handling, administrative activities and inventory carrying costs. The two solution providers are optimistic that these goals can be achieved. Evidence to support their perspective is already provided by the fact that Nonstop Solutions has already managed to reduce the inventory of the retail chain Longs Drugstores by 44 per cent and freed up $60 million in capital without reducing delivery service levels.

● E-Sourcing

For any company with limited experience in either integrated IT solutions or the operation of Internet systems, the task of building and implementing an e-commerce supply chain system can be extremely daunting. Furthermore, the capital costs of establishing such a system are often prohibitive. Yet if these obstacles cannot be overcome, and the company feels unable to move into e-commerce, it faces the risk of being outperformed by competitors. In recognition of this situation, companies have now become what is known as **application service providers** or **ASPs** (*those that bring together all of the hardware and software needed to operate an e-commerce supply chain, host the software on a central server, and permit customers access to the systems via browser software and an Internet link*) (anon. 2000). These companies charge clients a fee per transaction for using the system.

The new approach, known as **e-sourcing** (*using the Internet to manage all procurement activities*), means that companies can enter the world of e-commerce supply chains in a fraction of the time, and at the fraction of the cost, involved in building their own in-house system. The largest replicator of CDs and DVDs in the US, Technicolor, provides an example of the concept. Although this company is involved in leading-edge electronic technology, they have always relied on an essentially paper-based administration system. Recognizing that this operational philosophy had the potential to destroy the company, management turned to Vsource Inc. (*www.vsource.com*), an ASP based in Ventura, California. Using their Virtual Source Network system, in less than a month Ventura created an on-line system linking Technicolor with 28 key customers and 400 suppliers. The new Internet system has permitted the immediate automation of all aspects of processes associated with sending, receiving, approving and invoicing purchases and product sales.

● Summary

It has long been recognized that by using marketing information systems (MIS) to integrate external and internal information companies are able to ensure customer satisfaction. Creation of effective MIS operations require, however, that companies acquire and utilize data in a real time mode, and only very recently have advances in IT permitted that. In the 1980s, Pacific rim companies moved to exploit the opportunities offered by JIT to deliver greater customer satisfaction. To respond to this new threat, Western companies have been forced to re-think all their internal operational processes. They have in some cases been assisted in this by a technique known as process re-engineering. Another route by which both to enhance speed of response and reduce operating costs is to focus on the more effective management of supply chains. As with MIS achieving this aim has been frustrated by a lack of access to real time data and effective process management software. The advent of technologies such as EDI and ERP have contributed to resolving these problems. Further improvement in supply chain management has come by moving data management onto the Internet. To ensure data confidentiality, large firms are using extranets. On the basis of lessons learned by early users of extranets, guidance is provided on how to develop effective Internet-based supply chain systems.

STUDY QUESTIONS

1 Describe the components required to create and operate an effective MIS.

2 How can a JIT operating philosophy be utilized to enhance a company's marketing strategy?

3 How can e-commerce be utilized to enhance a JIT marketing strategy?

Case: *Removing Bottlenecks*

Design Solutions Ltd is a company founded ten years ago by Steve Wilson. For the first five years, the company specialized in the design and production of point of sale (POS) materials such as in-store display cards and 'dump bins' for small manufacturing firms. The problem faced by Design Solutions in operating as a regional supplier at the bottom end of the POS market was the high number of other small competitors in the same market sector, and the resulting price competition. After a few years, Steve recognized that to build a highly profitable business he would have to break with sector convention and cease to be a small regional supplier to small and medium-sized companies.

He decided that he would attempt to find a way of becoming a provider of POS materials to large national and multinational firms. These companies are interested in high quality, innovative solutions for their merchandising problems, and as a result are less likely to base purchase decisions purely on price. Steve recruited Les Adams to head up the company's product design group. Les had previously worked for a major POS design studio, and had an international reputation for creating extremely innovative display materials.

Steve also decided to invest in a machine for the forming, cutting, bending and folding of complex designs. The company had previously sub-contracted these activities, and was continually facing delays caused by the sub-contractor's poor quality control.

Initially, the move proved extremely successful. Les's reputation permitted access to f.m.c.g. companies in the confectionery, soft drinks, detergent, frozen food and pet food markets. However, as supermarket chains began to place more emphasis on their own label products, national and multinational branded goods companies found it increasingly difficult to get space in-store for their merchandising materials. Additionally, the very large POS manufacturers had been investing in new technology that permitted them to offer highly attractive prices. Steve realized that he would probably never achieve the scale advantages enjoyed by these larger printers, so he decided the only viable positioning was one based around rapid response, flexibility, and a willingness to solve complex design problems.

The sector of the market that Design Solutions decided to target was branded consumer computer and telecommunications products, because companies in this sector (1) are continually launching new products and (2) place major emphasis on in-store displays in the marketing of their latest offerings. Initially, the move proved highly successful, but in recent months the company has lost three major contracts. In all three cases the reason was that the company had failed to deliver the POS materials prior to the launch date for new products, and these customers were not willing to risk the same outcome again. In talking to these and other customers in the computer and telecommunications market, it became obvious to Steve that the speed with which new products are being brought to market means that lead times for the design and production of POS materials are now dramatically reduced.

Steve and Les realized that to survive, the company would have to find ways of reducing the company's design and production cycle. The start point in their review process was to map out the current processes. The outcome of this mapping exercise is shown in Fig. 10.5.

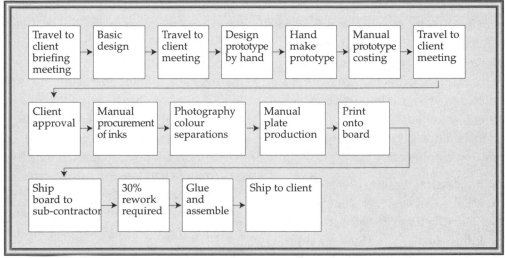

Figure 10.5 *The original process flow model at Design Solutions*

QUESTIONS

1 You have been appointed as a consultant to the company. Based upon the information shown in Fig. 10.5, identify where you believe bottlenecks are creating potential time delays within the described system.

2 By considering the exploitation of electronic technologies such as e-mail, videoconferencing, electronic data transfer, the Internet, computer aided design (CAD), computer aided manufacturing (CAM), robotics, computer-based job costing, and computerized production scheduling and procurement, develop recommendations for a new system to meet customer demands for a faster and more flexible response by Design Solutions.

Case: *Service Response Time*

Delco Systems is a distributor of office equipment and materials. The company acts as a supplier to large and medium-sized companies of branded computer products such as PCs, software, printers, servers, faxes and photocopiers. It services its market through ten national outlets based in major metropolitan areas. Each outlet consists of a sales office, showroom, administration department, warehouse, training centre, product installation group and a product servicing and repair team.

Graham Boydon has recently been recruited as the new Sales Director. In visiting the various outlets, he is impressed by the skills and capabilities of the staff. However, during introductory meetings with some major customers he is disturbed to find that Delco

has a reputation for taking a long time to undertake repairs. To obtain some more insights into this situation, he met with the Head of Customer Services, Frank Green. Frank's reaction was that he knew all about the problem, and for many months had been trying to get somebody in senior management to take some action. To explain what he felt was the cause of the problem, Frank showed Graham a flow-chart mapping the current process used by service engineers when undertaking a repair involving a replacement part (see Fig. 10.6). Frank's succinct summary of the situation was 'simplify the service engineers' lives, and customer dissatisfaction will disappear overnight'.

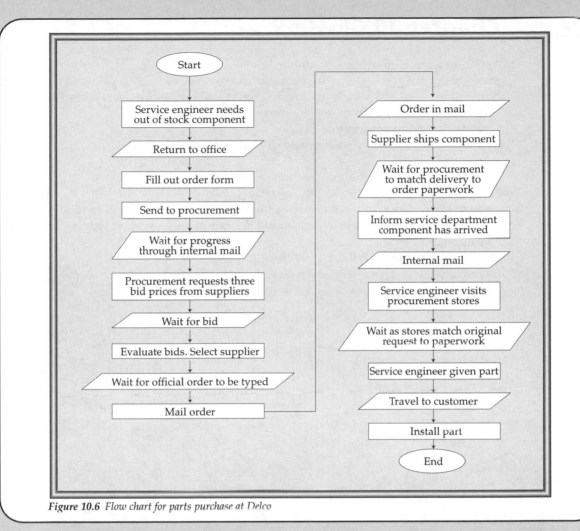

Figure 10.6 *Flow chart for parts purchase at Delco*

QUESTIONS

1 Use the information provided to prepare a report identifying why the repair process is taking so long.

2 Prepare a report that shows how, by using various aspects of e-commerce technology, delegation of authority, and procedure simplification, Delco can significantly reduce the repair cycle and thereby improve customer satisfaction.

Chapter 10 Glossary

Application service providers, or **ASPs** (p. 234)

Those that bring together all of the hardware and software needed to operate an e-commerce supply chain, host the software on a central server, and permit customers access to the systems via browser software and an Internet link.

Cross-functional communication (p. 225)

Information flows between different departments.

E-sourcing (p. 234)

Using the Internet to manage all procurement activities.

Enterprise resource planning, or **ERP**, **systems** (p. 225)

Software that links together all databases from marketing, logistics, manufacturing, procurement, accounting etc. to permit real time analysis of activities in progress across the organization.

Flexible manufacturing systems, or **FMS** (p. 224)

A combination of engineering design and production flexibility made possible by equipment such as robots, flexible machining centres and automated assembly machines.

Chapter 11

E-BUSINESS AND INSTITUTIONAL MARKETING

Learning Objectives

This chapter explains

◆ *The evolution of business-to-business marketing theory.*

◆ *The characteristics of business-to-business markets.*

◆ *Buyer–seller interactions in business-to-business markets.*

◆ *Management of supply chains.*

◆ *The impact of the Internet on business-to-business markets.*

◆ *The changing nature of institutional markets.*

◆ *The impact of the Internet on healthcare provision.*

◆ *Opportunities to exploit the Internet to deliver education.*

The early authors of business-to-business marketing texts often adopted an approach clearly rooted in a classical consumer goods, transactional marketing framework. Researchers seeking to validate the theories presented in such texts soon found, however, that actual marketing practices in the industrial sector were often very different from those espoused by many business school academics. Some researchers concentrated on determining whether differences in market structure influenced the marketing process, others concentrated on understanding buyer behaviour. By the early 1980s, academics were able to clarify differences that exist between consumer and business markets. Consequently, they were able to provide guidance on how such variations might influence the marketing process. Other academics, such as Sheth (1973) and Webster and Wind (1972) also began to construct and validate realistic buyer behaviour models reflecting the real nature of events that occur in industrial markets.

Meanwhile in Europe, the Nordic business schools were applying a grounded theory approach to researching industrial markets. Their studies raised questions about the validity of the theory that effective marketing involves application of classic confrontational, transactional strategic planning models of the type espoused by academics such as Michael Porter. Wider recognition of the Nordic school's thinking on alternative collaborative buyer–seller relationships in industrial markets was achieved through the formation of the pan-European IMP research group. Concurrently, some academics in the US, such as Jackson (1985), also began to question the correctness of rigidly adhering to purist transactional management approaches when studying industrial markets. The outcome of such research led to the conclusion that in many cases successful companies are more likely to achieve market leadership through the exploitation of relationship marketing principles.

By the end of the 1980s, most academics had accepted that certain fundamental aspects of the industrial marketing process are unique to the sector. Additional stimuli were provided through (1) the realization that many industrial marketers could be assisted by drawing upon theories and concepts being generated by research on service sector companies and (2), the way in which the advent of IT was producing massive changes in processes associated with the marketing of industrial goods.

Characteristics of Business-to-Business Markets

Business-to-business marketing has been described as 'the marketing of goods and services to commercial enterprises, governments and other non-profit institutions for use in the goods and services that they, in turn, produce for resale to other industrial customers' (Corey 1991). Implicit in this definition is the idea that the type of customer and nature of goods purchased are very different than that in consumer markets, where goods are bought for the purpose of final consumption. This will mean that business-to-business markets are likely to exhibit the following unique characteristics (Powers 1991; Rangan et al. 1995):

1   The nature of demand
    Supplier's products or services are incorporated into outputs for which the customer will seek to generate sales revenue. A resultant characteristic of business-to-business markets is that demand will be of a 'derived' nature. The implication of derived demand is that as customers purchase in response to what they perceive are the economic cycle trends in the final 'downstream' consumption market, industrial marketers often have to adopt a much longer range planning orientation than their counterparts in consumer goods markets.

2   The complexity of buying process
    In industrial markets, the sale of a product may involve the supplier in negotiations with the customer's purchasing, engineering, manufacturing, financial and legal departments before the purchase decision stage. Purchase negotiations between buyer and seller will probably involve complex discussions about product specifications, development lead times and the customization of design to suit specific applications.

3   Buyer power and location
    Business-to-business markets tend to have many fewer customers that individually purchase a large proportion of their suppliers' total output. Additionally, the specialist industrial sector infrastructure required by many manufacturing companies often causes them to be located in geographically concentrated areas (for example the large number of multinational electronics firms located in the area known as Silicon Glen in Scotland). The concentration of power and geographic clustering of customers means that direct marketing and one-to-one selling are economically viable propositions.

4   Buyer–seller relationships
    The small number of customers in business-to-business markets, and their potential to use their buying power to extract highly favourable terms from their suppliers does result in very closer buyer–seller relationships. Business-to-business marketers frequently find that the customer expects product offerings to be customized and that the marketing team must have the technical skills to handle customer concerns during both the pre and post-purchase phases. It is quite usual for the customer to expect (1) to be permitted to spend extensive periods in their suppliers' factories and (2) their supplier's engineering teams to spend a significant amount of time based at the customer's sites.

● Buyer–Seller Interaction

The research by the IMP group identified that the traditional model of the active seller and the passive buyer is just not born out by observations of actual processes in many industrial markets. The researchers concluded that the buyer–seller relationship is essentially one of active interaction. Ford (1990) posits that the repeated occurrence of 'buying episodes' over time leads to the development of longer-term, mutually dependent relationship between the employees within the participant organizations. This perspective on the importance of employee interaction is supported by the earlier work of Hakansson and Ostberg (1975). They conclude that the social exchanges that occur between individuals from the buyer and seller organizations during repeated execution of the order placement/order delivery cycle lead to the development of clear expectations about each other's capabilities and responsibilities.

Within the core of a buyer–seller interaction model, certain variables such as technology, strategy and individual employee behaviour can all contribute towards influencing the relationship. If both parties have a clear understanding of the technology upon which the seller's goods are based, this will simplify development of the market relationship. Where there is a major technology knowledge gap, the supplier will have to expend effort exhibiting organizational attributes capable of demonstrating their desire to establish a relationship with the customer founded upon mutual trust and commitment.

Ford (1990) groups the marketing management implications of the supplier–customer interaction model under the two headings of 'limitations' and 'handling problems'. Within the area of limitations he suggests the supplier 'cannot be all things to all people'. Thus a company specializing in the production of premium priced/premium quality components would face limitations if it also sought to meet the needs of customers seeking low price/low quality goods. Handling problems are those activities associated with ensuring information and output fulfil the specific requirements of the customer. Hakansson et al. (1976) use the interaction model as the basis for defining how perceptions of both the buyer and the seller will influence the marketing process. They think that possibly the most important variable is the degree of uncertainty that exists within the areas of customer need, market environment, and management of the actual transaction. The usual response of the buyer to need uncertainty is to specify carefully contractual requirements in relation to issues such as product performance and delivery dates. Market uncertainty may be seen to exist by the buyer in those cases in which there is a diversity of choice because supplier offerings are highly heterogeneous in product, quality and price. The buyer in this situation may need to consider carefully the implications of forming a long-term relationship with one supplier if it appears a better offering may become available from another source in the very near future. Transaction uncertainty centres on whether the product is delivered on time and meets the performance specifications agreed during the negotiations phase. Where high levels of uncertainty exist, the buyer may require lengthy contracts be signed that contain severe penalty clauses for any form of transaction error by the supplier.

As far as the supplier is concerned, it is also essential that the marketing management system contains elements designed to minimize the effects of uncertainty. Firstly, there is a need to ensure that the organization has the appropriate equipment, employee skills and production capacity to meet fully the buyer's specification. Where, for example, the contract involves a front-end period of extensive R&D to create a commercially viable product, the supplier must ensure that it can complete this first phase of the contract on time. Furthermore, in order to meet agreed delivery dates for the product, the final design must not subsequently create problems when the project enters the manufacturing phase. Another dimension of uncertainty management for the supplier is to handle effectively social interactions with the customer in order that mutual trust and commitment can develop. Typically, a critical element influencing this variable is the interchange of information. If this is handled efficiently, customer uncertainty will be reduced. Conversely, poor information management can rapidly cause mistrust to develop, and this can easily result in the customer beginning to consider alternative sources of supply.

Given the critical influence of uncertainty in industrial market scenarios, Ford (1980) proposes that effective management of the buyer–seller interaction demands that the supplier marketer exhibit a high level of relationship management competence. He

Cisco Systems (*www.cisco.com*)

An early player in the move to on-line execution of both the transaction and knowledge management aspects of business-to-business marketing processes was Cisco Systems. By 1997, its on-line operations had already evolved to the point where over 25 per cent of the total annual sales of $4.1 billion were via the company's website. The company is the leading supplier of routers and network switches, and in 1996 established an on-line facility permitting customers to configure products without the intervention of a Cisco sales engineer. The company's website contains an Internetworking Product Centre containing information on over 12 000 products. Cisco customers and resellers can use this facility to place orders 24-hours-a-day from anywhere in the world. A sophisticated sales-configuration software package actually evaluates the customer order for specification accuracy. In the fax-based order entry system, between 10 and 15 per cent of received orders are found to contain specification errors. This automation of on-line specification evaluation has helped Cisco to reduce lead times from order receipt to delivery by at least two or three days. (Bartholomew 1997).

Cisco offers customers access to its Calico software, which enables it to examine a diverse range of product options and select that configuration most likely to fulfil the desired product performance specification. This system also immediately confirms the actual price that would be charged for the specified configurations. Another aspect of the on-line system is the Status Agent software. This allows each customer to track an order at every stage, from original submission to identification of geographic location, during the delivery shipment cycle.

argues that to overcome any barriers that may exist between participant organizations, the supplier marketer must first carefully analyse market conditions to determine the exact nature of the relationship that each customer requires within a market sector. Having established which variables are critical, the marketer must decide how best to structure the organization's marketing operation to achieve delivery of buyer satisfaction. Furthermore, having created an initially effective buyer–seller relationship, the marketer will need to assess what ongoing activities further enhance customer loyalty.

Solberg (1995) proposes that development of effective industrial marketing strategies involves analysis of both opportunities to reduce uncertainty and the potential to form long-term functional relationships. Ways to reduce uncertainty include:

1 Marketing plans based on careful analysis of markets and customers.

2 The selection of appropriate distribution channels to service customer need.

3 A commitment to extensive social interaction with customer employee.

4 The careful management of communication flows.

5 The fulfilment of contractual obligations.

6 The building of customer loyalty, more important than generating new orders.

7 Organizational values compatible with customer values.

There is good potential for long-term relationships where:

1 Customers seek complex products.

2 Customers seek customized products.

3 Customers wish to negotiate high volume/long-term contracts.

4 Customers purchase on a frequent and regular basis.

5 Customers face high costs when changing suppliers.

6 Customers require extensive ongoing advisory support.

7 Customers seek ongoing post-purchase maintenance/service support.

8 Customers seek solutions demanding high levels of supplier R&D.

● E-Supply Chains

As Western companies in business-to-business markets became deeply immersed in total quality management (TQM) and just-in-time (JIT) management, they soon realized that these concepts could not succeed if suppliers and customers sustained traditional, adversarial relationships. Achieving quality goals and evolving a rapid, more flexible approach to the management of manufacturing processes has demanded the forging of new, closer links between all members of the market system. An eloquent proponent of this new orientation is Schonberger (1990) who tables the idea of forming 'customer chains'. With increased flexibility and speed of response a goal of most customers in business markets, the focus of their suppliers has been on finding new ways of speeding up all aspects of the transaction process whilst keeping control over operating costs.

In capital goods markets, most suppliers have tended to retain the classic business-to-business marketing process of a one-to-one personal interaction between supplier and customer to ensure effective management of transactions. However, in those market sectors in which the customers are interested in the ongoing procurement of standard products and services, suppliers have been able to adopt new approaches to the effective management of the customer purchase process. One of the earliest moves was to replace paper-based systems with electronic data interchange (EDI) links across all elements of the supply chain. Concurrently, suppliers began to examine the use of multiple channels, such that variations in customer purchase behaviour could be suitably matched with the most appropriate supply system.

One of the key drivers in this situation was the continuing rise in the cost of using personal selling to manage customer accounts. By assigning the selling role to intermediaries, suppliers were able to exploit the selling economies available to resellers representing the product lines of a number of manufacturers (Cespedes and Corey 1990). Customers that have adopted a JIT orientation often favour the use of resellers over buying direct from suppliers because resellers (1) are located near the customer's operations and (2) represent a number of suppliers, which reduces the risk of customers finding goods out-of-stock, or being locked into the price demands of a single supplier. The use of a reseller also offers the customer the opportunity to consolidate ordering, shipping, invoicing and stock replenishment through one, single point.

Resellers have not been unaware that a possible threat to their existence has been suppliers offering customers access to automated, electronic inventory-to-inventory links. In response to this threat, resellers themselves have evolved and developed computer-based systems. Two leaders in this process were McKesson Corporation and Bergen Brunswig, wholesalers operating in the US pharmaceutical market. Both companies supply drugs to retail pharmacies and hospitals. To retain customer loyalty, they have installed computers on their customers' premises. These permit customers to order on-line, and also gain access to other value-added services such as shelf labels and stickers of pre-priced products, automation of customer account receivables, and assistance in the management of the administrative processes demanded by medical insurance companies. The two companies have also established computer links with over 30 major suppliers, allowing for the provision of inventory management services, market data and order management processes to minimize the time between order placement and delivery (Cespedes and Corey 1990).

To further enhance customer service quality, business-to-business marketers have also led the move to adopt computer-based sales automation technology. This ensures that the sales force has detailed information, which can be used to guide the development of effective relationships with specific customers. Company databases permit rapid analysis of customer need and the formulation of recommendations on matters such as which products to emphasize, how to create new customer contact strategies, and the assessment of the actual performance of existing customers. By providing sales personnel with laptops, business-to-business suppliers are able to distribute data direct to the desk of the customer during one-to-one sales meetings (Hochhauser 1997).

Paralleling the move to computer technology to develop sales automation systems, business-to-business marketers have also recognized that the detailed databases created can be exploited through the operation of call centres to service customer needs. Although call centres are traditionally associated with consumer markets such as financial services and catalogue selling, over 75 per cent of total call centre revenues are attributable to business-to-business operations (Prabhaker et al. 1997). The big difference between the two sectors, however, is that the majority of business-to-business operations are outsourced to specialist service providers. The probable reason for this trend is that outsourcing provides access to the latest computer-based technology. This allows the call centre user to exploit features such as automatic number identification, dialled number identification, access to detailed customer databases offering immediate information on previous customer order patterns and instant access to data on orders being processed.

● The Internet

The wide breadth of experience that business-to-business marketers have acquired through activities such as using EDI, creating sales automation systems and serving customer needs through call centres, means that these individuals were some of the first in the marketing profession to recognize the major new opportunities offered by the Internet. The potential of the technology both to reduce operating costs and enhance the effectiveness of supply chain management processes is the reason for the Internet increasing global acceptance. It is expected that on-line sales will exceed half a trillion dollars by the end of 2002 (Smith 1999). Companies involved in optimizing supply chain performance have a natural affinity for exploiting the benefits offered by the Internet. It is for this reason, therefore, that business-to-business operations, not consumer goods companies, are expected to continue to dominate the world of on-line trading.

The feature of the Internet that seems of critical interest to business-to-business marketers is its interactivity. This means that in addition to the execution of automated order entry tasks in the past implemented through EDI, the business-to-business marketer is able to offer a wider breadth of on-line support services, such as assisting in the design of specialist components, permitting automated customization of product specifications, co-ordinating production schedules to avoid goods being out-of-stock, and offering on-line training in the application and exploitation of new technologies. Companies that were early entrants into business-to-business cyberspace marketing are now committed to the concept of eventually using the technology to manage all aspects of the customer transaction process, from initial enquiry to post-purchase product support.

In a study assessing the use of extranet-based systems, Anandarajan et al. (1998) identify a number of clear benefits associated with using the Internet in the management of supply chains. For inbound logistics, on-line data integration reduces costs through a consolidation of the total number of suppliers used and a reduction in the time taken to administer delivery processes. Inside the customer organization, cost-savings occur through reductions in the time taken by employees to administer the scheduling and operation of production processes. Outbound logistic efficiencies are improved, resulting in cost-savings for both absolute expenditure on freight services and the management of the delivery documentation process. With suppliers and customers in direct contact via an electronic medium, there is a significant saving of discussion time during the order-in-progress and transaction error processes. Additionally, with suppliers communicating promotional information via the Internet, customers can access these data at a workstation in their office. This ensures that customers can make the most of benefits offered by supplier marketing campaigns.

Another facet of the Internet is the ability of the technology to assist in the acquisition and dissemination of knowledge. In many business-to-business markets, customers have the option of purchasing the same product from a variety of sources. Customers seeking to determine whether supplies might be acquired at a lower price can use the Internet to assess rapidly the cheapest source of raw materials and components. Under these circumstances, possibly one of the few pathways to competitive advantage capable of retaining customer loyalty is a company's ability to acquire and apply new knowledge through the process of adopting a generative approach to organizational learning (Slater and Narver 1995). The benefits to be gained from exploiting new knowledge can include a diverse range of opportunities. These include the development of new products, the evolution of processes further to reduce order-to-

Lucent Technologies (*www.lucent.com*)

search

A major competitor of Cisco is Lucent Technologies, based in Murray Hills, New Jersey. This company is also committed to using the Internet as the core of its business-to-business marketing operations. To achieve this, the company is currently investing six per cent of total revenue to build ever more scaleable and flexible Web-based operating systems. Although the company recognizes the benefits of directing customers towards on-line order placement facilities, Lucent's marketing strategy seeks new ways of exploiting the Internet to enhance customer intimacy (Chen 1999). This has involved the construction of software systems that can be used by customers through every phase of the purchase process. The primary way this is achieved is through an integrated customer extranet system.

In 1999, Lucent electronically invoiced over $8 billion in sales via both extranets and EDI transactions. Nevertheless, a significant proportion of customers still prefer old technology, such as fax. It is a company philosophy not to apply any pressure to persuade this type of customer to change. Lucent also offers on-line facilities through which customers can view catalogues, configure products, order products, monitor the status of orders, and track shipments.

delivery times, and advice to customers on how to improve further the efficiency of their internal operations.

A major obstacle confronting companies wishing to base competitive advantage on superior knowledge is how ensure all sources of knowledge contained within the organization are made available to and exploited by both other employees and customers seeking to resolve operating problems. Although not evolved specifically to handle this issue, as companies have gained experience in the construction and exploitation of intranets and extranets it has become apparent that these systems provide an excellent platform for formalizing knowledge management practices across the entire organization. The outcome of this is that suppliers with electronic knowledge management platforms are finding that key customers perceive the existence of such systems as a key reason for remaining loyal to specific suppliers. This is because customers place an extremely high value on their ability to be able to access supplier knowledge platforms when confronted with the need to resolve complex operating problems (Chaston 2000).

The Cisco and Lucent examples (see boxes) both provide evidence that the Internet is being perceived as a way of creating and sustaining competitive advantage in industrial sector in which all companies have a full understanding of the manufacturing technologies upon which their industry is based, and consequently there is little opportunity to use tangible product performance to differentiate products from competition. Under these circumstances, in order to remain profitable, the more far-sighted members of sectoral supply chains are perceiving the Internet as a way to increase the service component of their product offering.

This is possibly best illustrated by the PC market, in which the PC manufacturer is merely acting as an integrator of technology, from chip producers such as Intel, and

Aerospace Goes On-Line

Given the global nature of the aerospace industry, and its long experience in pre-Internet technology such as EDI, it is not surprising to find this sector moving to create on-line supply chain systems (Kelly 2000). In the US, aeronautical communications specialists SITA have formed a joint venture with an aerospace inventory management company, AAR. Called *www.aerospan.com*, the website will initially focus on enabling customers to buy and sell air transport industry products and services on-line. In the longer term the site will also offer the facility to buy and sell aircraft and aircraft engines on the Internet.

United Technologies, Honeywell and i2Technologies are launching *www.myaircraft.com*, which specializes in the aerospace after-sales market, providing supply chain planning and procurement solutions for airlines, original equipment manufacturers and component suppliers. Boeing has also entered the market, creating New Ventures, a company that will use the Internet to offer aircraft parts, services and technical support.

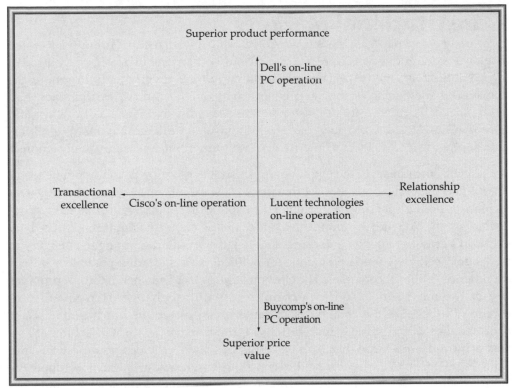

Figure 11.1 *Alternative Internet positionings in business-to-business markets*

operating systems, from software houses such as Microsoft. One of the first companies to recognize this was Dell. Its solution, having gained expertise in direct marketing, was to extend this operating philosophy by offering the Internet as an automated channel through which customers could ask Dell to assemble a customized PC to meet the specification requested by individual purchasers. As other PC manufacturers have moved onto the Internet at the bottom end of the market, an on-line price war has resulted. Success in this sector of the market requires the creation of Web-based trading operations responsive to the needs of those business-to-business customers for whom lowest possible price and minimal service is the basis for their purchase decision. To compete in this market, for example, Buycomp (*www.buycomp.com*) based in Santa Ana, US, has developed a software tool, that monitors competitor's on-line offerings and automatically revises Buycomp product specifications.

These case studies also support earlier observations in this text that the companies most successful in exploiting the technology are those that focus on using the technology to support and further enhance existing market positioning. Fig. 11.1 illustrates this point by using the case examples to describe the four types of positioning available to firms operating in business-to-business markets.

● Institutional Markets

In the early years following the Second World War, Western nation tax flows generated by global economic growth were sufficient to support an ever increasing expansion of the welfare state. Increasing tax revenues permitted governments to ignore the managerial inefficiencies that existed in many of the industries that they had nationalized. Furthermore, because nationalized industries such as railways and telecommunications were key underpinnings of a 'full employment' political philosophy, the inefficiencies of internal operating environments were usually ignored.

In the 1970s, the impact of the OPEC energy crisis, the growing power of public sector unions and the obligations on governments to sustain full employment through ever increasing deficit spending all combined to spark off a massive inflationary spiral within many Western economies. By the 1980s, some electorates, battered by inflation's erosion of personal incomes and lengthy strikes disrupting the delivery of public services, were prepared to vote for political parties offering possible solutions for rebuilding ailing economies. The election of Margaret Thatcher in the UK provides one of the most widely known examples of political change. Her government espoused a belief in the creation of an 'enterprise culture' in which public sector organizations would be made more effective through exposure to 'market forces'. This was achieved both through returning industries such as telecommunications and utilities to the private sector and attempting to engender a more competitive environment in those areas of the economy such as education and healthcare that apparently could not be privatized.

By the mid-1980s, many Western politicians had evolved the view that if public sector organizations were to become market-oriented, operational effectiveness would be significantly enhanced. Unfortunately, most senior managers were unwilling to incur the wrath of their political masters by openly expressing the view that classic marketing theory probably had little relevance in the sectors in which they are operating. Classic theories of marketing proved to have little relevance because inside the welfare state management is rarely in a position totally to fulfil the needs of 'customers'. Instead, welfare state managers in most developed economies were addressing a much more fundamental problem, namely how to manage resources against a background of ageing populations and declining economic performance, when these forces meant that funding the delivery of a full range of completely free services was no longer a realistic option.

Exacerbating this problem was the unfortunate phenomenon that until very recently few politicians were willing to jeopardize their chances of re-election by openly admitting the economic infeasibility of offering 'free services to all'. Nor were they prepared to tell electorates that, over time, citizens with sufficient incomes would have to take greater personal responsibility for funding their own consumption of services such as healthcare, education and pensions. One of the first politicians willing to propose a move towards a mixed private/public sector welfare economy was the New Zealand politician Roger Douglas (Walker 1989). His views have subsequently been adopted by other 'new socialists' such as UK Prime Minister, Tony Blair. Fortunately, such individuals have been willing to risk personal unpopularity by initiating the debate over the future inadequacy of public sector resources, and the role of the private citizen in the greater self-resourcing of services previously totally provided by the state. The re-discovery of integrity by some of the politicians responsible for determining welfare state policies now provides the institutional marketer with an environment in which it becomes feasible to evolve appropriate models for managing the marketing process within this sector of a nation's economy.

The fundamental constraint facing the institutional marketer is that resources will always be outstripped by demand for services. Under these circumstances, a primary objective must be that of seeking ways to optimize efficiencies in the ways available resources are used. A common characteristic of most welfare state services is that they involve the acquisition, storage and distribution of information. It is apparent, therefore, that given the ability of e-commerce to reduce dramatically the cost of all aspects of data management, this technology has significant potential for enhancing and improving the delivery of many public sector services. This fact is at last beginning to be recognized by governments around the world, many of which are now implementing initiatives designed to accelerate the rate at which e-commerce is incorporated into the diverse activities of the welfare state.

Government departments and agencies are now moving on-line as part of a strategy to improve the provision of information to the groups they serve both inside and outside the public sector. The New Jersey Police Department's Internet policy statement, for example, asserts that its presence on the Internet provides 'opportunities to improve communications and public service, extend government service hours and enhance the image of government'. The city of Fort Collins, Colorado believes that the dissemination of information via the Internet will (1) contribute to economic development of the city by providing favourable information to potential investors, (2) aid policy development and decision-making by giving employees immediate access to research materials and other technical and professional information, (3) conserve resources that would otherwise be consumed by the use of paper and fossil fuels, and by employee trips to conferences, and (4) improve service delivery by promoting and facilitating efficiency and innovation (Menzel 1998).

A recognized constraint on the optimization of efficiency in many public sector services is that important knowledge is often in the heads of a small number of key staff, and only a fraction becomes tangible through being written down. Moves to electronic information distribution platforms have acted as a catalyst for change (Soumi and Kastu-Haikio 1998). For example, in Finland the government has initiated a number of programmes aimed at improving the effectiveness of public services. A critical component of these reforms has been the adoption of electronic technology for the compilation and distribution of knowledge. A data communications network, Kuvernet, has been established using the TCP/IP protocol to exchange data on topics such as economic statistics, personnel records, document registration and the administration of local magistrates' courts. Distribution of funds, such as the payment of agriculture subsidies, have been greatly accelerated by an EDI file transfer system between the country's 450 municipalities.

Since the mid-1990s, various UK government departments and agencies have also launched initiatives aimed at enhancing service provision through exploitation of the Internet. These include websites offering general information about government activities, on-line provision of official forms and regulatory compliance information, and facilities for the on-line filing and payment of both direct and indirect taxes. A recent position assessment report concluded, however, that overall progress across the UK public sector has been slow and fragmented (Cabinet Office 1999). For example, it estimated that central government spends about £12 billion annually on the procurement of goods and services. Yet virtually all of this activity is paper-based and little has been done to exploit the opportunities offered by an electronic transactions system. Targets now state, therefore, that by 2008 all UK government service provision will be on-line. Linked to this aim, the Treasury Procurement Group set targets that by March 2001 90 per cent of all low-value purchases will be transacted electronically.

For virtually every Western government, the largest area of welfare state expenditure is on the provision of healthcare services. Possibly one of the commonest complaints about public sector healthcare is that too much money is consumed by staff buried in paperwork and forced to rely on antiquated record systems (McHugh 1998). In theory, therefore, e-commerce offers unprecedented opportunities to reduce operating costs and enhance the speed of service response (Cullen 1998). Areas in which information and communication technologies are being introduced include:

1 EDI systems to facilitate transfer of files between healthcare providers.
2 Computer-based hospital information systems (HISs) for the integration of patient records from different sources within a single distributable database.
3 Decision support systems to assist dialogue between doctors based at different locations (for example between general practitioners (GPs) in the surgery and hospital-based clinical specialists).
4 'Telediagnosis', in which telematic systems are used to carry out medical consultations remotely.
5 'Telemergency', in which telematics are used to co-ordinate emergency service interventions.
6 Medical imaging for the storage, retrieval and dissemination of images such as X-rays and CAT scans.
7 'Teleradiology' and 'telepathology', in which telecommunications are used respectively to distribute image data and the results of laboratory tests.

In the private healthcare sector, doctors have for some years faced pressures from medical insurers and health management organizations (HMOs) to take action to reduce costs and improve information flows. Hence it tends to be in this sector of the healthcare industry that e-commerce can be found to have affected the medical profession. Medical Logic in Oregon, for example, has made available to physicians a system that permits doctors to record and review patient information over the Internet, no matter what their location. The company ePhysicians in California has developed a pocket-sized computer that offer doctors the ability to communicate with laboratories and pharmacies (Schaffer 1999).

On-line pharmacies, pioneered in the US, are beginning to appear in other parts of the world. For example, in the UK, despite regulations that restrict the promotion and selling of prescription medicines on the Web, a company is Leeds, Pharmacy2U (*www.pharmacy2u.co.uk*), has opened for business (Gray 2000). The success of such projects will clearly be influenced by whether the UK medical regulatory authorities are willing to examine the implications of revising controls that at the moment restrict the marketing of prescription products to the medical profession.

In the meantime, websites featuring over-the-counter brands are beginning to emerge in the UK market. Pharmacia & Upjohn's website for the Nicorette product designed to help people stop smoking (*www.nicorette.co.uk*) includes desk-top diversion games for smokers to download as a distraction from wanting a cigarette. Another interesting approach is provided by Procter & Gamble's Vicks range of products (*www.vicks.com*), which allows visitors to e-mail get well postcards to friends and play interactive games, as well as offering advice on treating ailments. In the case of *www.clearasil.com*, as well as offering skin-care advice the site, aimed at teenager acne sufferers, features fashion tips and career guidance.

Within the public sector, progress to adopt e-commerce has been much slower. One of the reasons for the limited penetration of e-commerce into public sector healthcare is the lack of funds available to support the massive expenditures required to modernize existing computer systems and create an effective Internet data exchange

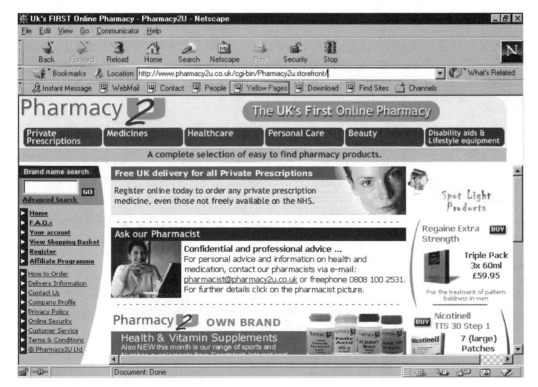

Cutting Costs

One of the largest expenses facing the drugs industry is the cost of the clinical trials required before a new treatment is approved by government regulatory authorities. An interesting approach to using the Internet to reduce medical industry costs is provided Health Decisions in North Carolina (Schoenberger 2000). The Swiss company Roche contracted that the company offer an Internet service to reduce costs of medical trials of the molecule lazabemide. Instead of having doctors produce handwritten notes on patients, these individuals sent their data electronically on a daily basis to Health Decisions. Here an optical reader entered the information. The system required a third of the number of people needed for traditional data entry.

The Internet system has the ability to send queries back to doctors where clarification is needed. The Health Decision system reduced queries from the industry's average of four per page of doctor's notes down to one per twenty. Additionally, the system has the capacity to identify immediately where errors are occurring in the trials. Although the study revealed the new molecule was performing as well as hoped, the method highlighted the problem in less than four years and saved Roche $32 million.

infrastructure. Regretably, however, the pace of change has also been slowed due to prevailing attitudes within the healthcare industry. Medical informatics has the potential to expand the knowledge and competences of non-specialist healthcare staff. This situation is perceived by senior doctors as having the potential to erode the power they have to direct the allocation of resources and set service provision priorities. The speed with which e-commerce is permitted to change public sector healthcare provision will to a large degree be controlled by the willingness of senior hospital consultants to relax demarcation lines between themselves and other staff such as nurses while also moving to establish a more collaborative attitude between different doctor practitioner disciplines (Cullen 1998).

A recent example of this attitude was provided by the medical profession's initial reaction to the UK government's launch of the NHS (National Health Service) Direct (*www.nhsdirect.nhs.uk*). This is an Internet system that provides general medical information on-line, and also offers access to call centres staffed by nurses. The idea

Medical Cost Reduction

Over 2 million injuries and 100 000 deaths occur every year as the result of the incorrect administration of medication. Beckton Dickenson has developed a system—using Riverbed technology and a palm-top computer with built-in scanner and wireless local area network—to verify that the correct medication is being given to patients. Adopting a small computer solution provides healthcare staff with the mobility required to use e-commerce technology where they work. The company expects that the system will reduce medication errors by at least 70 per cent (anon. 2000a).

> ### Reducing Fire Prevention Costs
>
> Los Angeles as a city needs to be very concerned about the prevention of brush fires. The city Fire Department conducts an annual brush inspection programme to ensure high risk areas are clear of fire hazards. Previously, fire inspectors hand wrote information that was then manually entered into the computer system.
>
> Using Puma technology and an SPT palm-top computer, this manual process was replaced with automated data entry. Back at the fire station the data is automatically loaded into the mainframe system. The saving on data entry costs are $123 000 per year, and even more importantly the city has much better records for managing fire prevention (Anon. 2000b).

behind the concept is to have more of the general population seeking guidance over common complaints such as colds and minor domestic accidents, thereby reducing the number of patient visits to GP surgeries. At the time of the launch in 1999, some doctors criticized the system because in their view it was not appropriate to delegate the provision of medical advice to nurses. As NHS Direct has begun to demonstrate the benefits of permitting the general public to get instant advice on medical issues (for example reducing pressure on GPs during the 2000 'flu epidemic), it does seem that the medical profession is beginning to accept that this highly innovative approach to welfare service provision is a cost-effective approach to the use of scarce resources.

Another area in which government expenditure is extremely high and the Internet offers major cost-saving opportunities is education. A large component of the total expenditure in education is on staff engaged in personal delivery of information to students in the classroom. To date, however, the teaching profession (anon. 1999) has been extremely reluctant to exploit this new technology, other than to use it as a powerful tool through which students can gain access to a much wider range of information databases. As in the healthcare sector, one obstacle has been the cost of updating computer systems in education. Government action before 2000 to ensure that all areas of the public sector were 'millennium bug' compliant does mean that many educational institutions now have the equipment infrastructure in place that would permit greater exploitation of the Internet. It seems reasonable to expect educators to move more rapidly to evolve new approaches to teaching using the Internet.

If one adopts an optimistic outlook, it seems reasonable to expect that over the next few years institutional marketers will begin fully to exploit the potential of e-commerce both to enhance service quality and reduce delivery cost. The speed with which this occurs, however, will be critically influenced by the attitudes of those who are now the providers of the core knowledge upon which services are based (for example the hospital consultants and school teachers) and their willingness to give others access and permit them to become responsible for using the information that can be made available on the Internet. It is probable that some countries will be more successful in achieving the cultural and organizational structural changes required. Those that succeed, however, will then be in a much better position to support the ongoing operation of an effective welfare state system.

● Summary

Early writings on business-to-business marketing tended to assume that management concepts could be evolved by drawing upon ideas and processes from the world of consumer goods marketing. Actual market studies then began to undermine this philosophy. Research revealed that business-to-business markets exhibit certain unique characteristics, such as derived demand and the influence of the purchasing power of individual customers. These characteristics require a somewhat different marketing strategies. Studies in both Europe and the US also revealed that effective management of the buyer–seller interaction has a critical impact on market performance. The advent of TQM and JIT have both highlighted the critical importance of effective supply chain management in business-to-business markets. The advent of e-commerce has significantly changed the degree to which suppliers are able to fulfil customer demands for speed and flexibility of response.

The growing importance of the welfare state in Western nations since the Second World War has meant that institutional (or public sector) markets also require special consideration by the marketer. Over recent years, as nations have begun to confront their increasing inability to fund many of their social welfare programmes, efforts are being made to discover new ways of sustaining service delivery while also lowering delivery costs. In areas such as healthcare and education, e-commerce offers some exciting ways of achieving these goals.

STUDY QUESTIONS

1 What are the characteristics of business-to-business markets?

2 What are the issues which need to be considered in the effective operation of an integrated supply chain?

3 How can e-commerce be used to enhance the effective operation of integrated supply chains?

E-BUSINESS AND INSTITUTIONAL MARKETING

Case: *E-Based Supply Chain Management*

Greenland Foods is a retail operation focussing on selling a diverse range of frozen food products. It operates over 100 stores, with procurement and warehousing operated from a central, single location. The company's most important category in terms of sales volume is the retailing of frozen fish and seafood. This is a very complex area of operation because, as can be seen from the market system diagram shown in Fig. 11.2, the company procures products from a wide range of both overseas and domestic sources.

Andy Benton is the Director of Greenland Foods procurement operation. Over the last few years he has become increasingly concerned about the effectiveness of fish and seafood procurement. Although the company has a computer system linking the central warehouse and in-store stock management

operations, all other aspects of the operation are still paper-based. He feels that as well as being very expensive to administer, opportunities to optimize total sales revenue are being missed due to factors such as slow recognition of low stock levels at either the warehouse or stores, time delays in the ordering / delivery cycle within the supply chain, and an inability to identify rapidly when changes in landings at the port might offer opportunities to offer different and / or new products to the customers.

He mentioned his concerns over a drink one evening with the company's IT Director. The next day he opened his e-mail to find that his colleague had forwarded the following extracts from two articles on e-commerce supply chain management.

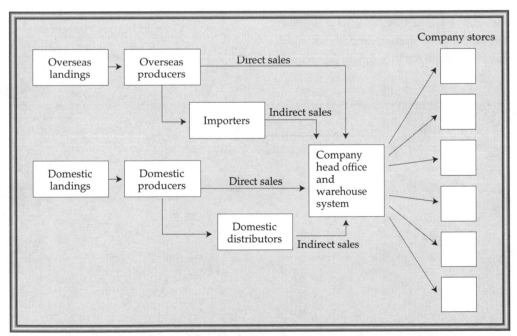

Figure 11.2 *The supply chain for frozen fish and seafoods*

Over the last ten years, there has been increasing recognition of the benefits of improving the flow of goods and information within supply chains. Planning production levels, sourcing materials, handling inventory and delivering product can represent anywhere between 10 and 25 per cent of total operating costs. Moving to the Internet to integrate supply chains offers advantages well beyond cutting paper and clerical costs. By automating purchasing and operating Web-based procurement huge savings in inventory costs, accompanied by increased customer satisfaction, can be achieved. In the US a leader in supply chain integration has been Wal-Mart. This company was the first retailer to pass responsibility for inventory management back to suppliers. To assist this process Wal-Mart has provided suppliers with access to the company's computer systems so that suppliers can gain instant information on product sales and on-hand stock levels. Another example is provided by IBM which has built Internet links to suppliers and distributors. This system supports the rapid assembly of customized PCs and the shipping of updated components to distributors involved in upgrading customers' machines.

Source: Moad (1997)

Supply chain models of the type pioneered by a hub organization such as Wal-Mart and IBM have more recently been followed by the formation of supply chain consortiums. On February 25th 2000, General Motors, Ford and Daimler Chrysler announced they were joining forces to create an e-commerce supply chain to manage their acquisition of $240 billion-worth of components from tens of thousands of suppliers. Within days Toyota, Renault and Nissan indicated an interest in joining the programme. On February 28th 2000, Sears Roebuck and France's Carrefour announced plans to create an e-commerce procurement consortium for the retail sector. The venture, known as GlobalNetXchange will manage the annual procurement of $80 billion-worth of products for stocking in retail stores. On March 1st 2000, Cargill, DuPont and Cenex Harvest said they will create Rooster.com to supply farmers and to sell their crops.

Source: *The Economist* (2000)

QUESTIONS

1 As a member of Andy Benton's operation you have been allocated the task of preparing a brief report for him on how, by developing an integrated e-commerce supply chain, Greenland Foods fish and seafood procurement and retailing operation might be made more efficient and more responsive to changing supply trends, thereby optimizing in-store customer satisfaction. It is recommended that you use the data provided in Fig. 11.2 to determine where e-commerce links and electronic trading relationships might be established. You will be expected to specify which aspects of Internet technology might be required within the proposed system.

2 Having completed your first report, you should prepare a second, somewhat briefer analysis, of whether Greenland Foods should seek to establish a single company system or adopt a consortium approach to e-commerce market management.

Case: *An Electronic Solution for Healthcare?*

Memorandum

To: Richard Green
From: Steven Bite

Research Unit Head
Minister of Health, Country X

I think we both accept that due to factors such as an ageing population and the continuing ability of medical technology to find successful cures for more illnesses, the country will find it increasingly difficult to fund the provision of healthcare to those who cannot afford private medical insurance. On the other hand, we as a government have a responsibility to attempt to deliver customer satisfaction to the general public by finding new ways of delivering the healthcare that they require. Having given some thought to the subject, I suspect that e-commerce might be able to contribute to cost stabilization in least three areas of healthcare provision, namely information management, procurement and patient education.

In the case of information management, I was struck by the ideas suggested in an article by Scharrer (1999). In the article, he describes the extremely inefficient way patient records are spread across a number of locations (the doctor's office, local hospitals etc.) and are still often in either a paper form or stored on old computer systems unable to communicate with other electronic databases. MedicaLogic in Hillsboro, Oregon has developed a system whereby doctors can record and review information over the Internet using any computer from any location in which they are operating (for example the office, the hospital, the patient's home). Another system being developed is AboutMyHealth, which permits patients to access their own records (*www.aboutmyhealth.com*). To enhance further doctor mobility, ePhysician of Mountain View, California has developed a palm-top computer to provide direct, mobile access to laboratories and pharmacies.

On the issue of procurement, the complex and diverse nature of medical equipment means that this is a time consuming and inefficient activity. An article by Schonfeld (1999) describes a new system being developed by Neoforma (*www.neoforma.com*) that can reduce procurement time significantly. The site is an on-line catalogue for the $150 billion-a-year clinical products industry. Medical procurement administrators can search the site for products. They can even gain floor plans of medical facilities and generate a list of the equipment required to equip the rooms in the facility.

In the case of patient education, although clearly we should never suggest that the government is seeking to replace the professional services of doctors, it is widely recognized that educating private citizens can reduce the ever increasing service provision demands that are being placed on the medical profession. Brown (1997) highlights the increasing benefits of offering private citizens access to medical information via the Internet. Commercial portals such as yahoo (*www.yahoo.com*) provide guidance to a vast range of bulletin boards and illness-specific patient support groups. Other sites are more medically specific (for example *www.healthatoz.com* or *www.achoo.com*). Major national organizations have also established on-line databases (for example the Centre for Disease Control, at *www.cdc.gov*, the National Cancer Institute, at *www.icic.nci.nih.gov*, and the Mayo Clinic, at *www.mayo.ivi.com*).

QUESTIONS

1 Assume the role of Richard Green and prepare a report for the Minister of Country X on how e-commerce might used to modernize healthcare systems and in that way assist the government in the achievement of its goal of seeking to enhance customer satisfaction over the quality of medical services being delivered across the entire country.

2 Develop a supplementary report for the Minister of Country X, pointing out where structural or attitudinal problems within the medical profession might create obstacles to the introduction of e-commerce systems that could enhance healthcare delivery.

Chapter 12

E-SERVICES MARKETING

Learning Objectives

This chapter explains

- *The evolution of service marketing theory.*

- *The characteristics of service products.*

- *The role of customer knowledge in service marketing.*

- *The impact of the Internet in the commoditization of service goods.*

- *Differentiation through adding value to service goods.*

- *The measurement of service quality and identification of service gaps.*

- *How e-companies can exceed customer service expectations.*

- *Automation of the service provision process.*

A characteristic of twentieth century Western economies was the increasing importance of service industries as both a contributor to Gross National Product (GNP) and a source of employment. In the 1980s, as many service markets became more competitive, organizations recognized the need to modernize their marketing philosophies. The popular solution was to employ transactionally-oriented managers from f.m.c.g. companies such as Procter & Gamble, General Foods and Nestlé. These individuals persuaded their new employers to adopt a highly conventional approach towards the management of the marketing process. This resulted in a major expansion of expenditure on various forms of mass marketing activity.

In some cases, these purist, conventional f.m.c.g. approaches were extremely successful (for example the global expansion of fast food chains such as Burger King, Pizza Hut and Kentucky Fried Chicken). Other areas of the service sector, however, were not similarly rewarded. The UK banks in the late 1980s, for example, having expended millions on TV advertising found that (1) the number of consumers opening current accounts remained virtually unchanged and (2) many of their new customers were dissatisfied transfers from other banks who continued to complain about the costs and/or quality of services delivered by the new bank.

This mixture of success and failure within the service sector prompted both academics and practitioners to revisit marketing theory. As a result, it has become widely accepted that the marketing of services probably demands a whole new range of marketing conventions and operating principles (Cowell 1984). Initially, much of the writing on this topic focused on purist service marketing in sectors such as financial services and retailing. More recently, however, there has been a growing recognition that in many manufacturing sectors companies can gain competitive advantage not by following the convention of marketing their ability to deliver a tangible core product, but through augmenting their offering with a portfolio of unconventional value-added services.

Quinn et al. (1990), for example, describe how many of the companies at the top end of the pharmaceutical industry have relied upon the use of unconventional value-added services to survive in the face of competitive threats from price-oriented generic drug producers. Companies such as Glaxo Wellcome (*www.glaxowellcome.com*) and Merck (*www.merck.com*) have added value to product lines through service activities such as R&D, the construction of legal and patent defences, the rapid progressing of new drugs through the clinical clearances demanded by regulatory bodies, support for clinicians in the use of new treatments, and the offer of advisory support in improvements to healthcare provided by customers such as large hospitals and health authorities. These authors argue that as manufacturing exploits IT to become more universally automated, increasingly adding value does not come from the conventional activities of converting raw materials into finished goods, but in areas of service such as styling, perceived quality, product customization, JIT distribution and post-purchase maintenance and repair services. They, in fact, would argue that the bastion of f.m.c.g. marketing, Procter & Gamble, is now a $15 billion service corporation that has achieved success by breaking with the sector convention of being perceived as a branded goods operation and repositioning itself as offering superior services across the core areas of R&D, manufacturing and logistics.

The Characterization of Service Goods

One of the primary reasons writers posit the view that service marketers must break with traditional, branded goods conventions is that service markets exhibit some very specific characteristics. One of these, **intangibility** (*that the item cannot be touched, smelt, seen or tasted*), is encompassed by Kotler's (1997) definition: 'a service is any act or performance that one party can offer to another that is essentially intangible and does not result in the ownership of anything. Its production may or may not be tied to a physical product.'

Favourites

It is necessary to recognize, however, that the degree of intangibility will vary across product sectors. At one extreme, service is a minor component of the product proposition (for example a new car may come with a three-year free repair and service guarantee). At the other extreme, service may be the dominant or sole product component (for example in the case of an on-line purchased car insurance policy). Intangibility means that a service, unlike physical products, cannot be seen, tasted, felt, heard or smelled before purchase. Thus one of the tasks of service marketers is to develop mechanisms to reduce customer uncertainty about intangibility. Typical solutions include exploiting variables such as:

1. Place, the physical setting in which services are provided.

2. People, the point of contact between the customer and the organization.

3. Equipment, which must be of the necessary standard to assist rapidly and efficiently service provision.

An example of managing the variables of place, people and equipment is provided by the UK car insurance industry. Up until the mid-1980s, the way that the industry handled these variables was to have branches in all major towns, complemented by local brokers paid on a commission-only basis. The entreprencurial company, Direct Line recognized that the advent of computer-based call centre technology permitted them to service customer needs electronically from a single location. The major lowering of operating costs associated with this idea allowed the company to charge much lower insurance premiums. Nevertheless, the company recognized that as customers would not visit its office, place could not be used as a variable through which to reduce customer insecurity. Their solution, therefore, was to invest heavily in staff training and the latest automated telesales systems to ensure the effective operation of these two variables were supportive of building customer trust. The company has now moved to market insurance products via the Internet. Here the key variable for building customer confidence is the hardware and software that constitute the on-line system. Hence the Direct Line website (*www.directline.com*) was only launched after a careful assessment had been made that the on-line interface was capable of ensuring that customers felt secure when using it.

● Understanding the Customer

The retail sector provides some of the earliest examples of moves to use e-commerce in the provision of services. Examples of both success and failure suggest, however, that just putting a store on-line is unlikely to be an effective strategy. A critical antecedent is that the supplier must give careful thought to the nature of the services being sought by its cyberspace customers. In the mid-1990s, for example, MCI and IBM respectively launched their Marketplace and World Avenue cyber-malls. These websites were an attempt at duplicating the successful US off-line retailing model of locating a diverse range of retail outlets in one large, out-of-town location. Evidence would suggest, however, that consumers were not impressed by either the apparently near-random selection of stores on these websites or the baffling procedures required to buy anything. The outcome was that most customers reverted to visiting more familiar, off-line shopping malls (anon. 1997).

search

In contrast, some on-line retailers undertook a very careful evaluation of the probable services sought by consumers and then constructed on-line provision models met these needs. One of the earliest successes was Peapod in the US (*www.peapod.com*). This company based its service model around meeting the needs of those customers prepared to pay extra for the convenience of being provided with an at-home shopping and delivery service (Pearce 1998). The essence of the Peapod approach is to partner grocery stores, acting as broker between the retailer and its customers. Peapod takes the order, staff select the requested items at the store and deliver these to the customer's home. The company's income is the service fee it receives from providing an on-line, at-home shopping service.

The provision of a time and convenience model has always been a key variable in the off-line success of mail-order catalogue operations. These companies have for some years been using call centre technology to optimise service delivery. Hence it is not surprising to find that firms such as Lands End (*www.landsend.com*) were very early movers into the world of on-line shopping. Another successful on-line retail model has been the one that sticks to particular sectors. Possibly the most well known example is Amazon, in book retailing. Companies that moved to exploit the fact that young people are disproportionately high users of the internet by offering music on-line have followed. Like Amazon, these music sites seek to add service value by incorporating music reviews, concert itineraries and sound samples. Where they are able to go further than book retailers, however, is in product delivery, because the MP3 data format means that customers can download the music they want to purchase. Customers can also order a customized CD carrying a mix of music chosen by themselves.

The 'wheel of retailing' theory suggests that once customers have gained sufficient confidence to dispense with the need for guidance from sales staff in a specific product sector, opportunity emerges for discount stores to exploit the cost-savings of bulk buying of top-selling lines in a self-service environment. In the off-line world, the megastore Wal-Mart in the US thrives by using bulk purchasing and supply chain efficiencies to out-price competitors. The company also uses IT to measure customer buying patterns on a daily basis. Now that the number of cyberspace shoppers has become a significant proportion of the total population, the wheel of retailing theory seems to be emerging in the world of on-line shopping. Two early players are NetMarket (*www.netmarket.com*) and Shopping.com (*www.shopping.com*). These operations operate on a membership basis, with on-line shoppers paying a fee for the privilege of access to available discounts. Both offer a broad portfolio of goods, ranging from CDs, books, videos, travel services and home furnishings at prices well below the specialist on-line retail stores. Another reason these companies can offer lower prices than specialist on-line stores is that both have avoided becoming owners or managers of inventory. Instead, once an on-line order is received it is forwarded to manufacturers or distributors, which are responsible for managing the delivery operation (anon. 1997).

● Other Service Market Characteristics

Another characteristic of services is **inseparability** (*the fact that many services are simultaneously produced and consumed*). The implication of this is that in many cases both the provider and the customer must be able to interact with each other. A further characteristic of services is **variability** (*the fact that no two offerings of the same service will ever be identical because both customer needs and employee abilities differ*). Unlike manufactured goods, which can be produced and inventoried for later use, another characteristic of many services is that they are highly perishable. For example, an inability to sell every seat on a specific airline flight on a specific day means that a proportion of total possible revenue has been lost forever. Sasser (1976) proposes a number of marketing strategies that over time have become the conventional methods for effectively matching supply and demand. These include:

1. Differential pricing, which moves demand from peak to off-peak periods.

2. Alternative service provision, which meets the varying needs of customers during peak periods.

3. Service modification, which ensures that during peak periods the needs of major purchasers receive priority.

4. Demand management systems, which permit the service provider rapidly to (1) identify current available capacity and (2) propose alternative solutions.

5. Temporary capacity expansion, whereby the provider can increase its ability to respond to customer needs during peak periods.

6. Service sharing, in which a number of organizations work together and are willing to cross-refer customers.

7. Customer participation, in which customers are encouraged to become self-providers.

● Commoditization

Services differ from tangible goods in the degree to which they possess search, experience and credence attributes. With tangible goods, the customer is able to examine the physical nature of the product during the search phase prior to purchase. In contrast, evaluation of services tends only to come from the experience of consumption and the market reputation, or credence, of the service provider. This situation, linked to the lack of physical differentiation among competing offerings, can often result in price being the key variable influencing purchase behaviour in service markets (Berry and Yadav 1996).

In an off-line world, many service providers can partially, or totally, avoid price-based competition because potential customers lack either the time or ability to undertake a detailed price comparison search prior to purchase. The advent of e-commerce has totally changed this situation, because at the touch of a button potential customers can

TC2 (*www.dama.tc2.com*)

TC2 is a clothes manufacturing consortium that has developed a virtual reality clothes customization system. The customer enters a booth in which six cameras take 48 photographs that a computer converts into a 300 000-point, three-dimensional map. Over 100 measurements can be extracted from these data, and these are used to cut and sew clothing that offers a better fit than an 'off-the-peg' purchase. Similar services are now being developed in the shoe industry. In the vitamin industry, companies such as GNC and Green-Tree are already offering on-line ordering of customized vitamin packs formulated to meet each customer's individual nutritional requirements.

> ### American Airlines (*www.americanair.com*)
> An organization's ability to manage marketing variables clearly affects customer perceptions of service quality. An example of a service provider which recognized that IT could be used to exploit this opportunity is American Airlines. Led by a technology visionary, Max Hopper, in the 1980s the company developed the Sabre computer-based flight reservation system (Hopper 1990). The system was initially created in order that American Airlines could track bookings and offer customers a more rapid response to their flight reservation enquiries. An added advantage of the system was that by providing management with electronic data concerning pricing, routing, staffing and other scheduling issues the airline was able to deliver a much higher level of service quality. In fact the system was so successful, through being marketed to other airlines, that it became a whole new revenue stream for the company. Once the Internet became accessible to a significant proportion of American's customers, the company invested heavily in the creation of a website that would permit customers to become even more involved in the self-management of their flights. By providing pricing information and details of other airlines' flights, the website very effectively matches demand against available supply.

price compare, either by visiting different websites or the growing number of on-line intermediaries providing information on price variations between service suppliers. Commenting on this situation, Loewe and Boncher (1999) conclude that in an on-line world power in the transaction process has passed from supplier to customer. They propose that on-line customers are now in a position to influence behaviour within service supply chains. This means that firms have to be more price competitive, or find new ways of differentiating themselves from competition. The author's conclusion is that in many markets, especially where there are minimal opportunities to differentiate services (for example in home insurance, consumer banking and air travel), as price becomes the dominant purchase decision factor, many services become commodity goods.

Determining how to respond to the commoditization of a market sector requires a careful re-assessment of the on-line marketing strategies of many e-business operations. In the event that the company cannot identify a mechanism by which to differentiate its offering from competition, it is extremely likely that the long-term survivors in the inevitable price wars will be those companies able to exploit existing well developed technological infrastructures to achieve economies of scale (for example those telecommunications companies such as AT&T and British Telecom) or have invested in developing internal process operations that deliver significantly lower operating costs than the competition (for example the leading provider of low cost, on-line share dealing services, Charles Schwab).

For those companies that decide to implement a strategy designed to avoid participation in price wars, there are a number of options available that have already been validated in the world of off-line service provision (Berry and Yadav 1996). One approach is to recognize that one company's price war is often another's opportunity to help customers search more effectively for the best price proposition. MediaCom, based in Bedford Massachusetts, for example, has developed a software system, PhoneMiser (***www.phonemiser.com***), that permits customers automatically to search a database of 200 long-distance telephone companies to find the cheapest carrier for each number dialled. The software routes the call in less than a second and provides a typical saving of more than 50 per cent (Loewe and Boncher 1999).

Another way to differentiate a company from competition is to offer the on-line purchaser the ability to customize the purchase to suit his or her specific personal requirements. Computer manufacturers Dell and Gateway 2000 are pioneers in the provision of e-commerce customization.

Another approach to avoiding price wars is to shift the market sector away from being transactionally-oriented by attempting to build a relationship with individual customers. One way of relationship building is to seek to enter into a long-term contract with the customer. This approach is relatively common in business-to-business service markets. The aim of the supplier is to use the stability of the contract period to invest in new technology to enhance and improve service delivery. Both Federal Express and UPS now use this approach with large corporate customers, which benefit because over the life of such contracts both suppliers commit to improving service in areas such as reducing delivery times and the customer's need to carry large inventories.

Most service market customers are willing to form relationships with providers that offer convenience and time saving as core components of the service offering. To exploit this strategy, a number of the larger service providers across various market sectors are moving to deliver convenience through creating 'bundles' of services. Price bundling has been common in off-line service markets for many years (for example in consumer banking, where banks pass along operational cost-savings in the form of reduced fees when the customer agrees to open an account composed of both financial transaction and savings components). Many companies that do this tend to retain and expand their price bundling as they enter the world of on-line service marketing (for example the Virgin Group's, which bundles an ISP, a diverse range of financial services, travel booking and on-line music purchasing). Potentially the largest on-line bundling proposition is the package expected to emerge following AOL's January 2000 takeover of the cable and media conglomerate, Time Warner.

Given the very clear risk of price competition and commoditization in on-line service markets, it is critical than the e-marketer undertakes a regular assessment of the company's price/value market position. One way to achieve this is to consider that there are two dimensions influencing positioning. One is the pricing of the on-line service proposition relative to prevailing prices within a market. It is suggested that this can be classified into either low, average or high. The second dimension is customer perceptions of the relative value of the company's service proposition. Again this can be classified as low, average or high. Having acquired data on these two dimensions, the marketer can assess the company's on-line positioning by creating a matrix of the type shown in Fig. 12.1.

In using a price/value matrix of the type shown in Fig. 12.1, it can be assumed that if the company's offerings fall somewhere along the three diagonal cells, this will usually mean a correct decision has been made over the nature of the service package and price offered to the customer. If a company's position is above the diagonal, immediate attention is necessary, because it would appear that customers perceive the service offering as over-priced. Alternatively if actual positioning falls below the diagonal, the company needs to determine whether the position results from an intention to support a 'superior value' service proposition, or whether a pricing error has been made. Should the latter be the explanation, the company must assess whether a pricing move or a revision in the nature of the service proposition should be initiated.

● Customer Satisfaction and Service Gap Theory

A number of writers posit that the objective of service satisfaction is to minimize the gap between customers' desires and actual experience. To permit service marketers to understand and manage service gaps requires access to plausible techniques for the measurement and analysis of customer expectations and perceptions. This need has been met through the activities of Parasuraman et al. (1988, 1990), who since 1983 have conducted a carefully sequenced research project aimed at delivering an

		Customer perception of value service proposition		
		Low	Average	High
Price	High	Extremely over-priced service offering	Over-priced service offering	Superior performance service package
	Average	Over-priced service offering	Average value service package	Superior value **or** poorly priced service package
	Low	Economy service package	Superior value or poorly priced service package	Extreme value **or** very poorly priced service package

Figure 12.1 An e-commerce price/value matrix

effective model for assessing the effectiveness and quality of the service provision process.

The first stage of their research was to identify some common variables that could be used to categorize customer expectations. By the use of focus groups, they identified the following five variables:

<u>1</u>   Reliability, the ability to perform the promised service dependably and accurately.

<u>2</u>   Tangibles , the images created by the appearance of physical facilities, equipment, personnel and communication materials.

<u>3</u>   Responsiveness, the willingness to help customers and provide prompt service.

<u>4</u>   Assurance, the process by which the knowledge, ability and courtesy of employees engenders customer trust and confidence in the service provider.

<u>5</u>   Empathy, created by the caring, individualized attention that employees offer the customer.

Having identified these generic expectations, Parasuraman et al. then created the Servqual model, which defined the following types of gap that organizations must ensure do not exist between expectations and perceptions:

1. Gap 1, between the customer's expectations and the organization's perceptions of customer need.

2. Gap 2, between the organization's perceptions of what it should offer and the definition of appropriate quality of service standards.

3. Gap 3, between the specified standards of service and the actual performance of the organization's employees.

4. Gap 4, between actual service delivered and the nature of the promise made in any communication with the customer.

5. Gap 5, between customer expectations and perceptions, created by combining the previous four gaps.

The magnitude and influence of the five service gaps can be measured using the Servqual tool. The technique involves surveying customers to determine their expectations and perceptions, by asking them to compare their perspectives of desired service with experience of actual service received. Other gap dimensions are measured by surveying employee attitudes about various aspects of operations within their organization (for example the existence of quality standards and mechanisms for integrating all aspects of the service delivery process across the entire organization).

Managing Gap 1: Dell

Dell is a leader in ensuring information flow between customer and supplier contributes towards building positive customer expectations. From the first day the company opened for business it recognized that direct marketing requires an overwhelming commitment to maximizing the effectiveness of the interface between company and customer. The company was one of the first to enter the world of Internet trading, and rapidly realized the importance of ensuring that information management in this medium is critical in influencing customer service expectations (Thurm 1998).

Over time, Dell has evolved a website that does much more than just take orders. Customers can access thousands of pages of information, tap into the technical guides used by Dell technicians, and use the site to track the progress of orders from submission to shipment. The company has found that these types of service improve their selling efficiency. For example, the traditional purchaser makes five phone calls before buying, whereas users of the website browse and then place their order during their first telephone call. Dell sales staff can also interrogate the site to determine whether there is a need to follow up a customer's search activities with a one-to-one telephone conversation.

For corporate clients, the company has now developed Premier Pages. This permits the corporate customer to specify the creation of a confidential home page to which it can direct its employees seeking information on what product specifications the employer authorizes. The Premium Page also allows these clients to access databases showing what type of computers have been purchased by their colleagues and their location.

Managing Gap 2: Federal Express

As a service business expands its customer-base and the proportion of world markets covered, the clear specification of service standards and monitoring of actual performance against those standards becomes an increasingly complex task. Such is the situation confronting firms in the global parcel delivery business, because these organizations need to monitor the progress of thousands of items moving between and within countries on a daily basis. The leading service provider, Federal Express, has recognized that to sustain service standards under these circumstances requires a solution that has to be based on exploiting the latest advances in IT (Grossman 1993).

The core of the solution is the Cosmos software, which tracks items using real time data. Monitoring commences when a courier first collects a package, and continues through every stage in the distribution cycle. This is achieved using a hand-held SuperTracker computer, which scans the package's barcode. At time of final delivery, the courier undertakes the final scan to record safe receipt by the customer. SuperTracker automatically records the time and date of each scan, and downloads the information to Cosmos. When a customer contacts Federal Express to ask questions such as 'where is my package', 'what time was it collected' or 'who signed the delivery slip', a customer service agent can provide an immediate on-line response by accessing the Cosmos database. The system also permits the organization to gather and track employee performance across areas such as length of service call, speed of response and delivery time. To avoid negative response amongst employees to the collation of such data, employees are encouraged to interrogate the database and use available information to determine how they might improve their performance in the future.

To further monitor and manage service standards, Federal Express has now given its major customers an on-line operating system called Powerships. These are kits that store addresses and shipping data, print mailing slips, and monitor package location. By integrating the customer more closely into Federal Express's data management system, the company has been able both to improve delivery times and further upgrade performance standards across all aspects of its package delivery operations.

The typical response to results from Servqual-type research studies is for companies to find ways of minimizing the identified gap between perceptions and expectations. Very successful service firms, however, recognize that the ultimate objective is to find ways of completely closing any identified gap. This is usually achieved by acting to ensure that the actual service experience totally exceeds customer expectations.

● Service Automation

The very diverse demands of customers in service markets often mean that, unlike with many tangible goods, it is extremely difficult to separate the marketing activity from all other functions undertaken within the company. Furthermore, the efficiency of

Managing Gap 3: US Automobile Association (USAA)

An issue confronting organizations seeking to excel at exceeding customer expectations is how to organize both the workforce and work processes in such a way that the customer receives a rapid, yet apparently personalized, response to their demands for service. Companies seeking to improve internal capability have over recent years increasingly come to rely upon new, computer-based, technologies. USAA, a San Antonio insurance company, specializes in the provision of services to military personnel and their families. Both to upgrade its operation and be able to personalize its contacts with customers, the company joined with IBM to create a computer imaging system that could eliminate all paper-based materials, and offered the associated ability to track the physical progress of bulky customer files through the organization's various departments (Teal 1991).

Employees are able to scan millions of pieces of incoming mail into electronic dossiers that are much easier to manage. The system is even able to record photographs from damage claims onto an optical disc, which means this data can be retrieved for use in other documents. Furthermore, because telephone personnel can immediately call up a customer's file, they have all the necessary information in front of them when speaking to the customer. As a result, the company, which rarely has any face-to-face contact with a highly dispersed customer base, is perceived by its clients as an organization which cares, because it is deeply informed about personal insurance needs. Having established a technology platform that effectively automates internal processes, the company has now further enhanced customer service provision by linking these internal systems to a highly interactive on-line purchase and insurance service delivery system. This move has been important in permitting the company to expand into new market sectors over recent years.

the buyer–seller interaction at the production/consumption interface can have significant impact on the customer's repeat buying decisions. For example, when a customer makes an hotel reservation using an on-line booking service and arrives to find the hotel has filled all the bedrooms and has no record of the booking, it is probable this customer will be 'lost forever'.

In off-line service environments, Eigler and Langeard propose that there are three main categories of resource involved in the buyer–seller interaction, namely:

1   Contact personnel, who interact directly with the customer.
2   Physical resources, which comprise the human and technical resources used by the organization in the production, delivery and consumption of the service offering.
3   The customer, who is forming a repeat purchase, loyalty decision based on the quality of service received to date.

Gronroos (1984) proposes that management of these three variables is a marketing task that differs from conventional f.m.c.g. marketing because it involves assets, not usually part of the mainstream marketing operation, but instead drawn from the entire production resources of the organization. Gronroos proposes that in service companies

> ## Managing Gap 4: Car Buying
>
> All aspects of the interface between the customer and supplier communicate implicit or explicit statements about an organization's service promise: advertising, sales peoples' comments, switchboard operators' responses to customer enquiries on any subject, and the physical facilities of the operation. Information provided influences the development of the customer's expectations of the quality of service to be received from the supplier. The car market is the one in which consumers express the greatest discontent about the discrepancy between expectations created by supplier information and the quality of the actual service received. In recent years a number of companies have recognized the credibility gap created by traditional car dealerships, and have acted to exploit this opportunity (Business Week 1996). The first moves were in relation to pricing information. Enterprises such as CompuServe's Auto Net have created websites where the buyer can obtain detailed information on the alternative deals being offered by suppliers prior to starting their car search. Even more assistance is provided by AutoByTel (*www.autobytel.com*), which operates a referral service to locate the best deal available for the customer.

there exist three marketing tasks. He describes these as **external marketing** (*the normal formal processes associated with the management of the four Ps*), **interactive marketing** (*the activities which occur at the buyer–seller interface*) and **internal marketing** (*the internal processes associated with ensuring that all aspects of the business operation, including automated, computer-based systems are (1) customer-conscious and (2) supportive of a philosophy that every action is oriented towards achieving total customer satisfaction*).

Given that errors at either the buyer–seller interface or during the execution of the internal processes associated with service delivery can affect customer satisfaction, there has been widespread debate on how best to manage service sector organizations. In two classic articles, Levitt (1972, 1976) eloquently argued for the adoption of a manufacturing orientation in the management of services. He believes that this approach is required because it allows for (1) simplification of tasks, (2) clear division of labour, (3) substitution of equipment and systems for employees, and (4) minimal decision-making by employees.

Early entrepreneurs in the fast food chain industry, such as Ray Croc of McDonalds, very effectively demonstrated the validity of Levitt's proposals. To this day within the McDonalds operation, employees are taught how to greet the customer and ask for their order in a scripted way designed to suggest the purchase of additional items. Clearly defined procedures are laid down for assembling the order, placing them on the tray, positioning the tray on the counter and collecting the money. Meanwhile in the 'back room', other employees are executing tasks, developed through the application of time-and-motion studies, designed rapidly and efficiently to produce food of uniform quality. The net result is that this production line approach permits the operation of an efficient, low cost, high volume food service operation that delivers customer satisfaction.

The concept of the industrialization of service operations has not been without its critics. Such individuals argue that the approach is not only dehumanizing, but also results in an inability to respond to heterogeneous customer needs, because employees are forced to respond to all situations by adhering to the rigid guidelines laid down in the organization's operating policy manual. Zemke and Schaaf (1989) argue that service excellence is more likely to be achieved by 'empowerment', which involves encouraging and rewarding employees for exercising initiative and imagination. Jan Carlzon (1987), the chief executive given credit for successfully turning around Scandinavian Airlines, expresses similar views. He states that 'to free someone from the rigorous control by instructions, policies and orders, and to give that person freedom to take responsibility for his ideas, decisions and actions, is to release hidden resources that would otherwise remain inaccessible to both the individuals and the organization'.

Bowen and Lawler (1992) present a somewhat more balanced view of the debate between industrialization and employee empowerment. They point to the example of two very contrasting and yet successful US companies in the international package delivery business, the highly entrepreneurial Federal Express (*www.fedex.com*) and their very conventional competitor, United Parcel Service (UPS) (*www.ups.com*). The Federal Express company motto, 'people, service and profits' is the foundation stone for an organization built around self-managed teams and empowered employees as a mechanism through which to offer a flexible and creative service to customers with varying needs. In contrast, UPS, with a philosophy of 'best service at low rates', uses controls, rules, a detailed union contract and rigidly defined operational guidelines to guarantee customers will receive a reliable, low cost service.

The advent of on-line service provision has added a new dimension to the debate about structuring organizational processes to optimize service quality. Possibly the best way to illustrate the debate's implications is to examine the banking sector. Since the deregulation of financial services around the world in last 20 years, competition between financial service providers has become extremely intense. The outcome in the banking sector is that organizations have been forced to examine ways of improving service quality while reducing operating costs. Technology has been a very effective route through which to achieve these dual goals. One of the earliest examples of the use of IT was the advent of automated teller machines (ATMs). The introduction of EDI to automate both bank-to-bank and bank-to-commercial customer financial transactions followed. In the mid-1990s, led by companies such as Wells Fargo in the US, banks moved to create on-line banking operations (Woolley 1998). The benefit of such moves is illustrated by the estimates issued by Wells Fargo (*www.wellsfargo.com*) that on-line customers generate 50 per cent more revenue than off-line customers, hold 20 per cent higher balances, use 50 per cent more of the bank's financial services portfolio, and that service provision costs are 14 per cent lower than those associated with satisfying off-line customer needs (Timewell and Young 1999).

The major challenge facing bankers wishing to use e-commerce to reduce service provision costs is the degree to which customers are willing to accept automated transaction processes as a replacement for services that in the past were delivered by one-to-one interaction between customers and bank employees. One possible way to determine whether customers will accept this replacement of people by machines is to assess the situation using a service positioning matrix (SPM). Collier and Meyer (1998) suggest that an effective SPM model should encompass both a measurement of customer perception and an assessment of the nature of the service process being undertaken.

In the context of e-commerce service provision, this can be achieved using the two variables of (1) customer perception of transaction complexity, and (2) the number of alternative service provision channels offered to the customer. In relation to the latter variable, at one extreme a bank can opt to restrict service provision to a very small number of channels (for example customers can only access banking services via ATMs or a website). At the other extreme, customers may be offered a wide variety of channels including, ATMs, a website, a call centre, over-the-counter services in traditional branch outlets and access to a personal banker.

The diversity of channel offerings may vary both by service provider (for example some banks are purely on-line operations) and by type of customer (for example fee structures can be designed to direct customers seeking basic transactions to use only on-line services, whereas customers with a diverse portfolio of financial service needs can be offered access to their own personal banker). Quantification of the two variables of customer perceptions of technology and service provision channels can be achieved using some form of numerical scale that permits classification into the three categories of low, average and high. An illustration of applying these measurements to evolve an e-commerce service provision matrix is provided in Fig. 12.2.

The model in Fig. 12.2 assumes that as customer perceptions of transaction complexity increases, they will require access to a higher number of channel provision options and an increasing level of involvement by service provider employees. Those organizations that find their analysis of provision reveals that they are positioned along the diagonal in the matrix can conclude that they have achieved the goal of matching the number of channel provision options to customer expectations. Those organizations positioned below the diagonal will need to examine how service channel provision can be improved so that customers are provided with a level of channel choice compatible with their perceptions of transaction complexity. If an organization finds the analysis reveals that it is positioned above the diagonal, then they can actually save operating costs by reducing the degree of channel choice offered to customers.

On the basis of the factors of influence shown in Table 12.1, it seems reasonable to suggest than as customer requirements move from a transactional to a relationship orientation, a service provider will need increasingly to complement automated on-line service provision with access to service delivery by employees. In the case of banking, Young (1999) suggests that in the next few years the main focus of new technology exploitation will be directed at developing a seamless service by integrating Internet and call centre technologies. A typical scenario would be an Internet site providing basic information, an automated banking transactions services and a 'call me' button. The customer facing problems or needing more detailed

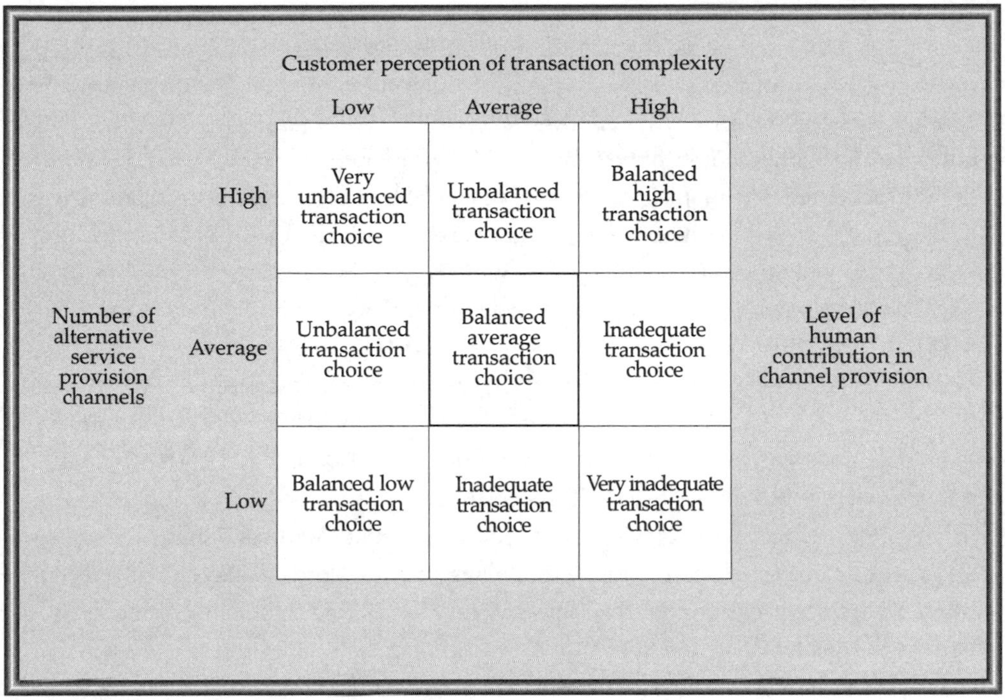

Figure 12.2 *An e-commerce service provision matrix*

information would use the call facility to be automatically routed, via the same line as the Internet connection using Voice-over Internet protocol (VoIP), to a bank employee. Voice degradation over the Internet is a major obstacle to the use of VoIP, so at the moment customers seeking human help tend to be offered a 'call me back' button. Here again there is a technology constraint, namely that for the system to work effectively the customer needs two telephone lines, one for the telephone, the other for the Internet. Dannenburg and Kellner (1998) express similar views on the evolution of technology that can satisfy the needs of both transactional and relationship-oriented

Table 12.1 *Factors influencing the service style decision*

Factor	Range of responses to factors	
	Transactional customer orientation	**Relationship customer orientation**
Service product need	Standard solutions	New, innovative solutions
Business environment	Predictable, stable	Changing, unstable
Service delivery technology	Simple	Complex
Company's closeness to customer orientation	Low	High
Company's service solution orientation	Established, well known	Applying new approaches
Average skills of workforce	Adequate for executing standard tasks	Capable of executing complex tasks
Managerial orientation	Directive	Delegative

In Europe, the Scandinavian banks were much earlier into Internet banking than their counterparts elsewhere in Europe (Brown-Humes 2000). A key reason for this is that their customers are early adopters of new technology. The region, for example, has one of the highest penetration of mobile telephones (no doubt due to the presence there of two leading manufacturers of mobile telephones, Nokia and Ericsson) and Internet usage is high, due to widespread computer ownership.

PC banking was launched in Finland as early as 1984, and the first Internet trades were made in 1988. The Nordic banks perceived the Internet as an opportunity, not a threat. Their focus has been on using the technology not to persuade customers to switch to them, but as a platform for enhancing services offered to existing customers. MeritaNordbanken, the Swedish–Finnish bank, has 1.1 million Internet customers out of a total customer-base of 6.5 million. On-line customers can check their accounts, switch money between accounts, apply for loans, pay bills, and buy and sell shares.

To encourage customers to migrate to the Internet, the Nordic banks charge a fee for using branch services, but offer the same service at no charge to on-line customers. It is also much cheaper to use the Internet for share trading. SEB, for example, offers a 50 per cent discount on share trading commission if customers opt to trade on-line. To date, the Nordic banks have been unable to demonstrate that the adoption of new technology has significantly reduced operating costs or increased revenues. However, the move has resulted in branches becoming centres for advice rather than a location for customer transactions. At MeritaNordbanken, for example, the Internet has permitted a reduction in the number of branches by two thirds over the last eight years. There is also some evidence to suggest that the revenue per Internet customer is higher than that generated by traditional, off-line, customers.

customers. In their view, however, the next really important advance in this area will be the use of picture telephony and videoconferencing to upgrade the quality of human intervention in the on-line customer–supplier interaction process.

● New Organizational Forms

In an excellent review of the myths surrounding the management of services, Zeithmal and Bitner (1996) propose that, contrary to popular belief, it is feasible simultaneously to deliver lower cost outputs and maximize personalization and customization of customer services. Achieving these joint goals, however, demands both the creative use of leading-edge technologies and the acceptance of new, entrepreneurial organizational configurations.

Quinn and Paquette (1990) argue that it is merely strategic dogma that conflicts exist between low cost and high flexibility in service sector scenarios. In their view, the secret

Banks and Parcel Delivery Firms Facing a Channel Threat?

In Japan, convenience stores are used by their customers to pay routine bills, and to collect delivered goods. Ito-Yokado Corporation, a retailing giant that owns the 7-Eleven chain in Japan and 72 per cent of the US 7-Eleven operation, has been experimenting with installing in its Japanese stores ATM machines linked to the Internet. These personal transaction terminals offer both financial services and a product delivery system (Fulford 2000).

The success of the initial experiment has caused the company to start testing the concept in 250 stores in the Dallas–Forth Worth area of Texas. Customers will be able to use the machines to pay bills, cash cheques, wire money to people and purchase tickets for entertainment events and travel. The next step in the planned programme is that websites will be able to use the 7-Eleven distribution network to deliver their on-line customers' orders to local stores. As well as reducing shipping costs, the service will be a real boon to those at work, who are unable to be at home to accept delivery of products. Evidence from experiments with the concept in Japan have already demonstrated market appeal. For example, at Esbooks, a Japanese on-line bookstore, 93 per cent of customers elected to have purchases shipped to their nearest 7-Elevens instead of delivered to their homes.

Bowen and Lawler (1992) posit that the appropriateness of a service philosophy is a contingency issue: an industrialization or empowerment orientation will be dependent upon the market in which the company operates and the influence of overall corporate strategy on the selection of appropriate internal organizational processes. By building upon their views it is possible in Table 12.1 to define factors that may have influence over determining which are likely to be the most effective service products and/or delivery processes for achieving the goal of customer satisfaction.

lies in (1) designing service systems as micro-units located close to the customer (for example the insurance advisor using a laptop-based project costing system to execute an on-site review of a manufacturing company's need for coverage appropriate to current trading circumstances) and (2) using technology to permit inexperienced people to perform very sophisticated tasks (for example front-line staff in a travel agency using on-line reservations systems to create complex, customized holiday packages). In the process of achieving these goals, the organization will probably recognize that new organizational forms are now demanded in order to optimize employee productivity.

Computer-based information systems appear to offer virtually limitless control operatives by supervisors. This means that on-line service organizations can safely consider moving to create 'infinitely flat' organizations in which authority is delegated to the lowest possible level, and all employees are empowered to make the best possible decision to satisfy changing customer needs. Federal Express, for example, has over 42 000 employees in more than 300 cities world-wide, but has a maximum of only five organizational layers between operatives and senior management.

> ### Hall-Kimbrell
>
> One approach to the process of optimizing productivity and reducing costs is simultaneously to exploit both technology and customer involvement. Hall-Kimbrell is an environmental services consulting business (Solomon 1989) that faced the problem of how to reduce costs for smaller clients of standard environmental audits. Clients are now sent a videotape covering the relevant environmental regulations and an accompanying detailed questionnaire. Hall-Kimbrell analyse the survey data electronically and automatically generate a report specifying areas in which the client must take action in order to comply with relevant regulations.

Co-ordination of service provision activities is achieved by permitting all employees to have access to computerized management information systems.

As large international organizations, such as accounting and consultancy firms offering complex client-specific services, act to sustain localized customer contact by opening offices around the world, the problems of updating staff on technological advances, and thereby sustaining leading-edge service quality, becomes an ever increasing problem. Fortunately, the advent of technologies such Lotus Notes (a software application allowing comprehensive communication) and videoconferencing has permitted these organizations to re-orient themselves into networked structures that use electronic media to ensure the dispersed nodes of their service operation can continually remain in touch with each other. Once an organization has created such internal systems, it does not require much of a leap in strategic thinking to extend the system to service the needs of clients. Ernst and Young (*www.ey.com*), for example, has created an on-line service for small companies that is capable of answering questions on issues such as how to train employees, the issues associated with letters of credit and the tracking of items through a continuous process manufacturing line. (Cavanaugh 1996). E-mailed queries are screened electronically, and routed to a 'knowledge provider', who is assigned the responsibility of responding within a specified time. The system also features a news clippings service and a frequently asked questions (FAQ) database that can be accessed for more immediate information.

● Summary

The growing importance of the service sector as a contributor to GNP in developed economies has resulted over the last two decades in an increasing interest in evolving marketing theories appropriate for the management of service products. Service goods exhibit specific characteristics, such as intangibility and perishability. These have significant influence over the implementation of sector marketing strategies. The advent of the Internet in sectors such as retailing and financial services has contributed to the commoditization of many service products. To overcome the impact of this trend, many service firms are seeking to differentiate themselves from competition by adding additional value to their on-line service offerings. The other critical factor in service markets is the influence of customer perceptions over the quality of delivered services. Effective on-line operations demand that firms identify potential gaps in service quality and ensure that delivered services exceed customer expectations.

STUDY QUESTIONS

1 What are the characteristics of service markets?

2 Why is the Internet likely to cause commoditization in some service markets?

3 How can an understanding of service gap theory be used to determine whether on-line customers are receiving an excellent level of service?

Case: *The Changing World of Banking*

Even at the end of the 1990s, in the UK the primary channel for the delivery of banking services to small companies remains the traditional local branch. Nevertheless, the following data from the Building Societies Association does suggest a declining use of branches in the delivery of services:

Delivery Channel	1995	1998
Bank branches	65%	50%
ATMs	23%	28%
Home banking	4%	8%
Telephone banking	3%	3%
Other	5%	8%

To a large degree this trend can probably be explained by the fact that over recent years the major UK high street banks have sought to reduce operating costs by closing many smaller branches. For example, at the start of the 1990s the total number of branches operated by Barclays, HSBC, Lloyds TSB and NatWest was 12 000. By the end of the decade the figure had fallen to 8000. However, at the same time there has been rapid growth in electronic service delivery channels such as ATMs, PC , Internet and telephone banking.

This change in service delivery has been driven both by the need to reduce operating costs and by a desire to use new technology to offer customers access to 24-hour, 365-day-a-year service. Unfortunately, the trends may be detrimental to small companies, which often require intensive cash handling services in their day-to-day running. They also rely on their banker having an in-depth knowledge of their business, and expect regular one-to-one contact. These two factors are seen by some as a limits on the potential for traditional branches to be replaced by alternative channels in the small business sector.

The increasing number of ATMs, which by 1999 had reached 26 000, with 6000 located at sites other than branches, has been seen to benefit small companies. Furthermore, the opening of self-service kiosks that allow customers to withdraw money and deposit cheques or cash has reduced the need for small companies to visit branches. Telephone banking is also becoming more attractive to those small companies that require service outside normal banking hours.

PC banking, and more recently Internet banking, allows small businesses instant access to accounts, and all banks can be expected to offer on-line banking services to small business customers in the near future. A significant catalyst for this trend is that nearly half of UK small companies now have access to the Internet, and this figure is expected to continue to grow over the next three years.

The traditional UK banks need to recognize, however, that other organizations are casting envious eyes over the small business market. The UK Post Office offers a basic corporate banking service through an alliance with the Alliance and Leicester. The former building societies (the equivalent of savings and loans organizations in the US) have extensive branch networks, and are beginning to offer a limited range of services to small businesses. Supermarket chains, although currently limiting their services to consumer banking, are known to be researching the small business market. This same trend can be expected in the case of the new e-banking organizations entering the UK market.

Source: Bank of England (2000)

QUESTIONS

1 What are the current trends in the UK banking market?

2 Compared to the personal banking sector, what are the additional services required by small firms? (Developing an answer to this question may be helped by a visit to some UK banks to obtain promotional materials on services offered to small companies.)

3 Assume you are the Small Companies Marketing Manager for a traditional bank. Prepare a report for the Board on how electronic banking services can be used in the future to enhance the delivery of services to small company customers.

Case: *On-Line Retail Strategies*

Over the last few years, the leading UK supermarket chains have all entered the world of e-commerce by offering customers an on-line shopping service. Verdict Research forecasts that in five years this market will be worth £2.3bn, but that virtually all of these sales will come from consumers reducing store visits and purchasing an increasing proportion of grocery products via the Internet. Currently, however, it does appear that UK retailers are using very different strategies to service the needs of on-line shoppers.

Tesco is the largest supermarket chain, and currently uses 100 of its stores, mainly in the south east of England, as the base from which to service the needs of on-line customers. Using its existing store base, Tesco believes it can avoid building new order-picking centres and be able to offer customers the store's entire range of almost 25 000 products.

Sainsbury, the UK number two food retailer, has opened a warehouse in Park Royal, North London dedicated to on-line order-picking. The warehouse will stock 15 000 products for Sainsbury's Orderline telephone, fax and Internet service. The company has restricted the operation to customers in the London area. It believes that a dedicated warehouse is the only way to ensure high service levels.

Asda, the UK's number three supermarket, operates its Asda@Home service from picking centres in Croydon and Watford. Two further centres are due to be built in the south east of England by the end of 2000, and 11 more are planned for a national roll-out over the next three-to-five years. Like Sainsbury, the company thinks that dedicated warehouse operations are the only way to service on-line customer needs.

Safeway, the number four supermarket chain, has a very different operating model. It does not offer either on-line ordering or home delivery. Instead, the company operates a customer collection service from eight stores, with ordering via telephone or fax. At its Basingstoke store and Hayes head office, shoppers can purchase any of its 22 000 products using a hand-held computer that uses Safeway's Easi-Order software. Over the longer term, the company plans to make Easi-Order available via digital TV and mobile telephones, but has no plans to offer a home delivery service.

Somerfields has supplemented its '24–7' telephone and fax home shopping facility with Open, an interactive satellite TV service that offers a choice of a 2200 products. The company is testing the provision of an Internet shopping service that will be supported by the opening of new order-picking warehouses. The plan is to offer a national home delivery service within two-to-three years.

Iceland was the first supermarket chain to offer national Internet ordering and free home delivery on 2750 products, subject to a minimum spend of £40. Other retailers charge somewhere between £3.50 and £5 for home delivery. The company makes about 10 000 home deliveries per week to service in-store, telephone and on-line orders. Order picking is done at local stores. Waitrose, a John Lewis subsidiary, offers delivery of more than 10 000 lines, but to workplace carparks rather than homes. The company's view is that home delivery is not an economically viable proposition.

Source: Stewart (2000)

QUESTIONS

1 Compare and contrast the differing strategies of UK supermarkets. Use the materials in the above case, supplemented by visits to the relevant supermarket websites (*www.j-sainsbury.co.uk; www.tesco.co.uk; www.asda.co.uk; www.safeway.co.uk; www.somerfield.co.uk; www.iceland.co.uk; www.waitrose.com*).

2 Prepare a report that determines the most effective strategy through which a supermarket chain can optimize the provision of a high quality service to on-line shoppers.

Chapter 12 Glossary

External marketing (p. 278)

The normal formal processes associated with the management of the four Ps.

Inseparability (p. 269)

The fact that many services are simultaneously produced and consumed.

Intangibility (p. 267)

That the item cannot be touched, smelt, seen or tasted.

Interactive marketing (p. 278)

The activities which occur at the buyer–seller interface.

Internal marketing (p. 278)

The internal processes associated with ensuring that all aspects of the business operation, including automated, computer-based systems are (1) customer-conscious and (2) supportive of a philosophy that every action is oriented towards achieving total customer satisfaction.

Variability (p. 269)

The fact that no two offerings of the same service will ever be identical because both customer needs and employee abilities differ.

References

Chapter 1 References

Adler, C. (1999), 'Going online, don't sacrifice marketing for technology', *Fortune*, 25 October, pp. 358–359.

Andersen Consulting (1999), 'Study finds European business at crossroads of e-commerce', **www.ac.ac.com**/showcase/ecommerce/ecom_estudy98.html

Anon. (1997), 'In search of the perfect market', *The Economist* (US), 10 May, pp. 3–5.

Anon. (2000), 'A thinker's guide', *The Economist*, 1 April, pp. 64–68.

Bicknell, D. (2000), 'E-commerce outpaces strategy', *Computer Weekly*, 24 February, pp. 20–21.

Boston Consulting Group (1999), 'Online retailing to reach $36 Billion', **www.bcg.com**/features/shop/main_shop.html.

Brooker, K. (1999), 'E-rivals seem to have Home Depot awfully nervous', *Fortune*, 8 August, pp. 28–29.

Churbuck, D. (1995), 'Where's the money?' *Forbes*, 30 January, pp. 100–105.

Cross, R. and Smith, J. (1995), 'Internet marketing that works for customers', *Direct Marketing*, vol. 58, no 4, pp. 22–25.

Eckman, M. (1996), 'Are you ready to do business on the Internet?' *Journal of Accountancy*, vol. 181, no 1, pp. 10–11.

Gielgud, R.E. (1998), *How to Succeed in Internet Business by Employing Real-World Strategies*, Actium Publishing, New York.

Gurley, J.W. (1998), 'Above the crowd: creating a great e-commerce business', *Fortune*, 16 March.

Internet Indicators (1999), 'The Internet economy indicators', **www.internetindicators.com**/features.html, 22 June, pp. 1–5.

McGovern, J.M. (1998), 'Logistics on the internet', *Transportation & Distribution*, vol. 39, no 7, pp. 68–72.

Mintzberg, H. (1994), *The Rise and Fall of Strategic Planning*, Prentice Hall, Englewood Cliffs, New Jersey.

Mintzberg, H. and Waters, J.A. (1982), 'Tracking study in an entrepreneurial firm', *Academy of Management Journal*, vol. XXV, no 3, pp. 465–499.

Poniewozik, J. (1998), 'Its not just a breath mint', *Fortune*, 17 August, pp. 40–41.

Romano, C. (1995), 'The new gold rush?' *Management Review*, November, pp. 119–124.

Seybold, P.B. and Marshak, R.T. (1998), *Customer.com: How to Create a Profitable Business Strategy for the Internet and Beyond*, Random House, New York.

Sugar, A. (1999), 'Show us the money', *Computer Weekly*, 4 March, pp. 34–35.

Chapter 2 References

Anon. (1998a), *The Economist*, 21 March, pp. 78–81.

Anon. (1998b), 'Cisco exploits Web sales channels to net mega savings', *Computer Weekly*, 26 March, p. 4.

Anon. (1999), 'The privacy lobby is starting to sting', *Business Week*, 15 November, pp. 57–58.

Anon. (2000), 'Babes in virtual toyland', *Business Week*, 13 March, pp. 62–64.

Booth, E. (1999), 'Will the web replace the telephone?' *Marketing*, 4 February, pp. 25–27.

Browning, B. (1999), 'Electronic commerce tutorial', *Web Developers Journal*, 2 September, www.webdevelopersjournal.com/columns/ecommerce3.html

Chaston, I. (1999), *New Marketing Strategies*, Sage, London.

East, R. (1990), *Changing Consumer Behaviour*, Cassell, London.

Engel, J.F., Blackwell, R.D. and Miniard, P.W. (1986), *Consumer Behaviour*, 5th ed., Dryden Press, Chicago.

Friel, D. (1999), 'Electronic commerce on the Web: digital drivers for 1999', *Business Economics*, January, pp. 67–69.

Ford, D. (1990), *Understanding Business Markets: Interaction Relationships and Networks*, Academic Press, London.

Garton, S. (1999), 'Global medium, global measure: an assessment of Internet users across and within regions of the world', *Marketing and Research Today*, Esomar, vol. 28, no 2, pp. 77–83.

Hicks, M. (1999), 'A matter of trust', *PC Week*, 25 October, pp. 67–68

Hunt, S.D. and Morgan, R.M. (1994), 'The commitment–trust theory of relationship marketing', *Journal of Marketing*, vol. 58, July, pp. 20–38

Judge, P.C. (1998), 'Are tech buyers different?' *Business Week*, 26 January, p. 65.

Kafka, P. (2000), 'Talk is cheap', *Forbes*, 17 April, pp. 150–151.

Kover, A. and Warner, M. (1999), 'Who's reading your e-mail?' *Fortune*, 3 February, pp. 56–62.

Kreps, D.M. (1996), 'Corporate culture and economic theory' in Buckley, P.J. and Mitchie, J. (eds) *Firms, Organisations and Contracts*, Oxford University Press, Oxford, pp. 221–275.

Kristensen, K., Matensen, A. and Gronholdt, L. (1999), *Total Quality Management*, July, pp. 602–616.

McHugh, J. (2000), 'Hall of mirrors', *Forbes*, 7 February, pp. 120–121.

Mardesich, J. (1999), 'E-shopping nightmare', **Fortune.com**, 3 November, www.pathfinder.com.fortune/technology/daily

Mohr, J. and Nevin, J.R. (1990), 'Communication strategies in marketing channels: a theoretical perspective', *Journal of Marketing*, vol. 54, October, pp. 36–51.

Munch, A. and Hunt, S.D. (1984), 'Consumer Involvement: Definition Issues and Research Directions' in Kinear, T. (ed.), *Advances in Consumer Research*, vol. 11, Association for Consumer Research, Provo, Utah, pp. 1–56.

Olsen, S. (2000), 'Fogdog email hounds customers' friends', **Cnetnews.com**, 15 March, 2.20 p.m.

Robinson, P.J., Faris, C.W. and Wind, Y. (1967), *Industrial Buying and Creative Marketing*, Allyn & Bacon, Boston.

S.R.I. Consulting (1998), 'iVALS segments', **www.future.sri.com**.

Sefton, D. (2000), 'Teen girls feel the Net effect sites let them feel like somebody is listening', *USA Today*, 14 March, pp. 3D–4D.

Seybold, P.B. and Marshak, R.T. (1998), *Customer.com: How to Create a Profitable Business Strategy for the Internet and Beyond*, Random House, New York.

Spar, D. and Bussgang, J. (1996), 'Ruling the net', *Harvard Business Review*, May–June, pp. 125–133.

Sterrett, C. and Shah, A. (1998), 'Going global on the information super highway', *SAM Advanced Management Journal*, vol. 63, no 1, pp. 43–49.

Strauss, G. (2000), 'Crop of start-ups compete to recruit military Web surfers', *USA Today*, 15 March, pp. 10b.

Webster, F.E. (1963), 'Modelling the industrial buying process', *Journal of Marketing Research*, vol. 2, no 3, pp. 251–260.

Webster, F.E. and Wind, Y. (1972), *Organizational Buying Behaviour*, Prentice Hall, Englewood Cliffs, NJ.

Weinberg, N. (1996), 'Getting granny to surf the Net', *Forbes*, 6 May, no 9, pp. 119–120.

Werner, T. (1999), 'EDI meets the Internet', *Transportation and Distribution*, vol. 40, no 6, pp. 36–41.

Chapter 3 References

Anon. (1998), 'Traveller's Aid', *Fortune*, Summer Special, 6 June, pp. 233–239.

Anon., (1999a), 'Net stock rules: masters of the parallel universe', *Fortune*, 7 June, pp. 66–73.

Anon., (1999b), 'Sporting goods in the North Woods', *Business Week*, 24 May, p. 20.

Anon. (2000), 'First America, then the world', *Business Week*, 26 February, pp. 159–162.

Baer, W.S. (1998), 'Will the Internet bring electronic services to the home?' *Business Strategy Review*, vol. 9, no 1, pp. 29–37.

Benjamin, R. and Wigand, R. (1995), 'Electronic markets and virtual value chains on the information superhighway', *Sloan Management Review*, Winter, pp. 62–72.

Bloch, M., Pigneur, R., and Segev, A. (1996), 'On the road to electronic commerce: A business value, framework, gaining competitive advantage and some research issues', **www.stern.nyu.edu/-mbloch/docs/roadtoec/ec.htm**.

Chen, A. and Hicks, M. (2000), 'Going global? Avoid culture clashes', *PC Week*, 3 April, pp. 65–67.

Hamel, G. and Sampler, J. (1998), 'The E-Corporation', *Fortune*, 7 December, pp. 80–81.

Hatlesstad, L. (2000), 'Can the Web fix education?' *Red Herring*, March, pp. 130–143.

James, D. (1999), 'Merr-e Christmas!' *Marketing News*, 8 November, pp. 1–3.

Jaworski, B., Kohli, A.K. and Sahay, A. (2000), 'Market-driven versus driving markets', *Journal of the Academy of Marketing Science*, vol. 28, no 1, pp. 45–54.

Kalin, S. (1998), 'Conflict resolution', *CIO Web Business*, February, pp. 28–36.

Kleindl, B. (1999), 'Competitive dynamics and opportunities for SMEs in the virtual market place', *Proceedings of the AMA Entrepreneurship SIG, University of Illinois at Chicago*, Chicago, pp. 21–27.

Kotler, P. (1997), *Marketing Management: Analysis, Planning, Implementation and Control*, 9th ed., Prentice Hall, Upper Saddle River, NJ.

Porter, M.E. (1980), *Competitive Strategy: Techniques for Analysing Industries and Competition*, The Free Press, New York,

Puente, M. (2000), 'Art discovers the Internet', *USA Today*, 10 January, pp. 5–6.

Rosato, D. and Khan, S. (2000), 'Net surfing nets savings for business travellers', *USA Today*, 7 March, pp. 3b–4B.

Sandovai, G. (2000), 'Drinks.com works around intrastate sales laws', **Cnetnews.com**, 15 March, 1.20 p.m.

Storey, J. (ed.) (1994), *New Wave Manufacturing Strategies: Organisational and Human Resource Management Dimensions*, Paul Chapman Publishing, London.

Weinberg, N. (2000), 'Not.coms', *Forbes*, 17 April, pp. 424–425.

Chapter 4 References

Anderson, J.C. and Narus, J.A. (1991), 'Partnering as a focused market strategy', *California Management Review*, Spring, pp. 95–113.

Anon. (1999a), 'Inside IBM: Internet business machines', *Business Week*, 13 December, pp. 20–24.

Anon. (1999b), 'Barriers in e-commerce', *Today* (New York), 6 August, pp. 8–9.

Bartholomew, D. (2000), 'Service to order', *Industry Week*, 3 April, pp. 19–20.

Berry, L.L. (1982), 'Relationship Marketing' in Berry, L.L., Shostack, G.L. and Upah, G.D. (eds), *Emerging Perspectives on Service Marketing*, American Marketing Association, Chicago, pp. 25–28.

Brickau, R. (1994), 'Responding to the Single Market: A comparative study of UK and German food firms', unpublished PhD dissertation, University of Plymouth.

Burns, P. (1994), 'Keynote Address', *Proceedings of the 17th ISBA Sheffield Conference*, ISBA, Leeds.

Chaston, I. (1999a), *New Marketing Strategies*, Sage, London.

Chaston, I. (1999b), *Entrepreneurial Marketing*, MacMillan Business, London.

Chaston, I. and Mangles, T. (1997), 'Core capabilities as predictors of growth potential in small manufacturing firms', *Journal of Small Business Management*, vol. 35, no 1, pp. 47–57.

Coopers & Lybrand, (1994), *Made in the UK: The Middle Market Survey*, Coopers & Lybrand, London.

Ghosh (1998), 'Making sense of the Internet', *Harvard Business Review*, March–April, pp. 127–135.

Goddard, J. (1997), 'The architecture of core competence', *Business Strategy Review*, vol. 8, no 1, pp. 43–53.

Gronroos, C. (1994), 'From marketing mix to relationship marketing', *Journal of Academic Marketing Science*, vol. 23, no 4, pp. 252–254.

Grossman, L.M. (1993), 'Federal Express, UPS face off over computers', *Wall Street Journal*, 17 September, pp. B1.

Gummesson, E. (1987), 'The new marketing: Developing long-term interactive relationships', *Long Range Planning*, vol. 20, no 4, pp. 10–20.

Harrington, A. and Solovar, G. (1998), 'America's most admired companies', *Fortune*, 2 March, pp. 70–74.

Hitt, M.A. and Ireland, R.D. (1985), 'Corporate distinctive competence, strategy, industry and performance', *Strategic Management Journal*, vol. 6, pp. 273–293.

Hornell, E. (1992), *Improving Productivity for Competitive Advantage: Lessons from the Best in the World*, Pitman, London.

Internet Indicators (1999), 'The Internet economy indicators', **www.internetindicators.com**/ features.html, 22 June, pp. 1–5.

Jackson, B.B. (1985), *Winning and Keeping Industrial Customers: The Dynamics of Customer Relationships*, D.C. Heath, Lexington, MA.

Lindsay, V., (1990), *Export Manufacturing: Framework For Success*, New Zealand Trade Development Board, Wellington.

Mahoney, J.T. and Pandian, J.R. (1992), 'The resource-based view within the conversation of strategic management', *Strategic Management Journal*, vol. 13, pp. 363–380.

Mardesich, J. (1999), 'The Web is no shopper's paradise', *Fortune*, 8 November, pp. 9–11.

Nevin, J.R. (1994), 'Relationship marketing and distribution channels: exploring fundamental issues', *Journal of the Academy of Marketing Science*, vol. 23, no 4, pp. 334–337.

Parasuraman, A., Zeithmal, V.A. and Berry, L.L. (1988), 'A conceptual model of service quality and its implications for future research', *Journal of Marketing*, vol. 49, Fall, pp. 34–45.

Peters, T. (1992), *Liberation Management*, A.F. Knopf, New York.

Prahalad, C.K. and Hamel, G. (1990), 'The core competence of the corporation', *Harvard Business Review*, May–June, pp. 79–91.

Reichfeld, F.F. and Sasser, W. (1990), 'Zero defections: quality comes to services', *Harvard Business Review*, September–October, pp. 301–7.

Schonberger, R.J. (1990), *Building a Chain of Customers: Linking Business Functions to Create the World Class Company*, Hutchinson, London.

Sellers, P. (1999), 'Inside the first e-christmas', *Fortune*, 1 February, pp. 52–55.

Seybold, P.B. and Marshak, R.T. (1998), *Customer.com: How to Create a Profitable Business Strategy for the Internet and Beyond*, Random House, New York.

Shapiro, C. and Varian, H.R. (1999), *Information Rules*, Harvard Business School Press, Boston, MA.

Tedlow, R.S., (1990), *New and Improved: The Story of Mass Marketing in America*, Heinemann, Oxford.

Webster, F.E. (1992), 'The changing role of marketing in the corporation', *Journal of Marketing*, vol. 56, October, pp. 1–17.

Young, K.M., El Sawy, O.A, Malhotra, A. and Gosain, S. (1997), 'The relentless pursuit of "Free Perfect Now": IT enabled value innovation at Marshall Industries', 1997 SIM International Papers Award Competition, **www.simnet.ord**/public/programs/capital/97papers/paper1.html.

Chapter 5 References

Anderson, J.C. and Narus, J.A. (1991), 'Partnering as a focused market strategy', *California Management Review*, Spring, pp. 95–113.

Anon. (1999), 'The information gold mine', *Business Week*, 26 July, pp. 10–12.

Anon. (2000), 'All yours', *The Economist*, 1 April, pp. 57–61.

Baker, S and Baker, K. (1998), 'Mind over matter', *Journal of Business Strategy*, vol. 19, no 4, pp. 22–27.

Bird, J. (1999), 'Time to get real and get out there with the big boys', E-Business supplement, *Sunday Times*, 14 November, pp. 8–9.

Bonoma, T.V. and Shapiro, B.P. (1983), *Segmenting the Industrial Market*, Lexington Books, Lexington, MA.

Chaston, I. (1999), *New Marketing Strategies*, Sage, London

Christensen, C.M. and Tedlow, R.S. (2000), 'Patterns of disruption in retailing', *Harvard Business Review*, January–February, pp. 42–46.

Garvin, D.A. (1987), 'Competing on the 8 dimensions of quality', *Harvard Business Review*, November–December, pp. 101–109.

Glazer, R. (1999), 'Winning in smart markets', *Sloan Management Review*, vol. 40, no 4, pp. 59–73.

Haley, R.J. (1963), 'Benefit segmentation: a decision orientated research tool', *Journal of Marketing*, July, pp. 30–35.

Hammer, M. and Champy, J. (1993), *Re-engineering the Corporation: A Manifesto for Business Revolution*, HarperCollins, New York.

Harari, O. (1997), 'Closing around the customer', *Management Review*, vol. 86, no 11, pp. 29–34.

Kotler, P. (1999), *Marketing Management: The Millennium Edition*, Prentice Hall, Upper Saddle River, NJ.

Marsh, H. (1999), 'Children's choice', *Marketing*, 15 July, pp. 27–29.

Noto, A. (2000), 'Vertical vs. broadline e-retailers: Which will survive?' **Cnetnews.com**, 2 March.

Porter, M. (1985), *Competitive Advantage: Creating and Sustaining Superior Performance*, The Free Press, San Francisco.

Porter, M. and Miller, V.E. (1985), 'How information technology gives you competitive advantage', *Harvard Business Review*, July–August, pp. 149–160.

Robertson, T.S. and Barich, H. (1992), 'A successful approach to segmenting industrial markets', *Journal of Marketing*, December, pp. 5–11.

Stackpole, B. (1999), 'A foothold on the Web: Industry-specific Net markets', *PC Week*, 10 May, pp. 78–80.

Tedlow, R.S., (1990), *New and Improved: The Story of Mass Marketing in America*, Heinemann, Oxford.

Vowler, J. (1999), *Computer Weekly*, 14 October, pp. 28–33.

Chapter 6 References

Anon. (1997), 'Relaunching Organics', *Marketing*, 17 April, p. 4.

Anon. (2000), 'Reuters', *The Economist*, 12 February, pp. 67–71.

Bradbury, D. (1999), '10 steps to e-business', *Computer Weekly*, 28 October, pp. 42–43.

Chaston, I. (1996), 'Critical events and process gaps in the D.T.I. SME structured networking model', *International Small Business Journal*, vol. 14, no 3, pp. 71–84.

Day, G.S. (1994), 'The capabilities of market-driven organisations', *Journal of Marketing*, vol. 58, no 4, pp. 37–53.

Hamel, G. and Prahalad (1994), *Competing for the Future: Breakthrough Strategies for Seizing Control of your Industry and Creating the Markets of Tomorrow*, Harvard Business School Press, Boston, MA.

Hunt, S.D. and Morgan, R.M. (1995), 'The comparative advantage theory of competition', *Journal of Marketing*, vol. 59, no 2, pp. 1–15.

Hunt, S.D. and Morgan, R.M. (1996), 'The resource-advantage theory of competition: dynamics, path dependencies and evolutionary dimensions', *Journal of Marketing*, vol. 60, no 4, pp. 107–115.

Jarillo, J.C. (1993), *Strategic Networks: Creating the Borderless Organization*, Butterworth-Heinemann, Oxford.

Kobayashi, K. (1986), *Computers and Communication: A Vision of C&C*, translation, MIT Press, Cambridge, MA.

Leibs, S. (2000), 'World of difference', *Industry Week*, 7 February, pp. 23–25.

Porter, M. (1985), *Competitive Advantage: Creating and Sustaining Superior Performance*, The Free Press, San Francisco.

Chapter 7 References

Anon. (1999a), 'PC makers think beyond the box', *Business Week*, 19 April, pp. 148–152.

Anon. (1999b), 'Beyond the PC', *Business Week*, 8 March , pp. 78–85.

Anon. (2000a), 'E-bonds, licensed to kill', *The Economist*, 15 January, pp. 73–74.

Anon. (2000b), 'The new Intel', *Business Week*, 13 March, pp. 110–114.

Bowonder, B. and Miyake, T. (1992), 'A model of corporate innovation management: Some recent high tech innovations in Japan', *R&D Management*, vol. 22, no 3, pp. 319–336.

Buzan, T. (1993), *The Mindmap Book*, BBC Publications, London.

Chaston, I. (1999), *New Marketing Strategies*, Sage Publications, London.

Christensen, C.M. (1997), *The Innovator's Dilemma: When New Technologies Cause Great Firms to Fail*, Harvard Press, Boston, MA.

Cooper, R.G. (1975), 'Why new industrial products fail', *Industrial Marketing Management*, vol. 4, pp. 315–326.

Cooper, R.G. (1986), *Winning at New Products*, Wesley, Reading, MA.

Cooper, R.G. (1988), 'The new product process: a decision guide for managers', *Journal of Marketing Management*, vol. 3, no 3, pp. 255–285.

Cooper, R.G. (1990), 'Stage-gate systems: A new tool for managing new products', *Business Horizons*, vol. 33, no 3, pp. 44–54.

Cooper, R.G. (1994), 'Third-generation new product processes', *Journal of Product Innovation Management*, vol. 11, pp. 3–14.

Cooper, R.G. and Kleinschmidt, E.J. (1990), *New Products: The Key Factors of Success*, American Marketing Association, Chicago.

Crawford, C.M. (1994), *New Products Management*, 4th ed., Irwin, Burr Ridge, IL.

Fisher, A. (2000), 'Here's your complete guide to getting MP3', *Web Guide*, vol. 3, no 6, pp. 32–34.

Gatignon, H. and Robertson, T.S. (1985), 'A proposition inventory for new diffusion research', *Journal of Consumer Research*, March, pp. 849–867.

Heldey, B. (1977), 'Strategy and the business portfolio', *Long Range Planning*, February, pp. 1–14.

Klein, K.J. and Sorra, J.S. (1996), 'The challenge of innovation implementation', *Academy of Science Review*, vol. 21, no 4, pp. 1055–1081.

Moore, G.A. (1991), *Crossing the Chasm*, HarperBusiness, New York.

Nanaka, C. and Sivakumar, K. (1996), 'National culture and new product development: an integrative review', *Journal of Marketing*, vol. 60, no 1, pp. 61–73.

Reed, M. (2000), 'Why the future might be wireless', *Marketing*, 3 February, pp. 22–24.

Robinson, W.T. and Fornell, C. (1985), 'Sources of market pioneer advantage in consumer goods industries', *Journal of Marketing Research*, August, pp. 305–17.

Rogers, M. (1983), *Diffusion of Innovation*, Free Press, New York.

Schaffer, R.A. (2000), 'The Internet's new revolution photography', *Fortune*, 20 March, pp. 222–223.

Chapter 8 References

Alexander, G. (1999), 'Advertising fever grips e-commerce', Business Section, *Sunday Times*, 21 November, p. 9.

Anderson, R. (1994), *Essentials of Personal Selling: The New Professionalism*, Prentice Hall, Englewood Cliffs, NJ.

Anon. (1999a), 'To the victors belong the ads', *Business Week*, 4 October, p. 39.

Anon. (1999b), 'Advertising that clicks', *The Economist*, 9 October, pp. 71–75.

Berthon, P. (1996), 'Marketing communication and the world wide web', *Business Horizons*, vol. 39, no 5, pp. 24–33.

Briggs, R. and Hollis, N. (1997), 'Advertising on the Web: is there response before click-through', *Journal of Advertising Research*, vol. 37, no 2, pp. 33–46.

Brown, E. (1999), 'The silicon valley heart of internet advertising: DoubleClick has made itself a key player in Madison Avenue's hottest niche', *Fortune*, 6 December, pp. 166–170.

Campbell, L. (1999), 'Ford's US arm swaps print for Internet advertising', *Campaign*, 20 August, p. 16.

Cartellieri, C., Parsons, A.J., Rao, V. and Zeisser, M.P. (1997), 'The real impact of Internet advertising', *The McKinsey Quarterly*, Summer, no 3, pp. 44–63.

Chaston, I. (1993), *Customer-focused Marketing*, McGraw-Hill, Maidenhead.

Chaston, I. (1999), *New Marketing Strategies*, Sage, London.

Crowley, A.E. and Hoyer, W.D. (1994), 'An integrative framework for understanding two-sided persuasion', *Journal of Consumer Research*, March, pp. 44–55.

Drez, X. and Zufryden, F.(1998), 'Is Internet advertising ready for prime time?' *Journal of Advertising Research*, May–June, pp. 31–46.

Garvin, D.A. (1987), 'Competing on the eight dimensions of quality', *Harvard Business Review*, November–December, pp. 101–109.

Hertz, S. (1996), 'Drifting closer and drifting away in networks' in Icacobucci, D. (ed.), *Networks in Marketing*, Sage, Thousand Oaks, CA, pp. 179–204.

James, D. (2000), 'Broadband Horizons', *Marketing News*, 13 March, pp. 1–9.

Kotler, P. (1997), *Marketing Management: Analysis, Planning, Implementation and Control*, 9th ed., Prentice Hall, Upper Saddle River, NJ.

Leckenby, J.D. and Hong, J. (1998), 'Using reach/frequency for Web media planning', *Journal of Advertising Research*, vol. 38, no 1, pp. 7–23.

Leong, E.K.F., Huang, X. and Stanner, P.J. (1998), 'Comparing the effectiveness of the Web site with traditional media', *Journal of Advertising Research*, vol. 38, no 5, pp. 44–53.

Lindsay, G. (2000), 'Buying without spending', *Fortune*, 6 March, pp. 386–387.

McLuhan, R. (2000), 'A lesson in online brand promotion', *Marketing*, 23 March, pp. 31–32.

Nash, E.L. (1995), *Direct Marketing: Strategy, Planning, Execution*, 3rd ed., McGraw-Hill, New York.

Nash, R. (1994), *How to Transform Marketing Through IT*, Management Today Publications, London.

Peters, T. (1987), *Thriving on Chaos*, Alfred Knopf, New York.

Ray, M.L. (1982), *Advertising and Communications Management*, Prentice Hall, Saddle River, NJ.

Reed, M. (1999), 'Going beyond the banner ad', *Marketing*, 29 April, pp. 25–27.

Rosier, B. (1999), 'The future of FMCG.com', *Marketing*, 21 October, pp. 21–24.

Schultz, D.E., Tannenbaum, S.I. and Lauterborn, R.F. (1993), *Integrated Marketing Communications*, NTC Business Books, Lincolnwood, IL.

Stauffer, D. (1999), 'Sales strategies for the Internet age', *Harvard Business Review*, July–August, pp. 3–5.

Van De Ven, A. (1976), 'On the nature, formation and maintenance of relations among organisations', *Academy of Management Review*, October, pp. 24–36.

Wasson, C.R. (1978), *Dynamic Competitive Strategy and Product Life Cycles*, Austin Press, Austin, TA.

Wolf, J. (2000), 'Coupons and rebates', *Web Guide*, April, pp. 64–65.

Wood, L. (1998), 'Internet ad buys: what reach and frequency do they deliver?' *Journal of Advertising Research*, vol. 38, no 1, pp. 21–29.

Woolgar, T. (1998), 'Measuring the net', *Campaign*, 30 October, pp. 13–14.

Chapter 9 References

Anon. (1997), 'Going, going…on-line auctions', *The Economist*, 31 May, pp. 61–62.

Anon. (1998), 'Web commerce shopping', *Fortune*, 16 November, pp. 244–245.

Anon. (1999), 'Going, going, gone', *Business Week*, 12 April, pp. 30–31.

Anon. (2000), 'Mail order jackpot', *Start Your Own Business*, Spring, pp. 22–36.

Berry, L.L. and Yadav, M.S. (1996), 'Capture and communicate value in the pricing of services', *Sloan Management Review*, vol. 37, no 4, pp. 41–52.

Business Week (1994), 'The Schwab revolution', *Business Week*, 19 December, p. 89.

Cronin, M.J. (1997), 'To sell or not to sell on the World Wide Web', *Fortune*, 9 June, pp. 144–146.

Day, G.S. (1981), 'The product life cycle: analysis and applications issues', *Journal of Marketing*, vol. 45, Fall, pp. 60–70.

Eddy, P.(1999), 'The selfish giants', *Sunday Times* Magazine, London, 14 March, pp. 43–48.

Garda, R.A. and Marn, M.V. (1993), 'Price wars', *McKinsey Quarterly*, Summer, no 3, pp. 87–101.

Glasser, P. (2000), 'Kicking virtual tyres', *Web Guide*, April, pp. 18–24.

James, D., (2000), 'Broadband horizons', *Marketing News*, 13 March, pp. 1–9.

Kirkpatrick, D. (1998), 'Microsoft: Is your company the next meal?' *Fortune*, 27 April, pp. 92–97.

Kirkpatrick, D. (2000), 'Can Compaq be revived?' *Fortune*, 6 March, pp. 64–65.

Knol, A.S. (2000), 'Take this job and love it', *eBay Magazine*, April, pp. 47–50.

McGarvey, R. (2000), 'Connect the dots', *Entrepreneur*, March, pp. 78–82.

Moriaty, R.W. and Moran, U. (1990), 'Managing hybrid marketing systems', *Harvard Business Review*, November–December, pp. 146–155.

Nakache, P. (1998), 'Secrets of the new brand builders', *Fortune*, 22 June, pp. 167–172.

Pitt, L., Berthon, P. and Berthon, J. (1999), 'Changing channels: The impact of the Internet on distribution strategy', *Business Horizons*, vol. 42, no 2, pp. 19–34.

Pitta, J. (1998), 'Competitive shopping', *Forbes*, 9 February, pp. 92–94.

Plotkin, H. (1998), 'Art net', *Forbes*, 6 April, pp. 29–32.

Rangan, V.K., Moriaty, R.T. and Swartz, G. (1993), 'Transaction cost theory: Inferences from field research on downstream vertical integration', *Organization Science*, vol. 4, no 3, pp. 454–477.

Shapiro, C. and Varian, H.R. (1999), *Information Rules*, Harvard Business School Press, Boston, MA.

Sinha, I. (2000), 'Cost transparency: The Net's real threat to process and brands', *Harvard Business Review*, March–April, pp. 43–52.

Stern, L.W. and El-Ansary, A.I. (1988), *Marketing Channels*, 3rd ed., Prentice Hall, Englewood Cliffs, NJ.

Stross, R. (1998), 'Netscape: inside the big software giveaway', *Fortune*, 30 March, pp. 150–153.

Tetzeli, R and Puri, S. (1996), 'What's it really like to be Marc Andreessen?' *Fortune*, 12 September, pp. 34–35.

Thurm, S. (1998), 'Leading the PC pack', *Wall Street Journal*, 7 December, p. 4.

Wayne, L. (1994), 'The next giant in mutual funds?' *New York Times*, 20 March, Section 3, pp. 8–9.

Wilson, S. (1999), 'Going once, going twice', *Intelligent Business*, December, pp. 84–89.

Chapter 10 References

Anon. (1998), 'No factory is an island', *The Economist*, 20 June, pp. 8–11.

Anon. (2000), 'E-sourcing the corporation', *Fortune*, 13 March, pp. S4–S12.

Aragon, L. (1997), 'Finding middle ground', *PC Week*, 15 September, pp. 91–92.

Blyinsky, R. (1999), 'ERP, a question of delivery and promise', *PC Week*, 6 September, pp. 11–13.

Brown, S. (1998), 'Giving more jobs to electronic eyes', *Fortune*, 16 February, pp. 49–50.

Buzzell, R.D. and Ortmeyer, G. (1995), 'Channel partnerships streamline distribution', *Sloan Management Review*, vol. 36, no 3, pp. 85–97.

Davis, S.M. (1987), *Future Perfect*, Addison-Wesley, Reading, MA.

Dyck, T. (1997), 'Match made in corporate heaven', *PC Week*, 15 September, pp. 82–83.

Goldhar, J.D. and Lei, D. (1995), 'Variety is free: manufacturing in the twenty-first century', *Academy of Management Executives*, vol. 9, no 4, pp. 73–91.

Hammer, M. (1995), *The Re-engineering Revolution: The Handbook*, HarperBusiness, New York.

Hammer, M. and Champy, J. (1993), *Re-engineering the Corporation: A Manifesto for Business Revolution*, Brealey Publishing, London.

Hasek, G. (1997), 'Missing links: extranets act as bridge for online business relationships', *Industry Week*, 3 March, pp. 47–50.

Jones, T.Y. (1999), 'Looking for Nirvana', *Forbes*, 8 March, 1999, p. 15.

Kano, C and Rao, R.M. (1995), 'New management secrets from Japan', *Fortune*, 27 November, pp. 45–52.

McGrath, A. (1996), 'Managing distribution channels', *Business Quarterly*, vol. 60, no 3, pp. 56–64.

Moad, J. (1999), 'The top 100 innovators in manufacturing', *PC Week*, 9 August, pp. 59–64.

Oliver, R.W. (1999), 'ERP is dead! Long live ERP!' *Management Review*, pp. 12–17.

O'Reilly, B. (2000), 'They've got mail!' *Fortune*, 7 February, pp. 100–104.

Pender, L. and Madden, J. (2000), 'Business grapples with how to take relationships online', *PC Week*, 28 February, pp. 1–2.

Ross, P.E. 'Virtual robots', *Forbes*, 8 March 1999, p. 32.

Schonfeld, E. (1998), 'The customised, digitized, have-it-your-way economy', *Fortune*, 28 September, pp. 31–36.

Schwarz, B. (2000), 'E-business: new distribution models coming to a site near you', *Transportation & Distribution*, vol. 41, no 2, pp. 3–4.

Seybold, P.B. and Marshak, R.T. (1998), *Customer.com: How to Create a Profitable Business Strategy for the Internet and Beyond*, Random House, New York.

Storey, J. (1994), *New Wave Manufacturing Strategies*, P. Chapman, London.

Tucker, R.B. (1991), *Managing the Future: Ten Driving Forces of Change for the 90s*, Putnam, New York.

Urbaczewski, A., Jessup, L.M. and Wheeler, B.C. (1998), 'A manager's primer in electronic commerce', *Business Horizons*, vol. 41, no 5, pp. 5–17.

Vaas, L. (1999), 'Big as an 18-wheeler, fast as a Ferrari', *PC Week*, 15 November, pp. 87–88.

Welles, E.O. (1992), 'Built on speed', *Inc. Magazine*, Goldhirsh Group, Boston, p. 82.

Zuckerman, A. (1999), 'Part 1 ERP: pathway to the future of yesterday's buzz?' *Transportation and Distribution*, vol. 40, no 8, pp. 37–43.

Chapter 11 References

Anandarajan, M., Anandarajan, A. and Wen, H.J. (1998), 'Extranets: Tools for cost control in a value chain framework', *Industrial and Management Systems*, vol. 98, no 3, pp. 29–38.

Anon. (1999), 'The Internet economy: the world's next growth engine', *Business Week*, 4 October, pp. 72–79.

Anon. (2000a), 'Beckton Dickenson', *Pen Computing*, vol. 7, no 23, p. 18.

Anon. (2000b), 'Los Angeles Fire Department', *Pen Computing*, vol. 7, no 23, p. 20.

Bartholomew, D. (1997), 'Trawling for $1 billion', *Industry Week*, 21 April, pp. 68–72.

Cabinet Office (1999), *E-Commerce@Its.Best.UK*, HMSO, London.

Cespedes, F.V. and Corey, E.V. (1990), 'Managing multiple channels', *Business Horizons*, vol. 33, no 4, pp. 67–78.

Chaston, I. (2000), *Entrepreneurial Marketing*, MacMillan, London.

Chen, A. (1999), 'Lucent builds its own IT revolution', *PC Week*, 15 November, pp. 87–88.

Corey, E.R. (1991), *Industrial Marketing Cases and Concepts*, 4th ed., Prentice Hall, Englewood Cliffs, NJ.

Cullen, J. (1998), 'The needle and damage done: Research, action research, and the organisational and social construction of health in the "information society"', *Human Relations*, vol. 51, no 12, pp. 1543–1563.

The Economist (2000), 'Seller beware', *The Economist*, 4 March, pp. 61–62.

Ford, D. (1980), 'The development of buyer–seller relationships in industrial markets', *European Journal of Marketing*, vol. 14, no 5, pp. 339–354.

Ford, D. (1990), *Understanding Business Markets: Interaction, Relationships and Networks*, Academic Press, London.

Gray, R. (2000), 'Web treatment', *Campaign*, 3 March, pp. 6–7.

Hakansson, H. (1987), *Industrial Technologies Development: A Network Approach*, Croom Helm, London.

Hakansson, H. and Ostberg, C. (1975), 'Industrial marketing: An organisational problem?' *Industrial Marketing Management*, vol. 4, pp. 113–123.

Hakansson, H., Johanson, J. and Wootz, B. (1976), 'Influence tactics in the buyer–seller processes', *Industrial Marketing Management*, vol. 4, no 6, pp. 316–332.

Hochhauser, R. (1997), 'How B–B direct marketing and direct response advertisers will succeed in the new millennium', *Direct Marketing*, vol. 60, no 3, pp. 50–54.

Jackson, B.B. (1985), *Winning and Keeping Customers: The Dynamics of Customer Relationships*, Lexington Books, Lexington, MA.

Kelly, E. (2000), 'Aerospace companies join e-commerce stampede', *Flight International*, 29 February, pp. 7–8.

Lee, H.L. and Billington, C. (1992), 'Managing supply chain inventory: Pitfalls and opportunities', *Sloan Management Review*, Spring, pp. 65–73.

Loewe, B. and Boncher, T. (1999), 'Taking control of your phone costs', *PC Week*, 7 June, pp. 23–24.

McHugh, J. (1998), 'Digital medicine men', *Forbes*, 1 June, pp. 46–50.

Menzel, D.C. (1998), 'www.ethics.gov: Issues and challenges facing public managers', *Public Administration Review*, vol. 58, no 5, pp. 445–453.

Moad, J. (1997), 'Forging flexible links', *PC Week*, 15 September, pp. 74–76.

Moskal, B.S. (1990), 'Logistics gets some respect', *Industry Week*, vol. 18, June, pp. 14–22.

Powers, T.L. (1991), *Modern Business Marketing: A Strategic Planning Approach to Business and Industrial Markets*, West Publishing, St Paul.

Prabhaker, P.R., Sheehan, M.J. and Coppett, J.I. (1997), 'The power of technology in business selling: Call centers', *Journal of Business & Industrial Marketing*, vol. 12, no 3–4, pp. 220–232.

Rangan, V.K., Shapiro, B.P. and Moriarty, R.T. (1995), *Business Marketing Strategy: Concepts and Applications*, Irwin, Chicago.

Schaffer, R.A. (1999), 'The Internet may finally cure what ails America's healthcare system', *Fortune*, 27 September, pp. 274–275.

Scharrer, R.A. (1999), 'The Internet may finally cure what ails America', *Fortune*, 29 September, pp. 274–275.

Schoenberger, C.R. (2000), 'An Alzheimer's drug goes on trial', *Forbes*, 20 March, pp. 94–95.

Schonberger, R.J. (1990), *Building a Chain of Customers: Linking Business Functions to Create the World Class Company*, Hutchinson Business Books, London.

Schonfeld, E. (1999), 'A site where hospitals can click to shop', *Fortune*, 4 December, p. 150.

Sheth, J. (1973), 'A model of industrial buying behaviour', *Journal of Marketing*, vol. 37, pp. 50–56.

Slater, S.F. and Narver, J.C. (1995), 'Market orientation and the learning organisation', *Journal of Marketing*, vol. 59, no 3, pp. 63–75.

Smith, D.S. (1999), 'The business revolution', *Sunday Times Enterprise Report*, no 3, pp. 3–4.

Solberg, C.A. (1995), 'Defining the role of the representative and the exporter in international industrial markets', *Proceedings of the 11th IMP Group Conference: Interactions, Relationships and Networks*, Manchester Business School, Manchester, pp. 1077–1099.

Soumi, T. and Kastu-Haikio, M. (1998), 'Cost and service-effectiveness solutions for local administration: The Finnish case', *Total Quality Management*, vol. 9, no 2–3, pp. 335–347.

Walker, S. (1989), *Rogernomics: Reshaping New Zealand's Economy*, GP Books, Auckland.

Webster F. and Wind, Y. (1972), 'A general model for understanding organisational buying behaviour', *Journal of Marketing*, vol. 36, pp. 12–19.

Chapter 12 References

Anon. (1997), 'The once and future mall: Internet shopping', *The Economist*, 1 November, pp. 64–67.

Bank of England (2000), *Finance for Small Firms*, Bank of England, London, pp. 24–26.

Berry, L.L. and Yadav, M.S. (1996), 'Capture and communicate value in the pricing of services', *Sloan Management Review*, vol. 37, no 4, pp. 41–52.

Bowen, D.E. and Lawler, E.E. (1992), 'The empowerment of service workers: What, why, how and when', *Sloan Management Review*, Spring, pp. 31–39.

Brown-Humes, C. (2000), 'The dinosaurs are not going to die', *The Banker*, March, pp. 13–15.

Business Week, (1996), 'The revolution in the showroom', *Business Week*, 19 February, p. 17.

Carlzon, J. (1987), *Moments of Truth*, Ballinger, New York.

Cavanaugh, K. (1996), 'Big 6 to launch an on-line consulting service', *New York Times*, 31 May, p. 17.

Collier, D.A. and Meyer, S.M. (1998), 'A service positioning matrix', *International Journal of Operations and Production Management*, vol. 18, no 12, pp. 1–15.

Cowell, D. (1984), *The Marketing of Services*, Heinemann, London.

Dannenberg, M. and Kellner, D. (1998), 'The bank of tomorrow with today's technology', *International Journal of Bank Marketing*, vol. 16, no 2, pp. 8–16.

Eigler, P. and Langeard, E. (1977), 'Services as systems: Marketing implications' in Eiglier, P. and Langeard, E. (eds), *Marketing Consumer Services*, Marketing Science Institute, Cambridge, MA, pp. 89–91.

Fulford, B. (2000), 'I got it @ 7-Eleven', *Forbes*, 3 April, pp. 53–54.

Gronroos, C. (1984), 'A service quality model and its marketing implications', *European Journal of Marketing*, vol. 18, no 4, pp. 36–44.

Grossman, L.M. (1993), 'Federal Express, UPS face off over computers', *Wall Street Journal*, 17 September, p. B1.

Hansell, S. (1998), 'Is this the factory of the future?', *New York Times*, 26 July, pp. 9–13.

Hicks, M. (2000), 'Going online for services rendered', *PC Week*, 7 February, pp. 65–66.

Hopper, M. (1990), 'Rattling SABRE: new ways to compete on information', *Harvard Business Review*, May–June, pp. 118–125.

Levitt, T. (1972), 'Production-line approach to service', *Harvard Business Review*, September–October, pp. 41–52.

Levitt, T. (1976), 'Industrialisation of services', *Harvard Business Review*, September–October, pp. 63–74.

Kotler, P. (1997), *Marketing Management: Analysis, Planning, Implementation and Control*, 9th ed., Prentice Hall, Upper Saddle River, NJ.

Parasuraman, A., Zeithmal, V.A. and Berry, L.L. (1988), 'SERVQUAL: A multiple item scale for measuring consumer perceptions of service quality', *Journal of Retailing*, vol. 64, no 1, pp. 12–23.

Parasuraman, A., Zeithmal, V.A. and Berry, L.L. (1990), 'A conceptual model of service quality and its implications for future research', *Journal of Marketing*, vol. 49, Fall, pp. 34–45.

Pearce, M.R. (1998), 'From carts to clicks', *Ivey Business Quarterly*, vol. 53, no 1, pp. 69–72.

Quinn, J.B., Doorley, T.L. and Paquette, P.C. (1990), 'Technology in services: rethinking strategic focus', *Sloan Management Review*, Winter, pp. 79–87.

Quinn, J.B. and Paquette, P.C. (1990), 'Technology in services: creating organisational revolutions', *Sloan Management Review*, Winter, pp. 67–78.

Sasser, W.E. (1976), 'Match supply and demand in service industries', *Harvard Business Review*, November–December, pp. 133–140.

Solomon, S.D. (1989), 'Growth strategies: Cleaning up', *Inc. Magazine*, Goldhirsh, Boston, December, pp. 137.

Stewart, A. (2000), 'Inside track: Diverging routes to the on-line buyer's heart', *Financial Times*, 15 March.

Teal, T. (1991), 'Service comes first: An interview with USA's Robert McDermott', *Harvard Business Review*, September–October, pp. 56–61.

Teitelbaum, R. (1997), 'The Wal-Mart of Wall Street', *Fortune*, 13 October, pp. 22–24.

Thurm, S. (1998), 'Leading the PC pack', *Wall Street Journal*, 7 December, p. 4.

Timewell, S. and Young, K. (1999), 'How the Internet redefines banking', *The Banker*, June, pp. 27–31.

Wiersma, F. (1996), *Customer Intimacy*, HarperCollins, London.

Woolley, S. (1998), 'Virtual banker', *Forbes*, 15 June, pp. 1272–1274.

Young, K. (1999), 'Customer care centres on profit', *The Banker*, October, pp. 132–134.

Zeithmal, V.A., Parasuraman, A. and Berry, L.L. (1990), *Delivering Quality Service: Balancing Customer Perceptions and Expectations*, The Free Press, New York.

Zeithmal, V.A. and Bitner, M.J. (1996), *Services Marketing*, McGraw-Hill, New York.

Zemke, R. and Schaaf (1989), *The Service Edge: 101 Companies that Profit from Customer Care*, New American Library, New York.

General Glossary

Applications services market (p. 6)

A market in which expensive, complex software is located on a remote computer server and users, instead of installing the software themselves, access the server and pay a usage fee when running these expensive programmes.

Application service providers, or **ASPs** (p. 234)

Those that bring together all of the hardware and software needed to operate an e-commerce supply chain, host the software on a central server, and permit customers access to the systems via browser software and an Internet link.

Back office staff (p. 78)

The off-line administrative activities of an organization.

Banner advertising (p. 16)

Small advertisements embedded into Web pages.

Batch processing (p. 133)

Storing received data and then entering this new information into the computer regularly, such as once or twice a day.

Brand differentiation (p. 82)

Differences between a brand and competitive offerings which can be used to attract the customer.

Business-to-business markets (p. 4)

Markets in which companies trade with each other rather than with consumers.

Communicability (p. 158)

The degree to which the benefit claims can be easily described to potential users.

Core competences (p. 72)

Internal capabilities critical to supporting key activities.

Correction-based quality management (p. 80)

Waiting until something goes wrong and then initiating remedial actions to correct the fault.

Cross-docking inventory management technique (p. 74)

A just-in-time stock control system that keeps inventory on the move throughout the value chain.

Cross-functional communication (p. 225)

Information flows between different departments.

Customer interface (p. 82)

The contact point between the company and the customer.

Customer relationship management, or **CRM** (p. 101)

Using data about customers to ensure a company offers an optimal product proposition, prices the product to meet specific customer expectations, and tailors all aspects of service quality such that every point of contact from initial enquiry to post-purchase service is perceived by the customer as a trouble-free, 'seamless' service).

Data warehousing, or **data mining** (p. 99)

Using computer-based statistical analysis to identify clusters and trends in large volumes of customer purchase data.

Differentiation (p. 30)

The creation of clear difference between a company's product and competition.

Divisibility (p. 158)

The degree to which the product can be tried on a limited basis.

E-sourcing (p. 234)

Using the Internet to manage all procurement activities.

Economic order quantity, or **EOQ** (p. 83)

The size of production run that optimizes manufacturing costs.

Economies of scale (p. 11)

The reduction in operating costs that occur as a company becomes larger.

Electronic data interchange, or EDI (p. 6)

A pre-Internet concept which uses specially developed computer software permitting companies to exchange electronically large volumes of data between their respective computers.

Enterprise resource planning, or **ERP, systems** (p. 225)

Software that links together all databases from marketing, logistics, manufacturing, procurement, accounting etc. to permit real time analysis of activities in progress across the organization.

External marketing (p. 278)

The normal formal processes associated with the management of the four Ps.

Extranets (p. 63)

Websites closed to the general public and can only be accessed via passwords by approved users.

Flexible manufacturing systems, or **FMS** (p. 224)

A combination of engineering design and production flexibility made possible by equipment such as robots, flexible machining centres and automated assembly machines.

Four Ps (p. 24)

The variables of product, price, promotion and place.

Frequency (p. 178)

How many times the average viewer sees the advertisement in a specified time period.

Fulfillment house (p. 60)

An operation responsible for processing orders, packing goods and managing deliveries.

Fuzzy logic (p. 182)

A type of software that analyses data, drawing conclusions and thereby 'learning' in a way similar to the processes found within the human mind.

Generic market (p. 54)

Made up of both potential and actual users.

Groupware (p. 65)

Computer software such as Lotus Notes which permit a group of individuals to exchange and store electronic information.

Immigrants (p. 30)

People who are recent arrivals in cyberspace, only using the technology because they have been forced to by very specific circumstances at work.

Initial public offering, or **IPO** (p. 79)

The first time a company offers the general public the opportunity to buy shares in the operation.

Inseparability (p. 269)

The fact that many services are simultaneously produced and consumed.

Intangibility (p. 267)

That the item cannot be touched, smelt, seen or tasted.

Interactive marketing (p. 278)

The activities which occur at the buyer–seller interface.

Internal marketing (p. 278)

The internal processes associated with ensuring that all aspects of the business operation, including automated, computer-based systems are (1) customer-conscious and (2) supportive of a philosophy that every action is oriented towards achieving total customer satisfaction.

Internet call back (p. 28)

The customer uses the website to request a telephone call from the company.

Internet chat (p. 28)

An instant interactive written exchange with the supplier.

Inventory turn (p. 100)

The speed with which inventory is acquired and then sold on to the customer.

Lean manufacturing (p. 99)

The concept of operating highly flexible production facilities using machine tools programmable for a range of tasks.

Market segmentation (p. 55)

Dividing the market into sub-groups of customers with common, unique product needs.

Mass marketing (p. 24)

Making available a standard product to the market.

Number of impressions (p. 179)

The total number of times a page is visited.

Off-the-shelf-software (p. 76)

An existing computer programme that can be purchased from a software supplier.

On-line auctions (p. 7)

Websites where people can bid on-line for products and services featured on the site.

On-line only operations (p. 3)

Organizations with no premises for customers to visit.

One-to-one, or **mass customized, marketing** (p. 99)

A philosophy of creating products or services designed to meet the specific needs of an individual customer.

Original equipment manufacturers, or **OEMs** (p. 63)

Manufacturing companies such as IBM or Ford.

Outsource (p. 81)

Sub-contract a specific role to an external supplier.

Page impressions (p. 179)

The number of times a page carrying a banner advertisement is visited.

Purchase loyalty (p. 35)

The commitment of the customer to continue buying from a specific supplier.

Reach (p. 189)

The proportion of the viewing population exposed to the advertisement.

Relative resource costs (p. 119)

The degree to which a company's operating costs are higher or lower than competition.

Relative resource-produced value (p. 119)

The degree to which the company's financial performance is better or worse than competition.

Retention (p. 78)

Ensuring that employees, having joined the company, want to remain there.

Shopping trolley (p. 81)

A visual device that makes it appear that the user is placing products into a supermarket trolley.

Smart cards (p. 6)

Plastic cards that contain a microchip on which information is stored electronically, and can be used, for example, to pay for travel on public transport without the need to carry money, or to store a person's medical records.

Supply chain (p. 7)

The description applied to all of the members of a system in which raw materials are acquired and products manufactured, distributed and sold to the final customer.

TCP/IP (p. 2)

A computer operating protocol which enables different machines using different operating languages to communicate with each other.

Tacit knowledge (p. 72)

Understanding among employees of how to undertake effectively organizational tasks.

Transaction engines (p. 36)

The in-company software systems that manage the customer order placement, order picking, invoice and shipping activities.

Universal product codes, or **barcodes** (p. 99)

The numerical codes printed onto product packaging that permit automatic identification.

Variability (p. 269)

The fact that no two offerings of the same service will ever be identical because both customer needs and employee abilities differ.

Vertical integration (p. 11)

When a company becomes involved in operations either upstream or downstream from itself in its supply chain.

Video over net (p. 28)

A videoconference with a member of the supplier's staff.

Voice over net (p. 28)

An audio conversation while the customer is using a website.

Wizards (p. 30)

People who have complete mastery of the technology.

Index

INDEX